# ADMINISTRATIVE THINKERS

# ADMINISTRATIVE THINKERS

Ashutosh Kumar
Manoj Kr. Singh

ANMOL PUBLICATIONS PVT. LTD.
NEW DELHI-110 002 (INDIA)

**ANMOL PUBLICATIONS PVT. LTD.**
**Regd. Office:** 4360/4, Ansari Road, Daryaganj,
New Delhi-110002 (India)
Tel.: 23278000, 23261597, 23286875, 23255577
Fax: 91-11-23280289
*Email:* anmolpub@gmail.com
*Visit us at:* www.anmolpublications.com

**Branch Office:** No. 1015, Ist Main Road, BSK IIIrd Stage
IIIrd Phase, IIIrd Block, Bangalore-560 085 (India)
Tel.: 080-41723429 • Fax: 080-26723604
*Email:* anmolpublicationsbangalore@gmail.com

*Administrative Thinkers*



First Edition, 2010

ISBN 978-81-261-4564-5

PRINTED IN INDIA

Printed at Mehra Offset Press, Delhi.

# Contents

# Preface

Administrative Thinkers as a book is being taught at the graduate and post graduate level in public administration.

A very significant contribution in the growth of administrative thought in our modern time was made by political thinkers like Karl Marx who strongly pleaded that the workers who form vast majority of population in very country are being denied a share in the running of their own administration both in the government and industry. Karl Marx and many other intellectuals came forward with their ideas about administration and role of administrators in society.

The major ideas of the eminent thinkers have been examined in the context of their total administrative philosophy. Besides, a comparative analysis of the ideas of different scholars has also been attempted at appropriate places. Thinkers' contributions have been evaluated from the requirements of social science methodology as also from their relevance in the present time.

The book deals with the topics of—Abraham Maslow, Chester Barnard, Chris Argyris, Douglas McGregor, Frederick Herzberg, Frederick Winslow Taylor, Henri Fayol, Herbert Simon, Karl Marx, Luther Gulick, Lyndall Urwick, Mary Parker Follett, Max Weber, Peter Drucker, Robert K. Merton, Woodrow Wilson; etc.

—*Editor*

# 1

# Introduction

Public administration can be broadly described as the development, implementation and study of branches of government policy. The pursuit of the public good by enhancing civil society, ensuring a well-run, fair, and effective public service are some of the goals of the field.

Public administration is carried out by public servants who work in public departments and agencies, at all levels of government, and perform a wide range of tasks. Public administrators collect and analyse data (statistics), monitor budgets, draft legislation, develop policy, and execute legally mandated government activities. Public administrators serve in many roles: ranging from "front-line" positions serving the public (e.g., peace officers, parole officers, border guards); administrators (e.g., auditors); analysts (e.g., policy analysts); and managers and executives of government branches and agencies. Public administration is also an academic field. In comparison with related fields such as political science, public administration is relatively new, having emerged in the 19th century. Multidisciplinary in character, it draws on theories and concepts from political science, economics, sociology, administrative law, behavioural science, management and a range of related fields.

## History—Antiquity to the Early 19th Century

Classic scholars including Plato, Aristotle, Vishnu Gupta (Kautilya) and Machiavelli are the basis of subsequent generations of public administration. Until the birth of a national state, the governors principally emphasized moral and political human nature, as well as the on the organization of the governing bodies.

Operations were perceived to be secondary to establishing and clarifying the overall guiding theory of government. In Machiavelli's *The Prince,* European princes or governors were offered advice for properly administering their governments. This work represents one of the first Western expressions of the methodology of government. As the centuries moved past, scholars and governors persisted in their various endeavours explaining how one governs.

Though progress varied across the globe, 16th century Western Europe primarily ascribed to the "national-state" model of government and its corresponding administrative structures. Predominantly imperial Asia, tribal Africa, and the tribal/colonial Americas were each feeling the extent of Europe's diplomatic strategies whose emphasis was war, profit, and proselytizing. In any event, nation-states required a professional force and structure for carrying out the primary purposes of government: ensuring stability with through law, security with a military, and some measure of equity through taxation. Consequently, the need for expert civil servants whose ability to read and write formed the basis for developing expertise in such necessary activities as legal records, military prowess, and tax administration, and record keeping. As the European imperialist age progressed and the militarily dominant region extended its hold over other continents and people, the need for increasingly conventional administrative expertise grew.

Eighteenth century noble, King Frederick William I of Prussia, created professorates in Cameralism in an effort to service this need. The universities of Frankfurt an der Oder and University of Hallewere Prussian institutions emphasizing economic and social disciplines, with the goal of societal reform. Johann Heinrich Gottlob Justi was the most well-known professor of Cameralism. Thus, from a Western European perspective, classic, medieval, and enlightened scholars formed the foundation of the discipline that has come to be called public administration.

### *Mid-1800s-1930s*

Lorenz von Stein, an 1855 German professor from Vienna, is considered the founder of the science of public administration in many parts of the world. In the time of Von Stein, public administration was considered a form of administrative law, but Von Stein believed this concept too restrictive.

Von Stein taught:

- Public administration relies on many preestablished disciplines such as sociology, political science, administrative law and public finance. Further, public administration is an integrating science.
- Public administrators need be concerned with both theory and practice. Practical considerations are at the forefront of the field, but theory is the basis of best practices.
- Public administration is a science because knowledge is generated and evaluated according to the scientific method.

In the United States, Woodrow Wilson is considered the father of public administration. He first formally recognized public administration in an 1887 article entitled "The Study of Administration." The future president wrote that "it is the object of administrative study to discover, first, what government can properly and successfully do, and, secondly, how it can do these proper things with the utmost possible efficiency and at the least possible cost either of money or of energy." Wilson was more influential to the science of public administration than Von Stein, primarily due to an article Wilson wrote in 1887 in which he advocated four concepts:

- Separation of politics and administration
- Comparative analysis of political and private organizations
- Improving efficiency with business-like practices and attitudes toward daily operations
- Improving the effectiveness of public service through management and by training civil servants, merit-based assessment

The separation of politics and administration has been the subject of lasting debate. The different perspectives regarding this dichotomy contribute to differentiating characteristics of the suggested generations of public administration.

### *1940s*

The separation of politics and administration advocated by Wilson continues to play a significant role in public administration today. However, the dominance of this dichotomy was challenged by second generation scholars, beginning in the 1940s. Luther Gulick's fact-value dichotomy was a key contender for Wilson's allegedly impractical politics-administration dichotomy. In place of Wilson's first generation split, Gulick advocated a "seamless web of discretion and interaction" (Fry 1989, 80).

Luther Gulick and Lyndall Urwick are two second-generation scholars. Gulick, Urwick, and the new generation of administrators built on the work of contemporary behavioral, administrative, and organizational scholars including Henri Fayol, Fredrick Winslow Taylor, Paul Appleby, Frank Goodnow, and Willam Willoughby. The new generation of organizational theories no longer relied upon logical assumptions and generalizations about human nature like classical and enlightened theorists.

Gulick developed a comprehensive, generic theory of organization that emphasized the scientific method, efficiency, professionalism, structural reform, and executive control. Gulick summarized the duties of administrators with an acronym; POSDCORB, which stands for planning, organizing, staffing, directing, coordinating, reporting, and budgeting. Fayol developed a systematic, 14-point, treatment of private management. Second-generation theorists drew upon private management practices for administrative sciences.

A single, generic management theory bleeding the borders between the private and the public sector was thought to be possible. With the general theory, the administrative theory could be focused on governmental organizations.

### Post-World War II-1970s

The mid-1940s theorists challenged Wilson and Gulick. The politics-administration dichotomy remained the centre of criticism in the third generation. In addition to this area of criticism, government itself came under fire as ineffective, inefficient, and largely a wasted effort. The sometimes deceptive, and expensive American intervention in Vietnam along with domestic scandals including Watergate are two examples of self-destructive government behaviour during the third generation. There was a call by citizens for efficient administration to replace ineffective, wasteful bureaucracy. Public administration would have to distance itself from politics to answer this call and remain effective. Elected officials supported such reform. The Hoover Commission, chaired by University of Chicago professor Louis Brownlow, to examine reorganization of government. Dr. Brownlow subsequently founded the public administration service on the university, 1313 E. 60th Street. The organization PAS provided consulting services to governments at all levels of government until the 1970s.

### *1980s*

In the late 1980s, yet another generation of public administration theorists began to displace the last. What was called New Public Management was proposed by David Osborne and Ted Gaebler. The new model advocated the use of private sector innovation, resources, and organizational ideas to improve the public sector.

During the Clinton Administration (1992-2000), Vice President Al Gore adopted and reformed federal agencies accordingly. New public management there by became prevalent throughout the US bureaucracy. Some critics argue that the New Public Management concept of Americans as "customers" rather than "citizens" is an unacceptable abuse. That is, customers are a means to an end, profit, rather than part of the policy making process. Citizens are in fact the proprietors of government (the owners), opposed to merely the customers of a business (the patrons). In New Public Management, people are viewed as economic units not democratic participants. Nevertheless, the model is still widely accepted at all levels of government.

### *1990s*

In the late 1990s, Janet and Robert Denhardt proposed a new public service model. This model's chief contribution is a focus on Americans as "citizens" rather than "customers". Accordingly, the citizen is expected to participate in government and take an active role throughout the policy process. No longer are the proprietors considered an end to a mean. Whilse this remains feasible at the federal, state & local levels, where the concept of citizenship is commonly wedded, the emergence of 'transnational administration' with the growing number of international organizations and 'transnational executive networks' complicates the prospects for citizen engagement. One example of this is openforum.com.au, an Australian non-for-profit eDemocracy project which invites politicians, senior public servants, academics, business people and other key stakeholders to engage in high-level policy debate.

### *New Public Management (NPM)*

The critics of NPM claim that a successor to NPM is digital era governance, focusing on themes of reintegrating government responsibilities, needs-based holism (executing duties in cursive ways), and digitalization (exploiting the transformational capabilities of modern IT and digital storage).

### *Core Branches*

In academia, the fields of Public Administration, are contrived in five disciplines:

- Ethics in Public Administration serves as a normative approach to decision making.
- Policy Analysis serves as an empirical approach to decision making.
- Public Budgetingis the activity within a government that seeks to allocate scarce resources among unlimited demands.
- Organizational Theory in Public Administration is the study of the structure of governmental entities and the many particulars inculcated in them.
- Human Resource Management in Public Administration is an in-house structure that ensures unbiased treatment, ethical standards, and promotes a values-based system. The Basic functions of the HR system are:
    - o Employee Benefits, Employee health care, Compensation, etc.
    - o Leading Contributors: George H. Pendleton, Chester Barnard, Paul C. Light, and Volcker Commission.
    - o Legislation: *Pendleton Civil Service Reform Act* 1883, *Civil Service Reform Act* of 1978, *Hatch Act* of 1939, *Classification Act* of 1949, and Title VII from *Civil Rights Act* of 1964.

### *Decision-making Models*

Given the array of duties public administrators find themselves performing, the professional administrator might refer to a theoretical framework from which he or she might work. Indeed, many public and private administrative scholars have devised and modified decision-making models.

### *Niskanen's Budget-maximizing*

An relatively recent rational choice variation, proposed by William Niskanen in a 1971 article budget-maximizing model, argued that rational bureaucrats will universally seek to increase their budgets, thereby contributing to state growth, measured by expenditure.

Niskanen served on President Reagan's Council of Economic Advisors; his model underpinned what has been touted as curtailed public spending and increased privatization. However, budgeted expenditures and the growing deficit during the Reagan administration is evidence of a different reality. A range of pluralist authors have critiqued Niskanen's universalist approach. These scholars have argued that officials tend also to be motivated by considerations of the public interest.

### *Dunleavy's Bureau-shaping*

The bureau-shaping model, a modification of Niskanen, holds that rational bureaucrats only maximize the part of their budget that they spend on their own agency's operations or give to contractors and interest groups. Groups that are able to organize a "flowback" of benefits to senior officials would, according to this theory, receive increased budgetary attention. For instance, rational officials will get no benefit from paying out larger welfare checks to millions of low-income citizens because this does not serve a bureaucrats' goals.

Accordingly, one might should instead expect a jurisdiction to seek budget increases for defence and security purposes in place of domestic social programming. If we refer back to Reagan once again, Dunleavy's bureau shaping model accounts for the alleged decrease in the "size" of government while spending did not, in fact, decrease. Domestic entitlement programming was financially de-emphasized for military research and personnel.

### *Notable Scholars*

Notable scholars of public administration have come from a range of fields. In the period before public administration existed as its own independent discipline, scholars contributing to the field came from economics, sociology, management, political science, law, and, other related fields. More recently, scholars from public administration and public policy have contributed important studies and theories.

### *As An Academic Field*

In the United States, the academic field of public administration draws heavily on political science and law. Scholars such as John A. Rohr write of a long history behind the constitutional legitimacy of government bureaucracy. In Europe (notably in Britain and Germany), the divergence of the field from other disciplines can be traced to the 1720s continental university curriculum. Formally, official academic distinctions were made in the 1910s and 1890s, respectively. The goals of the field of public administration are related to the democratic values of improving equality, justice, security, efficiency, effectiveness of public services usually in a non-profit, non-taxable venue; business administration, on the other hand, is primarily concerned with taxable profit. For a field built on concepts (accountability, governance, decentralization, clientele), these concepts are often ill-defined and typologies often ignore certain aspects of these concepts.

One minor tradition that the more specific term "public management" refers to ordinary, routine or typical management concerns, in the context of achieving public good. Others argue that public management as a new, economically driven perspective on the operation of government. This latter view is often called "new public management" by its advocates. New Public Management represents a reform attempt, aimed at reemphasizing the professional nature of the field. This will replace the academic, moral or disciplinary emphasis. Some theorists advocate a bright line differentiation of the professional field from related academic disciplines like political science and sociology; it remains interdisciplinary in nature. As a field, public administration can be compared to business administration, and the master of public administration (MPA) viewed as similar to a master of business administration (MBA) for those wishing to pursue governmental or non-profit careers. An MPA often emphasizes substantially different ethical and sociological criteria that are traditionally secondary to that of profit for business administrators. The MPA is related to similar government studies including public affairs, public policy, and political science. Differences often include program emphases on policy analysis techniques or other topical focuses such as the study of international affairs as opposed to focuses on constitutional issues such as separation of powers, administrative law, problems of governance and power, and participatory democracy.

The Doctor of Public Administration (DPA) is an applied-research doctoral degree in the field of public administration, focusing on practice. The DPA requires a dissertation and significant coursework beyond the masters level. Upon successful completion of the doctoral requirements, the title of "Doctor" is awarded and the post-nominals of D.P.A. are often added. Public administration theory is the domain in which discussions of the meaning and purpose of government, bureaucracy, budgets, governance, and public affairs takes place. In recent years, public administration theory has periodically connoted a heavy orientation toward critical theory and postmodern philosophical notions of government, governance, and power. However, many public administration scholars support a classic definition of the term emphasizing constitutionality, service, bureaucratic forms of organization, and hierarchical government.

## Public Administration as an Academic Discipline

A Public Administrator can fill many voids. The academic field evolved in the United States from both academic political science and law as a separate study in the 1910s. In Europe, notably England and Germany (Max Weber), it started as a separate scholarly field in the 1890s, but it was first taught in Continental universities in the 1720s. The Federalist Papers several times referred to the importance of good administration, and scholars such as John A. Rohr see a long history behind the constitutional legitimacy of government bureaucracy. A few public administration theorists advocate a bright line differentiation of the professional field from related academic disciplines like political science and sociology. But, in general, the interdisciplinary nature of PA is acknowledged and it is viewed as a field of study rather than a discipline.

As a field, public administration can be compared to business administration, and the MPA viewed as similar to an MBA for those wishing to pursue governmental or non-profit careers. An MPA often entails substantial ethical and sociological aspects not usually found in business schools. There are derivative and related degrees that address public affairs, public policy, and the like. Differences often connote program emphases on policy analysis techniques or other topical focuses such as the study of international affairs as opposed to focuses on constitutional issues such as separation of powers, administrative law, problems of governance and power, and participatory democracy.

Public administration theory is the domain where discussions of the meaning and purpose of government, bureaucracy, budgets, governance, and public affairs take place in the field. In recent years, public administration theory has occasionally connoted a heavy orientation toward critical theory and postmodern philosophical notions of government, governance, and power, but many public administration scholars support a classic definition of the term which gives weight to constitutionality, service, bureaucratic forms of organization, and hierarchical government.

There is minor tradition that holds that the more specific term public management refers to ordinary, routine or typical management concerns, but in the context of achieving public good. Others see public management as a new, economically driven perspective on the operation of government. This latter view is often termed "new public management" by its advocates and can be seen as a reform attempt aimed at re-emphasizing the professional nature of the field versus its academic, moral or disciplinary characteristics.

### *Bureaucracy*

*Bureaucracy* is a concept in sociology and political science referring to the way that the administrative execution and enforcement of legal rules are socially organized. This office organization is characterized by standardized procedure (rule-following), formal division of responsibility, hierarchy, and impersonal relationships. Examples of everyday bureaucracies include governments, armed forces, corporations, hospitals, courts, ministries and schools. A few specific examples of bureaucracies are the Department of Motor Vehicles and the College Board.

### *Origin of the Concept*

Bureaucracy is derived from the word bureau, used from the early 18th century in Western Europe not just to refer to a writing desk, but to an office, i.e. a workplace, where officials worked. The original French meaning of the word *bureau* was the baize used to cover desks. The term bureaucracy came into use shortly before the French Revolution of 1789, and from there rapidly spread to other countries. The Greek suffix-*kratia* or *kratos*-means "power" or "rule". Bureaucracy thus basically means office power or office rule, the rule of the officialdom.

In a letter of July 1, 1764, the French Baron de Grimm declared: "We are obsessed by the idea of regulation, and our Masters of Requests refuse to understand that there is an infinity of things in a great state with which a government should not concern itself."

Jean Claude Marie Vincent de Gournay sometimes used to say, "We have an illness in France which bids fair to play havoc with us; this illness is called *bureaumania.*" Sometimes he used to invent a fourth or fifth form of government under the heading of "bureaucracy". In another letter of July 15, 1765 Baron Grimm wrote also, "The real spirit of the laws in France is that bureaucracy of which the late Monsieur de Gournay used to complain so greatly; here the offices, clerks, secretaries, inspectors and *intendants* are not appointed to benefit the public interest, indeed the public interest appears to have been established so that offices might exist."

This quote refers to a traditional controversy about bureaucracy, namely the perversion of means and ends so that means become ends in themselves, and the greater good is lost sight of; as a corollary, the substitution of *sectional* interests for the *general* interest. The suggestion here is that, left uncontrolled, the bureaucracy will become increasingly self-serving and corrupt, rather than serving society. However, bureaucracy existed long before words and theories were devised to describe it in detail.

The Chinese Song dynasty (960 AD) for example constructed a centralized bureaucracy staffed with civilian scholar-officials. This system of rule led to a much greater concentration of power in the hands of the emperor and his palace bureaucracy than was achieved in previous dynasties. The first occurrence of this was in Ancient China, during the Wang dynasty in 380 BC.

### *Karl Marx and Bureaucracy*

In Karl Marx's theory of historical materialism, the historical origin of bureaucracy is to be found in *four* sources: religion, the formation of the state, commerce and technology.

Thus, the earliest bureaucracies consisted of castes of *religious* clergy, officials and scribes operating various rituals, and armed functionaries specifically delegated to keep order. In the historical transition from primitive egalitarian communities to a civil society divided into social classes and estates, occurring from about 10,000 years ago, authority is increasingly centralized in, and enforced by a state apparatus existing separately from society. This state formulates, imposes and enforces laws, and levies taxes, giving rise to an officialdom enacting these functions. Thus, the state mediates in conflicts among the people and keeps those conflicts within acceptable bounds; it also organises the defence of territory. Most importantly, the right of ordinary people to carry and use weapons of force becomes increasingly restricted; forcing other people to do things becomes increasingly the legal right of the state authorities only.

But the growth of trade and commerce adds a new, distinctive dimension to bureaucracy, insofar as it requires the keeping of accounts and the processing/recording of transactions, as well as the enforcement of legal rules governing trade. If resources are increasingly distributed by prices in markets, this requires extensive and complex systems of record-keeping, management and calculation, conforming to legal standards. Eventually, this means that the total amount of work involved in commercial administration outgrows the total amount of work involved in government administration. In modern capitalist society, private sector bureaucracy is *larger* than government bureaucracy, if measured by the number of administrative workers in the division of labour as a whole. Some corporations nowadays have a turnover larger than the national income of whole countries, with large administrations supervising operations.

A fourth source of bureaucracy Marxists have commented on inheres in the technologies of mass production, which require many standardised routines and procedures to be performed. Even if mechanisation replaces people with machinery, people are still necessary to design, control, supervise and operate the machinery. The technologies chosen may not be the ones that are best for everybody, but which create *incomes* for a particular class of people or maintain their power. This type of bureaucracy is nowadays often called a technocracy, which owes its power to control over specialised technical knowledge or control over critical information.

In Marx's theory, bureaucracy rarely creates new wealth by itself, but rather controls, coordinates and governs the production, distribution and consumption of wealth. The bureaucracy as a social stratum derives its income from the appropriation of part of the social surplus product of human labour. Wealth is appropriated by the bureaucracy by law through fees, taxes, levies, tributes, licensing etc.

Bureaucracy is therefore always a *cost* to society, but this cost may be accepted insofar as it makes social order possible, and maintains it by enforcing the rule of law. Nevertheless there are constant conflicts about this cost, because it has the big effect on the distribution of incomes; all producers will try to get the maximum return from what they produce, and minimise administrative costs. Typically, in epochs of strong economic growth, bureaucracies proliferate; when economic growth declines, a fight breaks out to cut back bureaucratic costs.

Whether or not a bureaucracy as a social stratum can become a genuine ruling class depends greatly on the prevailing property relations and the mode of production of wealth. In capitalist society, the state typically lacks an independent economic base, finances many activities on credit, and is heavily dependent on levying taxes as a source of income. Therefore, its power is limited by the costs which private owners of the productive assets will tolerate. If, however, the state owns the means of production itself, defended by military power, the state bureaucracy can become much more powerful, and act as a ruling class or power elite. Because in that case, it directly controls the sources of new wealth, and manages or distributes the social product. This is the subject of Marxist theories of bureaucratic collectivism.

Marx himself however never theorised this possibility in detail, and it has been the subject of much controversy among Marxists. The core organisational issue in these disputes concerns the degree to which the *administrative* allocation of resources by government authorities and the *market* allocation of resources can achieve the social goal of creating a more free, just and prosperous society. Which decisions should be made by whom, at what level, so that an optimal allocation of resources results? This is just as much a moral-political issue as an economic issue.

Central to the Marxian concept of socialism is the idea of workers' self-management, which assumes the internalisation of a morality and self-discipline among people that would make bureaucratic supervision and control redundant, together with a drastic reorganisation of the division of labour in society. Bureaucracies emerge to mediate conflicts of interest on the basis of laws, but if those conflicts of interest disappear (because resources are allocated directly in a fair way), bureaucracies would also be redundant.

Marx's critics are however skeptical of the feasibility of this kind of socialism, given the continuing need for administration and the rule of law, as well as the propensity of people to put their own self-interest before the communal interest. That is, the argument is that self-interest and the communal interest might *never* coincide, or, at any rate, can always diverge significantly.

### *Max Weber on Bureaucracy*

Max Weber has probably been one of the most influential users of the word in its social science sense. He is well-known for his study of bureaucratization of society; many aspects of modern public administration go back to him; a classic, hierarchically organized civil service of the continental type is — if basically mistakenly — called *"Weberian civil service"*.

However, contrary to popular belief, "bureaucracy" was an English word before Weber; the Oxford English Dictionary cites usage in several different years between 1818 and 1860, prior to Weber's birth in 1864.

Weber described the ideal type bureaucracy in positive terms, considering it to be a more rational and efficient form of organization than the alternatives that preceded it, which he characterized as *charismatic domination* and *traditional domination*. According to his terminology, bureaucracy is part of legal domination.

However, he also emphasized that bureaucracy becomes inefficient when a decision must be adopted to an individual case. According to Weber, the attributes of modern bureaucracy include its impersonality, concentration of the means of administration, a levelling effect on social and economic differences and implementation of a system of authority that is practically indestructible.

Weber's analysis of bureaucracy concerns:

- the historical and administrative reasons for the process of bureaucratization (especially in the Western civilisation)
- the impact of the rule of law upon the functioning of bureaucratic organisations
- the typical personal orientation and occupational position of a bureaucratic officials as a status group
- the most important attributes and consequences of bureaucracy in the modern world

A bureaucratic organization is governed by the following seven principles:

1. official business is conducted on a continuous basis
2. official business is conducted with strict accordance to the following rules:
    1. the duty of each official to do certain types of work is delimited in terms of impersonal criteria
    2. the official is given the authority necessary to carry out his assigned functions
    3. the means of coercion at his disposal are strictly limited and conditions of their use strictly defined
3. every official's responsibilities and authority are part of a vertical hierarchy of authority, with respective rights of supervision and appeal

4. officials do not own the resources necessary for the performance of their assigned functions but are accountable for their use of these resources
5. official and private business and income are strictly separated
6. offices cannot be appropriated by their incumbents (inherited, sold, etc.)
7. official business is conducted on the basis of written documents

A bureaucratic official:

- is personally free and appointed to his position on the basis of conduct
- exercises the authority delegated to him in accordance with impersonal rules, and his loyalty is enlisted on behalf of the faithful execution of his official duties
- appointment and job placement are dependent upon his technical qualifications
- administrative work is a full-time occupation
- work is rewarded by a regular salary and prospects of advancement in a lifetime career

An official must exercise his judgment and his skills, but his duty is to place these at the service of a higher authority; ultimately he is responsible only for the impartial execution of assigned tasks and must sacrifice his personal judgment if it runs counter to his official duties. Weber's work has been continued by many, like Robert Michels with his Iron Law of Oligarchy.

***Street-level Bureaucracy***

Street-level bureaucracy is a term used to refer to a public agency employee who actually performs the actions that implement laws.

***Examples of Street-level Bureaucrats:*** Street-level bureaucrats include police officers, firefighters, and others who "walk the streets" with regular citizens, and provide services to protect, as well as uphold the laws.

***System Administrator***

A system administrator, or sysadmin, is a person employed

to maintain, and operate a computer system or network for a company or other organization. System administrators are often members of an information technology department.

The duties of a system administrator are wide-ranging, and vary widely from one organization to another. Sysadmins are usually charged with installing, supporting, and maintaining servers or other computer systems, and planning for and responding to service outages and other problems. Other duties may include scripting or light programming, project management for systems-related projects, supervising or training computer operators, and being the equivalent of a handyman for computer problems beyond the knowledge of technical support staff.

***Skills:*** The *subject matter* of systems administration includes computer systems and the ways people use them in an organization. This entails a knowledge of operating systems and applications, as well as hardware and software troubleshooting, but also knowledge of the purposes for which people in the organization use the computers.

However, perhaps the most important *skill* to a system administrator is problem solving—frequently under various sorts of constraints and stress. The sysadmin is on call when a computer system goes down or malfunctions, and must be able to quickly and correctly diagnose what is wrong and how best to fix it. System administrators are not software engineers or developers. It is not usually within their duties to design or write new applications software. However, sysadmins must understand the behaviour of software in order to deploy it and to troubleshoot problems, and generally know several programming languages used for scripting or automation of routine tasks.

Particularly when dealing with Internet-facing or business-critical systems, a sysadmin must have a strong grasp of computer security. This includes not merely deploying software patches, but also preventing break-ins and other security problems with preventative measures. In some organizations, computer security administration is a separate role responsible for overall security and the upkeep of firewalls and intrusion detection systems, but all sysadmins are generally responsible for the security of the systems in their keep.

***Related Fields:*** Many organizations staff other jobs related to systems administration. In a larger company, these may all be separate positions within a computer support or Information Services (IS) department. In a smaller group they may be shared by a few sysadmins, or even a single person.

- A database administrator (DBA) maintains a database system, and is responsible for the integrity of the data and the efficiency and performance of the system.
- A network administrator maintains network infrastructure such as switches and routers, and diagnoses problems with these or with the behaviour of network-attached computers.
- A security administrator is a specialist in computer and network security, including the administration of security devices such as firewalls, as well as consulting on general security measures.
- Technical support staff respond to individual users' difficulties with computer systems, provide instructions and sometimes training, and diagnose and solve common problems.
- A computer operator performs routine maintenance and upkeep, such as changing backup tapes or replacing failed drives in a RAID array. Such tasks usually require physical presence in the room with the computer; and while less skilled than sysadmin tasks require a similar level of trust, since the operator has access to possibly sensitive data.

In some organizations, a person may begin as a member of technical support staff or a computer operator, then gain experience on the job to be promoted to a sysadmin position and afterwards an IT Manager.

***Training:*** Unlike many other professions, there is no single path to becoming a system administrator. Few colleges or universities have specific programs for system administration, so many system administrators have a degree in generic fields: computer science, computer engineering, information system management, or even a trade school program. As of 2006, only four U.S. universities, Rochester Institute of Technology, Tufts, Florida State University, Miller-Motte Technical College in AAS in Microcomputer Applications Systems Network Engineer and Michigan Tech have postgraduate programs in system administration. In Europe, Norway, there is a special English-taught MSc programme organized by Oslo University College in cooperation with Oslo University, named "Masters programme in Network and System Administration". The founder of the programme is the creator of ofengine, Mark Burgess.

In addition, because of the practical nature of systems administration and the easy availability of open-source server software, many systems administrators enter the field self-taught. Generally, a prospective administrator will be required to have some experience with the computer system he or she is expected to manage. In some cases, candidates are expected to possess industry certifications such as the Microsoft MCSA or Red Hat RHCE. At the same time, some employers consider reliance on such certifications to be a sign of a poor candidate, or 'paper cert'-someone who has trade-school "book learning" rather than formal theoretical knowledge or hard practical experience.

Sometimes, almost exclusively in smaller sites, the role of system administrator may be given to a skilled user in addition to or in replacement of his or her duties.

***Duties of a System Administrator:*** A system administrator's responsibilities typically include:

- Morning checks of systems/software.
- Performing backups of data.
- Applying operating system updates, and configuration changes.
- Installing and configuring new hardware/software.
- Adding/deleting/creating/modifying user account information, resetting passwords, etc.
- Answering technical queries.
- Responsibility for security.
- Responsibility for documenting the configuration of the system.
- Troubleshooting any reported problems.
- System performance tuning.
- Keeping the network up and running.

In larger organizations, some tasks listed above may be divided among different system administrators or members of different organizational groups. For example, a dedicated individual may apply all system upgrades, a Quality Assurance (QA) team may perform testing and validation, and one or more technical writers may be responsible for all technical documentation written for a company.

In smaller organizations, the system administrator can also perform any number of duties elsewhere associated with other fields:

- Technical support
- Database administrator (DBA)
- Network administrator/analyst/specialist
- Application analyst
- Security administrator
- Programmer.

System administrators, in larger organizations, also tend not to be system architects, system engineers, or system designers, however, like many roles in this field, demarcations between systems administration and these other roles are often not well defined in smaller organizations. However, even in larger organizations, senior systems administrators often have skills in these other areas as a result of their working experience. In smaller organizations, IT/computing specialties are less often discerned in detail, and the term "system administrator" is used in a rather generic way — they are the people who know how the computer systems work and can respond when something fails.

### *Public Policy*

*Public policy* is a course of action or inaction chosen by public authorities to address a problem. Public policy is expressed in the body of laws, regulations, decisions and actions of government. Policy analysis may be used to formulate public policy and to evaluate its effectiveness. Many public policy analysts earn Ph.D., Master of Public Policy and Master of Public Administration degrees in public policy schools, while others earn specialized degrees, such as an M.Ed for specializing in educational policy or an MSW for specializing in social welfare policy.

***Various Definitions:*** According to William Jenkins in *Policy Analysis: A Political and Organizational Perspective* (1978), a Public Policy is 'a set of interrelated decisions taken by a political actor or group of actors concerning the selection of goals and the means of achieving them within a specified situation where those decisions should, in principle, be within the power of those actors to achieve'. Thus, Jenkins understands Public Policy making to be a process, and not simply a choice.

According to Thomas A. Birkland in *An Introduction to the Policy Process* (2001), there is a lack of a consensus on the definition of public policy. Birkland outlines a few definitions of public policy:

- Clarke E. Cochran, et al.: "The term public policy always refers to the actions of government and the intentions that determine those actions".
- Clarke E. Cochran, et al.: "Public policy is the outcome of the struggle in government over who gets what".
- Thomas Dye: Public policy is "Whatever governments choose to do or not do".
- Charles L. Cochran and Eloise F. Malone: "Public policy consists of political decisions for implementing programs to achieve societal goals".
- B. Guy Peters: "Stated most simply, public policy is the sum of government activities, whether acting directly or through agents, as it has an influence on the life of citizens".

Birkland indicates that the elements common to all definitions of public policy are as follows:

- The policy is made in the name of the "public".
- Policy is generally made or initiated by government.
- Policy is interpreted and implemented by public and private actors.
- Policy is what the government intends to do.
- Policy is what the government chooses not to do.

# 2

# Abraham Maslow

Abraham Maslow (April 1, 1908 – June 8, 1970) was an American psychologist. He is noted for his conceptualization of a "hierarchy of human needs", and is considered the founder of humanistic psychology.

***Biography***

Born and raised in Brooklyn, New York, Maslow was the oldest of seven children. His parents were uneducated Jews from Russia. He was slow and tidy, and remembered his childhood as lonely and rather unhappy, because, as he said, "I was the little Jewish boy in the non-Jewish neighbourhood. It was a little like being the first Negro enrolled in the all-white school. I was isolated and unhappy. I grew up in libraries and among books, without friends." He would pursue law, but he went to graduate school at the University of Wisconsin to study psychology. While there, he married his first cousin Bertha in December 1928, and found as his chief mentor, professor Harry Harlow. At Wisconsin he pursued an original line of research, investigating primate dominance behaviour and sexuality. He went on to further research at Columbia University, continuing similar studies; there he found another mentor in Alfred Adler, one of Sigmund Freud's early colleagues.

From 1937 to 1951, Maslow was on the faculty of Brooklyn College. In New York he found two more mentors, anthropologist Ruth Benedict and Gestalt psychologist Max Wertheimer, whom he admired both professionally and personally. These two were so accomplished in both realms, and such "wonderful human beings" as well, that Maslow began taking notes about them and their behaviour. This would be the basis of his lifelong research and thinking about mental health and human potential. He wrote extensively on the subject, borrowing ideas from other psychologists but adding significantly to them, especially the concepts of a hierarchy of needs, metaneeds, self-actualizing persons, and peak experiences. Maslow became the leader of the humanistic school of psychology that emerged in the 1950s and 1960s, which he referred to as the "third force" — beyond Freudian theory and behaviourism.

Maslow was a professor at Brandeis University from 1951 to 1969, and then became a resident fellow of the Laughlin Institute in California. He died of a heart attack on June 8, 1970. In 1967, the American Humanist Association named him Humanist of the Year.

### *Humanistic Theories of Self Actualization*

Many psychologists have made significant impacts on society's understanding of the world. Abraham Maslow was one of these; he brought a new face to the study of human behaviour. He was inspired by great minds, and his own gift of thought created a unique concept of Humanistic Psychology. His family life and his experiences influenced the ideas that created a whole new form of psychology. After World War II, Maslow began to question the way psychologists had come to their conclusions, and though he didn't completely disagree, he had his own ideas on how to understand the Human mind.

Humanistic Psychologists believe that every person has a strong desire to realize his or her full potential, to reach a level of Self-actualization. To prove that humans are not simply blindly reacting to situations, but trying to accomplish something greater, Maslow studied mentally healthy individuals instead of people with serious psychological issues. This enabled him to discover that people experience "peak experiences", high points in life when the individual is in harmony with himself and his surroundings. Self-actualized people can have many peak experiences throughout a day while others have those experiences less frequently.

A visual aid Maslow created to explain his theory, which he called the Hierarchy of Needs, is a pyramid depicting the levels of human needs, psychological and physical. When a human being ascends the steps of the pyramid he reaches self actualization. At the bottom of the pyramid are the "Basic needs" of a human being, food and water and touch. The next level is "Security and Stability." These two steps are important to the physical survival of the person. Once individuals have basic nutrition, shelter and safety, they attempt to accomplish more. The third level of need is "Love and Belonging," which are psychological needs; when individuals have taken care of themselves physically, they are ready to share themselves with others. The fourth level is achieved when individuals feel comfortable with what they have accomplished. This is the "Esteem" level, the level of success and status. The top of the pyramid, "Self-actualization," occurs when individuals reach a state of harmony and understanding.

Maslow based his study on magazines (e.g. "hello" and "Look") and the writings of other psychologists, including Albert Einstein, as well as people he knew who clearly met the standard of self actualization. Maslow used Einstein's writings and accomplishments to exemplify the characteristics of the self actualized person. He realized that all the individuals he studied had similar personality traits. All were "reality centred," able to differentiate what was fraudulent from what was genuine. They were also "problem centred," meaning that they treated life's difficulties as problems that demanded solutions. These individuals also were comfortable being alone and had healthy personal relationships. They had only a few close friends and family rather than a large number of shallow relationships. One historical figure Maslow found to be helpful in his journey to understanding self actualization was Lao Tzu, The Father of Taoism. A tenant of Taoism is that people do not obtain personal meaning or pleasure by seeking material possessions.

When Maslow introduced these ideas some weren't ready to understand them; others dismissed them as unscientific, a critique often levelled at Freud. Sometimes viewed as disagreeing with Freud and psychoanalytic theory, Maslow actually positioned his work as a vital complement to that of Freud. Maslow stated in his book, "It is as if Freud supplied us the sick half of psychology and we must now fill it out with the healthy half." (Toward a psychology of being, 1968) There are two faces of human nature—

the sick and the healthy—so there should be two faces of psychology.

Consequently, Maslow argued, the way in which essential needs are fulfilled is just as important as the needs themselves. Together, these define the human experience. To the extent a person finds cooperative social fulfilment, he establishes meaningful relationships with other people and the larger world. In other words, he establishes meaningful connections to an external reality—an essential component of self-actualization. In contrast, to the extent that vital needs find selfish and competitive fulfilment, a person acquires hostile emotions and limited external relationships—his awareness remains internal and limited.

Benedict and Wertheimer were Maslow's models of self-actualization. From them he generalized that, among other characteristics, self-actualizing people tend to focus on problems outside themselves; have a clear sense of what is true and what is false; are spontaneous and creative; and are not bound too strictly by social conventions. Beyond the routine of needs fulfilment, Maslow envisioned moments of extraordinary experience, known as Peak experiences, which are profound moments of love, understanding, happiness, or rapture, during which a person feels more whole, alive, self-sufficient and yet a part of the world, more aware of truth, justice, harmony, goodness, and so on. Self-actualizing people have many such peak experiences.

Maslow's thinking was surprisingly original—-most psychologists before him had been concerned with the abnormal and the ill. He wanted to know what constituted positive mental health. Humanistic psychology gave rise to several different therapies, all guided by the idea that people possess the inner resources for growth and healing and that the point of therapy is to help remove obstacles to individuals' achieving them. The most famous of these was client-centred therapy developed by Carl Rogers. Classical Adlerian Psychotherapy, based on the teachings of Alfred Adler, also encourages the optimal psychological development of the individual. Maslow's influence extended beyond psychology-his work on peak experiences is relevant to religious studies, while his work on management is applicable to transpersonal business studies.

### *Hierarchy of Needs*

Maslow has set up a hierarchy of five levels of basic needs. Beyond these needs, higher levels of needs exist. These include needs for understanding, aesthetic appreciation and purely spiritual needs. In the levels of the five basic needs, it is said that the person does not feel the second need until the demands of the first have been satisfied, nor the third until the second has been satisfied, and so on.

Maslow's hierarchy of needs is a theory in psychology, proposed by Abraham Maslow in his 1943 paper *A Theory of Human Motivation*. Maslow subsequently extended the idea to include his observations of humans' innate curiosity. Maslow studied what he called exemplary people such as Albert Einstein, Jane Addams, Eleanor Roosevelt, and Frederick Douglass rather than mentally ill or neurotic people, writing that "the study of crippled, stunted, immature, and unhealthy specimens can yield only a cripple psychology and a cripple philosophy." Maslow also studied the healthiest 1% of the college student population. Maslow's theory was fully expressed in his 1954 book *Motivation and Personality*.

### *Representations*

Maslow's hierarchy of needs is often portrayed in the shape of a pyramid, with the largest and lowest levels of needs at the bottom, and the need for self-actualization at the top, also the needs for people. The lower four layers of the pyramid contain what Maslow called "deficiency needs" or "d-needs": physiological (including sexuality), security of position, friendship and love, and esteem. With the exception of the lowest (physiological) needs, if these "deficiency needs" are not met, the body gives *no* physical indication but the individual feels anxious and tense.

### *Physiological Needs*

For the most part, physiological needs are obvious—they are the literal requirements for human survival. If these requirements are not met (with the exception of clothing and shelter), the human body simply cannot continue to function. Physiological needs include:

- Breathing

- Food
- Sexual activity
- Homeostasis.

Air, water, and food are metabolic requirements for survival in all animals, including humans. The intensity of the human sexual instinct is shaped more by sexual competition than maintaining a birth rate adequate to survival of the species. The urge to have sex is so powerful that it can drain psychic energy away from other necessary goals. Therefore every culture has to invest great efforts in rechanneling and restraining it, and many complex social institutions exist only in order to regulate this urge. The saying that "love makes the world go round" is a polite reference to the fact that most of our deeds are impelled, either directly or indirectly, by sexual needs. —Mihaly Csikszentmihalyi, *Flow: The Psychology of Optimal Experience*

### *Safety Needs*

With their physical needs relatively satisfied, the individual's safety needs take precedence and dominate behaviour. These needs have to do with people's yearning for a predictable, orderly world in which injustice and inconsistency are under control, the familiar frequent and the unfamiliar rare. In the world of work, these safety needs manifest themselves in such things as a preference for job security, grievance procedures for protecting the individual from unilateral authority, savings accounts, insurance policies, and the like.

For most of human history many individuals have found their safety needs unmet, but as of 2009 "First World" societies provide most with their satisfaction, although the poor—both those who are poor as a class and those who are temporarily poor (university students would be an example)—must often still address these needs.

Safety and Security needs include:

- Personal security
- Financial security
- Health and well-being
- Safety net against accidents/illness and their adverse impacts.

### *Love and Belonging*

After physiological and safety needs are fulfilled, the third layer of human needs are social and involve feelings of belongingness. This aspect of Maslow's hierarchy involves emotionally-based relationships in general, such as:

- Friendship
- Intimacy
- Family.

Humans need to feel a sense of belonging and acceptance, whether it comes from a large social group, such as clubs, office culture, religious groups, professional organizations, sports teams, gangs ("Safety in numbers"), or small social connections (family members, intimate partners, mentors, close colleagues, confidants). They need to love and be loved (sexually and non-sexually) by others. In the absence of these elements, many people become susceptible to loneliness, social anxiety, and clinical depression. This need for belonging can often overcome the physiological and security needs, depending on the strength of the peer pressure; an anorexic, for example, may ignore the need to eat and the security of health for a feeling of control and belonging.

### *Esteem*

All humans have a need to be respected and to have self-esteem and self-respect. Also known as the *belonging need*, esteem presents the normal human desire to be accepted and valued by others. People need to engage themselves to gain recognition and have an activity or activities that give the person a sense of contribution, to feel accepted and self-valued, be it in a profession or hobby. Imbalances at this level can result in low self-esteem or an inferiority complex. People with low self-esteem need respect from others. They may seek fame or glory, which again depends on others. Note, however, that many people with low self-esteem will not be able to improve their view of themselves simply by receiving fame, respect, and glory externally, but must first accept themselves internally. Psychological imbalances such as depression can also prevent one from obtaining self-esteem on both levels.

Most people have a need for a stable self-respect and self-esteem. Maslow noted two versions of esteem needs, a lower one and a higher one. The lower one is the need for the respect of others, the need for status, recognition, fame, prestige, and attention. The higher one is the need for self-respect, the need for strength, competence, mastery, self-confidence, independence and freedom. The latter one ranks higher because it rests more on inner competence won through experience. Deprivation of these needs can lead to an inferiority complex, weakness and helplessness. Maslow stresses the dangers associated with self-esteem based on fame and outer recognition instead of inner competence. He sees healthy self-respect as based on earned respect.

### *Self-actualization*

"What a man can be, he must be". This forms the basis of the perceived need for self-actualization. This level of need pertains to what a person's full potential is and realizing that potential. Maslow describes this desire as the desire to become more and more what one is, to become everything that one is capable of becoming.. This is a broad definition of the need for self-actualization, but when applied to individuals the need is specific. For example one individual may have the strong desire to become an ideal parent, in another it may be expressed athletically, and in another it may be expressed in painting, pictures, or inventions. As mentioned before, in order to reach a clear understanding of this level of need one must first not only achieve the previous needs, physiological, safety, love, and esteem, but master these needs. Below are Maslow's descriptions of a self-actualized person's different needs and personality traits.

Maslow was a professor of Dr. Wayne Dyer. Dyer suggests that Maslow taught him two ways of understanding self-actualization: 1) To be free of the good opinion of others. 2) To do things not simply for the outcome but because it's the reason you are here on earth.

### *Acceptance*

A self-actualized person "can accept their own human nature in the stoic style, with all its shortcomings, with all its discrepancies from the ideal image without feeling real concern". This means that a self-actualized person can clearly see human nature in all its good and evil without the distortion from false social norms.

Maslow uses basic animal acceptance to prove this point. He states that self-actualized people tend to be good and lusty animals, hearty in their appetites and enjoying them mightily without regret or shame. This involves a basic acceptance of nature and the way things are rather than trying to change things (for example: disgust with body functions or having a food aversion) to suit one's neuroses. This doesn't mean these people lack morals, guilt, shame, or anxiety; it means that they have the ability to remove all unnecessary forms of these processes.

### *Problem Centering*

Most people, when thinking of problems in their life, focus on what affects them and their own problems and issues; this applies particularly to insecure people. Self-actualized persons focus not on themselves, but for some greater good. These people attack problems as a "task they must do" and are concerned with "the good of mankind in general".

### *The Need for Privacy*

The self-actualized can be solitary, with no human contact, and do no harm to themselves. In fact most of the self-actualized like "solitude and privacy to a definitely greater degree than the average person". This gives them a level of detachment and an ability to remain calm and aloof even in situations where a personal problem or misfortune arises.

### *Discrimination between Means and Ends*

Maslow found that those who are self-actualized are very strong ethically. They have definite moral standards and do not experience the daily chaos of discerning right and wrong like most common people. When dealing with means and ends they have the ability to clearly distinguish between the two. Also, Maslow found that they enjoy the means to an end: unlike most people who just see it as a means and want to finish it as soon as possible.

For example, driving to a destination annoys most people but a self-actualized person would enjoy the drive, the experience of travel. It is also in their ability to take the most trivial and mundane activities or objects and turn them into a game or perhaps a dance.

### *Sense of Humour*

Maslow discovered that most self-actualized people do not have the same sense of humour as the average person. For example: they do not laugh at hostile humour (hurting someone to laugh), superiority humour (laughing at someone's short comings), or authority-rebellion humour (laughing at unfunny, smutty jokes). A self-actualizing person's sense of humour relates to philosophy and finding humour in humans who forget their place in the universe or when they act foolishly. It doesn't attack people, rather states a message that happens to be funny. Self-actualized people don't merely tell jokes to laugh, but to send a message or educate; "akin to parables or fables".

### *Understand*

This becomes the need after a person achieves self-actualization. Maslow understands the quest for knowledge can be the common man simply filling a basic need or the self-actualized man reaching his pinnacle, but these are only parts to the quest for knowledge not the entire picture. The list below shows Maslow's examples of when the quest for knowledge is to satisfy merely a curiosity and not merely to fill a lesser need:

1. Something like human curiosity can easily be observed in the higher animals. The monkey will pick things apart, will poke his finger into holes, will explore in all sorts of situations where it is improbable that hunger, fear, sex, comfort status, etc., are involved. Harlow's experiments (174) have amply demonstrated this in an acceptably experimental way.
2. The history of mankind supplies us with a satisfactory number of instances in which man looked for facts and created explanations in the face of the greatest danger, even to life itself. There have been innumerable humbler Galileos.
3. Studies of psychologically healthy people indicate that they are, as a defining characteristic, attracted to the mysterious, to the unknown, to the chaotic, unorganized, and unexplained. This seems to be a Per se attractiveness; these areas are in themselves and of their own right interesting. The contrasting reaction to the well known is one of boredom.

4. It may be found valid to extrapolate from the psychopathological. The compulsive-obsessive neurotic (and neurotic in general), Goldstein's brain-injured soldiers, Maier's fixated rats (285), all show (at the clinical level of observation) a compulsive and anxious clinging to the familiar and a dread of the unfamiliar, the anarchic, the unexpected, the un-domesticated. On the other hand, there are some phenomena that may turn out to nullify this possibility. Among these are forced unconventionality, a chronic rebellion against any authority whatsoever, Bohemianism, the desire to shock and to startle, all of which may be found in certain neurotic individuals, as well as in those in the process of deacculturation. Perhaps also relevant here are the perseverative detoxifications, which are, behaviorally at any rate, an attraction to the dreadful, to the not understood and to the mysterious.
5. Probably there are true psychopathological effects when the cognitive needs are frustrated (295, 314). The following clinical impression are also pertinent.
6. I have seen a few cases in which it seemed clear to me that the pathology (boredom, loss of zest in life, self-dislike, general depression of the bodily functions, steady deterioration of the intellectual life, of tastes, etc.) were produced in intelligent people leading stupid lives in stupid jobs. I have at least one case in which the appropriate cognitive therapy (resuming parttime studies, getting a position that was more intellectually demanding, insight) removed the symptoms. We have seen many women, intelligent, prosperous, and unoccupied, slowly develop these same symptoms of intellectual inanition. Those who followed my recommendation to immerse themselves in something worthy of them showed improvement or cure often enough to impress me with the reality of the cognitive needs. In those countries in which access to the news, to information, and to the facts were cut off, and in those where official theories were profoundly contradicted by obvious facts, at least some people responded with generalized cynicism, mistrust of all values, suspicion even of the obvious, a profound disruption of ordinary interpersonal relationships, hopelessness, loss of morale,

etc. Others seem to have responded in the more passive direction with dullness, submission, loss of capacity, coarctation, and loss of initiative.

7. The needs to know and to understand are seen in late infancy and childhood, perhaps even more strongly than in adulthood. Furthermore this seems to be a spontaneous product of maturation rather than of learning, however defined. Children do not have to be taught to be curious. But they may be taught, as by institutionalization, not to be curious, e.g., Goldfarb (158).
8. Finally, the gratification of the cognitive impulses is subjectively satisfying and yields end-experience. Though this aspect of insight and understanding has been neglected in favour of achieved results, learning, etc., it nevertheless remains true that insight is usually a bright, happy, emotional spot in any person's life, perhaps even a high spot in the life span.

Maslow also states that even though these are examples of how the quest for knowledge is separate from basic needs he warns that these "two hierarchies are interrelated rather than sharply separated" (Maslow 97). This means that this level of need as well as the next and highest level are not strict, separate, levels but closely related to others and this is possibly the reason that these two levels of need are left out of most textbooks.

### *Taoism and Zen Buddhism*

There are similarities between Maslow's hierarchy of needs and the final stages of Taoism and Zen Buddhism. The similarities deal directly with the higher needs, starting with the self-actualization need. Maslow regards self-actualizing people as largely free from the power of society's rules and making decisions based upon their beliefs not the accepted norms of society. In Taoism and Buddhism people free themselves of worldly possessions, thus freeing themselves from societal pressures and power. The self-actualized person most likely will not have the same freedom from society as the Zen Buddhist or Taoist, but all three beliefs find their "perfect" being as one who is independent and makes decisions based upon nature and not the external authority of society or man.

### *Marketing*

Courses in marketing teach Maslow's hierarchy as one of the first theories as a basis for understanding consumers' motives for action. Marketers have historically looked towards consumers' needs to define their actions in the market. If producers design products meeting consumer needs, consumers will more often choose those products over those of competitors. Whichever product better fulfils this void will be chosen more frequently, thus increasing sales. This makes the model relevant to transpersonal business studies.

### *Criticisms*

While Maslow's theory was regarded as an improvement over previous theories of personality and motivation, it had its detractors. For example, in their extensive review of research based on Maslow's theory, Wahba and Bridgewell found little evidence for the ranking of needs Maslow described, or even for the existence of a definite hierarchy at all. Chilean economist and philosopher Manfred Max-Neef has also argued fundamental human needs are non-hierarchical, and are ontologically universal and invariant in nature—part of the condition of being human; poverty, he argues, may result from any one of these needs being frustrated, denied or unfulfilled.

The order in which the hierarchy is arranged (with self-actualisation as the highest order need) has been criticised as being ethnocentric by Geert Hofstede. He was also heavily criticized for his limited testing of only 100 students.

# 3

# Chester Barnard

Chester Irving Barnard (1886 – 1961) was an American business executive, public administrator, and the author of pioneering work in management theory and organizational studies. His landmark 1938 book, *Functions of the Executive,* sets out a theory of organization and of the functions of executives in organizations. The book has been widely assigned in university courses in management theory and organizational sociology.

### *Biography*

In his youth, Barnard worked on a farm, then studied economics at Harvard University, earning money tuning pianos and operating a dance band. Harvard denied him a BA because of a technicality, but a number of universities later granted him honorary doctorates. Barnard joined the American Telephone and Telegraph Company (now AT&T) in 1909. In 1927, he became president of the New Jersey Bell Telephone Company. During the Great Depression, he directed the New Jersey state relief system. He was president of the United Service Organizations (USO), 1942-45. Upon retiring from business, he served as president of the Rockefeller Foundation, 1948-52, and as chairman of the National Science Foundation, 1952-54. End 1950s he was among the first members of the Society for General Systems Research.

### *Work*

Barnard looked at organizations as systems of cooperation of human activity, and noted that they are typically short-lived. It is rare for a firm to last more than a century. Similarly most nations last for less than a century. The only organization that can claim a substantial age is the Roman Catholic Church. According to Barnard, organizations are not long-lived because they do not meet the two criteria necessary for survival: effectiveness and efficiency. Effectiveness, is defined the usual way: as being able to accomplish stated goals. In contrast, Barnard's meaning of organizational efficiency differed substantially from the conventional use of the word. He defined efficiency of an organization as the degree to which that organization is able to satisfy the motives of the individuals. If an organization satisfies the motives of its members while attaining its explicit goals, cooperation among its members will last. Barnard was a great admirer of Talcott Parsons (1902-1979) and he and Parsons corresponded persistently. The two scholars would send manuscripts for commentary to each other and they would write long letters where they engage in a common theoretical discussion. The first correspondence between Barnard and Parsons began in the end of the 1930s and it persisted essentially to Barnard's death in 1961.

### *Functions of the Executive*

Barnard's classic 1938 book *Functions of the Executive* discusses, as the title suggests, the functions of the executive, but not from a merely intuitive point of view, but instead deriving them from his conception of cooperative systems. Barnard summarized the functions of the executive as follows:

- Establishing and maintaining a system of communication;
- Securing essential services from other members;
- Formulating organizational purposes and objectives.

### *Authority and Incentives*

Barnard formulated two interesting theories: one of authority and the other of incentives. Both are seen in the context of a communication system grounded in seven essential rules:

- The channels of communication should be definite;
- Everyone should know of the channels of communication;
- Everyone should have access to the formal channels of communication;
- Lines of communication should be as short and as direct as possible;

- Competence of persons serving as communication centres should be adequate;
- The line of communication should not be interrupted when the organization is functioning;
- Every communication should be authenticated.

Thus, what makes a communication authoritative rests with the subordinate rather than with his superior. Barnard's perspective had affinities to that of Mary Parker Follett and was very unusual for his time, and that has remained the case down to the present day. He seemed to argue that managers should obtain authority by treating subordinates with respect and competence. As for incentives, he proposed two ways of convincing subordinates to cooperate: tangible incentives and persuasion. He gives great importance to persuasion, much more than to economic incentives. He described four general and four specific incentives. The specific incentives were:

1. Money and other material inducements;
2. Personal non-material opportunities for distinction;
3. Desirable physical conditions of work;
4. Ideal benefactions, such as pride of workmanship etc.

## Management Theorist

Few theorists in the field of management have had such a broad and continuous affect on management thought, both in scholarly application and functional practice, as Chester Barnard. His theories revolve around the participation of executives in an organization and the functionally appropriate communication channels. However, Barnard's theories cover more than simple business acumen; they also cover sociological and psychological impacts of leadership and organizational design and the morality required as a core competency for management. Arguably one of the most apt management theorists of his time, Barnard was viewed as somewhat of an elitist who believed there were vast differences between executive management and the common employees. Throughout his professional life, Barnard articulated and demonstrated his ideas on leadership both in print, with The Functions of the Executive and numerous other writings, and in industry as a philanthropist, CEO, and former president of the charitable Rockefeller Foundation. The author views Chester Barnard as a corporate role model and his theories as a foundation for management scholarship.

*Chester Barnard – The Person*

Born in 1886 in Malden, MA, Chester Barnard was raised on a farm by a single father and later went on to attend Harvard University. From an early age, Barnard focused his professional efforts on improving management as he saw it. Starting with American Telephone and Telegraph in 1909, Barnard began a career that spanned almost five decades while creating theories that were generally regarded as "the most thought provoking... on organization and management ever written by a practicing executive."

AT&T, Barnard became the president of New Jersey Bell Telephone Company in 1927. In true tribute to his character, Barnard announced in 1933 a policy that was unheard of at the time and extremely admirable today – a no-layoff policy, (Mahoney, 2002) earning him credibility and stature with his employees. During the Great Depression, he directed the New Jersey State Relief System, or as it is more aptly titled, Emergency Relief Administration. From there, he became the president of the United Service Organization (USO) from 1942-1945. (Britannica, 2009) When he retired from business, he served as president of the Rockefeller Foundation from 1948 to 1952 and chairman of the National Science Foundation from 1952 to 1954. Chester Barnard died on June 7, 1961 in New York City.

While his life lasted three quarters of a century, it appears that Barnard's teachings will "resonate intensely with current students of management at various levels in our management educational system" for years to come. Many graduate level professors enjoy reflecting on the scholarship of his theories because of the favourable response and feedback from the graduate students. "Barnard inspires contemporary students because he provides them with an authentic sense of organization" and "combines the two cultures – the science of organization and the art of organizing." The combination of technical management sciences with the appealing aura of artistic organization that is widely used, yet rarely labelled, is a major draw to Barnard's theories and provides learners with a subtle cushion for assimilation. His style of deliverance is disarming, informative, and thought-provoking. Many times theorists, especially management theorists, deliver a large quantity of complex data for the undergraduate or graduate learner to comprehend, and as a result, the learner steers away from the material presented. His presentation and communication styles have earned him a solid reputation for procedural and functional managerial wisdom.

## Key Theories

"Barnard concluded that because of their position and expertise, managers had to be the actual rulers of modern society, even though others might govern it nominally. Managers were a new elite arising from the grassroots of American democracy." To understand how an executive fits in to an organization, the reader needs to define their roles and responsibilities. "(Executives) had to proselytize others on the behalf of their organization's values, missions, objectives, and purposes. Such was the substance of the executive responsibility..." The functional role of an executive is to coordinate the overall strategy, mission, and values of an organization while assembling the employees to participate willingly in the process of production or output. If the employees are unwilling to assist in the process of efficiency, the organization will not function in the long term. Barnard also states (The Functions of the Executive, 1938) that creating a solid system for communication between organizational and functional business individuals (units) is required for sustainable operations. This includes aligning business employees in a manner that their lines of communication are easily understood, followed, and repeatable.

Barnard also focuses on the topic that managerial authority needs to be constantly understood and accepted. This is accomplished in a number of ways, but most importantly, according to Barnard, (1938) "the competence of the persons serving as... officers, supervisory heads, must be adequate." His candor and openness regarding the possibility that current management and executives might be less than competent begs for criticism and further evaluation, but the intrinsic truthfulness validates the need for appraisal of all current and future managers and executives. "When a condition of honesty and sincerity is recognized to exist, errors of judgment, defects of ability, are sympathetically endured. They are expected... What disturbs (employees) is the insincerity and the appearance of insincerity when the facts are not in their possession." "Barnard warns of a tendency for personnel to avoid responsibility (due in part to the fear of criticism) and that an executive must distribute responsibility, or otherwise run the risk of being overwhelmed with the burdens of decision." Another aspect of this theory is that managerial authority is derived not from command-style leadership where orders are given by management and executed by staff, but "awarded" by the subordinate. This was a radical idea at the time that strayed greatly from the accepted norms in both production industry and the developing corporate America in the first half of the twentieth century. In today's business environment, there is little, if any, negative discourse to this theory. Simply put, Barnard believes that authority is gained by showing respect, appreciation, integrity, and confidence in his staff; and human resource professionals agree.

### *Managerial Communications*

Barnard is frequently credited with applying three distinct, yet valuable, criteria to managerial communication. First, Barnard stated in 1938 that all employees should know what the lines of communication are. This is imperative for businesses that require a high degree of input from management, such as creative or technical positions, or those that are frequently undergoing external changes or pressures and have to adapt quickly. Having such lines eliminates any confusion about who reports to whom, or where to go for directions. The second criterion is to make those lines of communication "as direct and as short as possible'. This expedites any transmission of the message to the receiving party and decreases the overall amount of time required to deliver messages to large groups. (The author acknowledges that email was not available at the time Barnard published and telephonic access was not as wide-spread as it is today) Finally, the third criterion is to ensure that everyone knows the proper channels of communication. Barnard (1938) states that "authority requires a definite formal channel of communication to every member of an organization". This maximizes the relevance of the message because it allows the "correct" person to be in receipt of the message when it is transmitted the first time. Although avoiding discussing non-repudiation or similar information assurance related concepts of communication because they did not exist at the time of publication, Barnard does assign a value (while not always quantifiable) to the loss of communications that were not properly received or transmitted. His theory on managerial communications stresses the importance of getting the information to the right people at the right time. From personal experience inside the defence sector and military, providing time-critical, mission-relevant information to the combatant commanders on the ground is imperative for operational success and sustainment.

### *Cooperative Systems and Organizations*

One of the theories that Barnard had is that of cooperative systems and formal organizations. Defined as "a system of consciously coordinated activities or forces of two or more persons", formal organizations in business structures are not normal, but abnormal. Barnard states (1938) that "In western civilization only one formal organization, the Roman Catholic Church, claims substantial 'age'" due to the fact that so many organizations fail after inception. When describing the corporate powerhouses of business and industry, "what are observed from day to day are successful survivors among innumerable failures." Barnard stated there are two main factors for cooperative success; effectiveness and efficiency. Barnard defined efficiency as "the satisfaction of individual motives" and defined effectiveness as "the ultimate objective of cooperative action". (1938) He is notable for correlating the relationship between employee's personal values and desires and the objectives of the organization. It is this symbiotic relationship which Barnard argues, is the premise for successful organizations. He advocates aligning the objectives of the individual with those of the organization to create a harmonious, yet productive, work environment. "Barnard speaks of the limited value of material incentives, and the necessity for adoption of certain methods of persuasion" (Chandran, 1998), and therefore, takes a more sociological approach to motivating his employees. Barnard states "Cooperation... means genuine restraint of self in many directions, it means actual service for no reward, (and) it means courage to fight for principles rather than for things..." (Scott, 1992) and subsequently, discovers alternative methods of compensation and motivation that are void of material objects such as confidence, validation, and acceptance.

### *Logical Fallacies and Errors*

Considering the theories were written by 1) an individual who is well known for not being an academic, and 2) written for functional use and reference as compared to scholarly evaluation, Barnard had relatively few logical fallacies. Most of his logical fallacies are based on his constant application of personal experience and self-representation as an expert in the field without the use of supporting citation and references. However, the author does not discount Barnard's material as logically flawed because Barnard uses the available knowledge at a time when modern management theory was being developed and applies that knowledge to applicable situations. His attention to nuances not yet identified (as of the early and mid 1900's) speaks volumes to his ability to independently analyse situations and areas of improvement within management. The fact that his book was written for functional use and education of other executives and managers needs to be considered when critics of his teachings assign a lower "scholarship value" to the material based on lack of accepted technical principles and other theorists work. The author finds Barnard's use of other's work adequate for what was described and Barnard's references understandable considering his background, education, and professional experience.

Another error that many scholars point out is the fact that the book, The Functions of the Executive, is not written in a linear, concise manner. Many of the quotes derived from the book need to be rearranged in order to validate a point or clarify a topic. The focus of the book shifts from direct comparison to abstract thought and back again too many times to be considered for modern acceptance as scholarly material. Chandran points out that "the discontinuity in chronology… is a common failing of the book." (1998) The author agrees that the chronology of the text is abstract and contend that alone does not disqualify it for being unscholarly.

### Alternative Viewpoints

Few theorists come to mind when discussing alternative and opposing viewpoints of Chester Barnard. The most prolific is Mary Parker Follett. Since Parker was known for her views on management as being reciprocal relationships, where respect is mutually exchanged and authority is granted on that basis, Barnard's theories on authority are a natural comparison and somewhat similar. Since Barnard's time, many management theorists have added to, or detracted from, Barnard's teachings. William G. Scott of the University of Washington has written several articles (Scott, 1982; 1992) on Barnard and generally praised his work as groundbreaking, while also seeking to deliver clarification on Barnard's principles and delineation on Barnard's theories.

"Even those who take vigorous exception to Barnard's views concede his vast influence in organizational theory." (Mahoney, 2002) Steven M. Dunphy and James Hoopes published an article critical of Barnard, Barnard's implied self-description as "elite", and of Barnard's moral appreciation which actually caused (the author) a renewed confidence in Barnard's theories. The conclusion of Dunphy and Hoopes article referred to Barnard's theories as having the ability to "create some measure of equal opportunity and foster greater societal synergy… by addressing and perhaps embracing (Barnard's) concepts and arguments which have been sifted through the filter of time." (Dunphy & Hoopes, 2002) After reading both works, the author further solidified his position that Barnard is one of the most influential management theorists of all time.

## Barnard's Relevance Today

Barnard has been enormously influential in the study and classification of management and management theories. In fact, Bedeian and Wren actually specified Chester Barnard's The Functions of the Executive as the 2nd most influential management book of the twentieth century. (2001) His explanations on organizing a group to follow clear cut lines of authority and communication are still in existence today. One segment of his theories outlined in The Functions of the Executive (1938) is specialization in organizations and away from the executive. "The immediate staff of the executive, consisting of deputies, or chief clerks, or adjutants, or auxiliaries with their assistants, constitute an executive unit of organization (, of which) only one member of which is an 'executive', that is, occupies the *position* of authority;

and technical matters are assigned to staff departments or organizations of experts." This is a crucial tasking for today's executive because of the enormous growth of technology and other specialized fields. As business sciences further stray towards specialization and subject matter experts, executives need to be willing to embrace and direct responsibility and authority to those with specific needs for it.

## Scholastic Value

While Chester Barnard did not receive formal education in the path many other business and academic theorists did, his teachings have long been used as a scholarly tool and drawn upon by other, more "educated" researchers. Much of his research is based in personal experience and trial and error. Barnard avoided (to the best of his ability) drawing on other's works and chose instead to focus on intrinsic beliefs and values. The author believes that his theories and concepts do have significant scholarly value and "his accomplishments were recognized by many universities. In fact, during his later years, he turned down a number of honorary degrees." Wolf states (1961) that Barnard was offered fifteen or twenty honorary doctorate degrees from universities such as: University of California, Chicago, Rutgers, Brown, Pennsylvania, and Princeton. While accepting some degrees, Barnard was a "self-educated, self-made man... a man of affairs and a philosopher."

Another surprisingly valuable aspect of Barnard's teachings is the fact that his theories "inspire(s) succeeding generations of both scholars and practitioners, remaining a wellspring for contemporary thinking" not only in scholarly areas, but also industrial ones. From researching Barnard, the author found that many of his writings, if not the majority of them, are based or stored on professional or industrial databases, as compared to academic ones. This only further advances the idea that Barnard was more than an academic theorist, but an established practitioner of management, business, and leadership.

### *Conclusion and Findings*

Defining the life and accomplishments of a theorist more intelligent and established than the author, is difficult. While the author accepts and understands opposing viewpoints, acknowledges certain theories no longer apply in the current management arena, and continually facilitates other theories, the author believes that Chester Barnard is one of the most specific and accurate management theorists of all time. The author appreciates the fact that Barnard addresses issues that are not politically correct in today's tense business environment and personally agree that executives are of a higher "status" than rank and file workers. He does a fantastic job outlining the fact that with greater status comes greater responsibility, while he did a fantastic job executing that belief in executive positions during his career. The author believes Barnard's theories are well rooted in management science and find that his thoughts on executive management, managerial communications, and cooperative systems are still very much applicable today. The author anticipates that Barnard's theories will continue to be used well in to the next century as a basis for management scholarship and examination.

# 4

# Chris Argyris

Chris Argyris (born July 16, 1923 in Newark, New Jersey, USA) is an American business theorist, Professor Emeritus at Harvard Business School, and a Thought Leader at Monitor Group. He is commonly known for seminal work in the area of "Learning Organizations".

*Action Science*, Argyris' collaborative work with Robert W. Putnam (not to be confused with Robert D. Putnam) and Diana McLain Smith, advocates an approach to research that focuses on generating knowledge that is useful in solving practical problems. Other key concepts developed by Argyris include Ladder of Inference, Double-Loop Learning, Theory of Action/Espoused Theory/Theory-in-use, High Advocacy/High Inquiry dialogue and Actionable Knowledge.

Chris Argyris' early research explored the impact of formal organizational structures, control systems and management on individuals and how they responded and adapted to them. This research resulted in the books *Personality and Organization*, 1957 and *Integrating the Individual and the Organization*, 1964. He then shifted his focus to organizational change, in particular exploring the behaviour of senior executives in organizations.

From there he moved onto an inquiry into the role of the social scientist as both researcher and actor. His fourth major area of research and theorizing – in significant part undertaken with Donald Schön – was in individual and organizational learning and the extent to which human reasoning, not just behaviour, can become the basis for diagnosis and action. He has also developed this thinking in *Overcoming Organizational Defenses*, 1990 and *Knowledge for Action*, 1993.

### *Action Science*

Argyris' concept of Action Science begins with the study of how human beings design their actions in difficult situations. Human actions are designed to achieve intended consequences and governed by a set of environment variables. How those governing variables are treated in designing actions are the key differences between single loop learning and double loop learning. When actions are designed to achieve the intended consequences and to suppress conflict about the governing variables, a single loop learning cycle usually ensues. On the other hand, when actions are taken, not only to achieve the intended consequences, but also to openly inquire about conflict and to possibly transform the governing variables, both single loop and double loop learning cycles usually ensue. (Argyris applies single loop and double loop learning concepts not only to personal behaviors but also to organizational behaviors in his models.)

### *Honorary degree*

Chris Argyris received an Honorary Doctor of Laws degree from the University of Toronto in 2006. The work of Chris Argyris (1923-) has influenced thinking about the relationship of people and organizations, organizational learning and action research. Here we examine some key aspects of his thinking. Chris Argyris has made a significant contribution to the development of our appreciation of organizational learning, and, almost in passing, deepened our understanding of experiential learning. On this page we examine the significance of the models he developed with Donald Schön of single-loop and double-loop learning, and how these translate into contrasting models of organizational learning systems.

### *Life*

Chris Argyris was born in Newark, New Jersey on July 16, 1923 and grew up in Irvington, New Jersey. During the Second World War he joined the Signal Corps in the U.S. Army eventually becoming a Second Lieutenant (Elkjaer 2000). He went to university at Clark, where he came into contact with Kurt Lewin (Lewin had begun the Research Centre for Group Dynamics at M.I.T.). He graduated with a degree in Psychology (1947). He went on to gain an MA in Psychology and Economics from Kansas University

(1949), and a Ph.D. in Organizational Behaviour from Cornell University (he was supervised by William F. Whyte) in 1951. In a distinguished career Chris Argyris has been a faculty member at Yale University (1951-1971) where he served as the Beach Professor of Administrative Science and Chairperson of the department; and the James Bryant Conant Professor of Education and Organizational Behaviour at Harvard University (1971-). Argyris is currently a director of the Monitor Company in Cambridge, Massachusetts.

Chris Argyris' early research explored the impact of formal organizational structures, control systems, and management on individuals (and how they responded and adapted to them). This research resulted in the books *Personality and Organization* (1957) and *Integrating the Individual and the Organization* (1964). He then shifted his focus to organizational change, in particular exploring the behaviour of senior executives in organizations. From there he moved onto a particularly fruitful inquiry into the role of the social scientist as both researcher and actor. Much of the focus on this page lies with his fourth major area of research and theorizing – in significant part undertaken with Donald Schön – around individual and organizational learning. Here the interest lies in the extent to which human reasoning, not just behaviour, can become the basis for diagnosis and action

As well as writing and researching, Chris Argyris has been an influential teacher. This is how Peter Senge (1990: 182-3) talks about his own experience of Argyris as a teacher.

Despite having read much of his writing, I was unprepared for what I learned when I first saw Chris Argyris practice his approach in an informal workshop... Ostensibly an academic presentation of Argyris's methods, it quickly evolved into a powerful demonstration of what action science practitioners call 'reflection in action'.... Within a matter of minutes, I watched the level of alertness and 'presentness' of the entire group rise ten notches – thanks not so much to Argyris's personal charisma, but to his skilful practice of drawing out... generalizations. As the afternoon moved on, all of us were led to see (sometimes for he first time in our lives) subtle patterns of reasoning which underlay our behaviour; and how those patterns continually got us into trouble. I had never had such a dramatic demonstration of own mental models in action... But even more interesting, it became clear that, with proper training, I could become much more aware of my mental models and how they operated. This was exciting. The ability, demonstrated here, to engage with others, to make links with the general and the particular, and to explore basic orientations and values is just what Argyris talks about when exploring the sorts of behaviours and beliefs that are necessary if organizations are to learn and develop.

## Theory in Use and Espoused Theory

Our starting point is Argyris and Schön's (1974) argument that people have mental maps with regard to how to act in situations. This involves the way they plan, implement and review their actions. Furthermore, they assert that it is these maps that guide people's actions rather than the theories they explicitly espouse. What is more, fewer people are aware of the maps or theories they do use (Argyris, 1980). One way of making sense of this is to say that there is split between theory and action. However, Argyris and Schön suggest that two *theories of action* are involved.

The notion of a theory of action can be seen as growing out of earlier research by Chris Argyris into the relationships between individuals and organizations. A theory of action is first a theory: 'its most general properties are properties that all theories share, and the most general criteria that apply to it – such as generality, centrality and simplicity-are criteria applied to all theories'. The distinction made between the two contrasting theories of action is between those theories that are implicit in what we do as practitioners and managers, and those on which we call to speak of our actions to others. The former can be described as *theories-in-use*. They govern actual behaviour and tend to be tacit structures. Their relation to action 'is like the relation of grammar-in-use to speech; they contain assumptions about self, others and environment-these assumptions constitute a microcosm of science in everyday life'. The words we use to convey what we, do or what we would like others to think we do, can then be called *espoused theory*.

When someone is asked how he would behave under certain circumstances, the answer he usually gives is his espoused theory of action for that situation. This is the theory of action to which he gives allegiance, and which, upon request, he communicates to others. However, the theory that actually governs his actions is this theory-in-use.

Making this distinction allows us to ask questions about the extent to which behaviour fits espoused theory; and whether inner feelings become expressed in actions. In other words, is there congruence between the two? Argyris (1980) makes the case that effectiveness results from developing congruence between theory-in-use and espoused theory. For example, in explaining our actions to a colleague we may call upon some convenient piece of theory. We might explain our sudden rush out of the office to others, or even to ourselves at some level, by saying that a 'crisis' had arisen with one of 'our' clients. The theory-in-use might be quite different. We may have become bored and tired by the paper work or meeting and felt that a quick trip out to an apparently difficult situation would bring welcome relief. A key role of reflection, we could argue, is to reveal the theory-in-use and to explore the nature of the 'fit'. Much of the business of supervision, where it is focused on the practitioner's thoughts, feelings and actions, is concerned with the gulf between espoused theory and theory-in-use or in bringing the later to the surface. This gulf is no bad thing. If it gets too wide then there is clearly a difficulty. But provided the two remain connected then the gap creates a dynamic for reflection and for dialogue.

To fully appreciate theory-in-use we require a model of the processes involved. To this end Argyris and Schön (1974) initially looked to three elements: Governing variables: those dimensions that people are trying to keep within acceptable limits. Any action is likely to impact upon a number of such variables – thus any situation can trigger a trade-off among governing variables.

Action strategies: the moves and plans used by people to keep their governing values within the acceptable range. Consequences: what happens as a result of an action. These can be both intended-those actor believe will result-and unintended. In addition those consequences can be for the self, and/or for others. (Anderson 1997). Where the consequences of the strategy used are what the person wanted, then the theory-in-use is confirmed. This is because there is a match between intention and outcome. There may be a mismatch between intention and outcome. In other words, the consequences may be unintended. They may also not match, or work against, the person's governing values. Argyris and Schön suggest two responses to this mismatch, and these are can be seen in the notion of single and double-loop learning.

### *Double-loop Learning*

For Argyris and Schön (1978: 2) learning involves the detection and correction of error. Where something goes wrong, it is suggested, an initial port of call for many people is to look for another strategy that will address and work within the governing variables. In other words, given or chosen goals, values, plans and rules are operationalized rather than questioned. According to Argyris and Schön (1974), this is *single-loop learning*. An alternative response is to question to governing variables themselves, to subject them to critical scrutiny. This they describe as *double-loop learning*. Such learning may then lead to an alteration in the governing variables and, thus, a shift in the way in which strategies and consequences are framed. Thus, when they came to explore the nature of organizational learning. This is how Argyris and Schön (1978: 2-3) described the process in the context of organizational learning:

When the error detected and corrected permits the organization to carry on its present policies or achieve its presents objectives, then that error-and-correction process is *single-loop* learning. Single-loop learning is like a thermostat that learns when it is too hot or too cold and turns the heat on or off. The thermostat can perform this task because it can receive information (the temperature of the room) and take corrective action. *Double-loop* learning occurs when error is detected and corrected in ways that involve the modification of an organization's underlying norms, policies and objectives.

Single-loop learning seems to be present when goals, values, frameworks and, to a significant extent, strategies are taken for granted. The emphasis is on 'techniques and making techniques more efficient' Any reflection is directed toward making the strategy more effective. Double-loop learning, in contrast, 'involves questioning the role of the framing and learning systems which underlie actual goals and strategies (*op. cit.)*. In many respects the distinction at work here is the one used by Aristotle, when exploring technical and practical thought. The former involves following routines and some sort of preset plan – and is both less risky for the individual and the organization, and affords greater control. The latter is more creative and reflexive, and involves consideration notions of the good. Reflection here is more fundamental: the basic assumptions behind ideas or policies are confronted... hypotheses are publicly tested... processes are disconfirmable not self-seeking.

The focus of much of Chris Argyris' intervention research has been to explore how organizations may increase their capacity for double-loop learning. He argues that double-loop learning is necessary if practitioners and organizations are to make informed decisions in rapidly changing and often uncertain contexts. As Edmondson and Moingeon (1999:160) put it:

The underlying theory, supported by years of empirical research, is that the reasoning processes employed by individuals in organizations inhibit the exchange of relevant information in ways that make double-loop learning difficult – and all but impossible in situations in which much is at stake. This creates a dilemma as these are the very organizational situations in which double-loop learning is most needed.

The next step that Argyris and Schön take is to set up two models that describe features of theories-in-use that either inhibit or enhance double-loop learning. The belief is that all people utilize a common theory-in-use in problematic situations. This they describe as Model I – and it can be said to inhibit double-loop learning. Model II is where the governing values associated with theories-in-use enhance double-loop learning.

## *Model I and Model II*

Argyris has claimed that just about all the participants in his studies operated from theories-in-use or values consistent with Model I (Argyris et al. 1985: 89). It involves 'making inferences about another person's behaviour without checking whether they are valid and advocating one's own views abstractly without explaining or illustrating one's reasoning'. The theories-in-use are shaped by an implicit disposition to winning (and to avoid embarrassment). The primary action strategy looks to the unilateral control of the environment and task plus the unilateral protection of self and others. As such Model I leads to often deeply entrenched defensive routines (Argyris 1990; 1993) – and these can operate at individual, group and organizational levels. Exposing actions, thoughts and feelings can make people vulnerable to the reaction of others. However, the assertion that Model I is predominantly defensive has a further consequence:

> Acting defensively can be viewed as moving away from something, usually some truth about ourselves. If our actions are driven by moving away from something then our actions are controlled and defined by whatever it is we are moving away from, not by us and what we would like to be moving towards. Therefore our potential for growth and learning is seriously impaired. If my behaviour is driven by my not wanting to be seen as incompetent, this may lead me to hide things from myself and others, in order to avoid feelings of incompetence. For example, if my behaviour is driven by wanting to be competent, honest evaluation of my behaviour by myself and others would be welcome and useful. (Anderson 1997)

It is only by interrogating and changing the governing values, the argument goes, is it possible to produce new action strategies that can address changing circumstances. Chris Argyris looks to move people from a Model I to a Model II orientation and practice – one that fosters double-loop learning. He suggests that most people, when asked, will *espouse* Model II. As Anderson (1997) has commented, Argyris offers no reason why most people espouse Model II. In addition, we need to note that the vast bulk of research around the models has been undertaken by Argyris or his associates.

The significant features of Model II include the ability to call upon good quality data and to make inferences. It looks to include the views and experiences of participants rather than seeking to impose a view upon the situation. Theories should be made explicit and tested, positions should be reasoned and open to exploration by others. In other words, Model II can be seen as dialogical – and more likely to be found in settings and organizations that look to shared leadership. As Edmondson and Moingeon (1999:162) comment, employing Model II in difficult interpersonal interactions 'requires profound attentiveness and skill for human beings socialized in a Model I world'. While they are not being asked to relinquish control altogether, they do need to share that control.

### *Organizational Learning*

Chris Argyris and Donald Schön suggest that each member of an organization constructs his or her own representation or image of the theory-in-use of the whole (1978: 16). The picture is always incomplete – and people, thus, are continually working to add pieces and to get a view of the whole. They need to know their place in the organization, it is argued. An organization is like an organism each of whose cells contains a particular, partial, changing image if itself in relation to the whole. And like such an organism, the organization's practice stems from those very images. Organization is an artifact of individual ways of representing organization.

Hence, our inquiry into organizational learning must concern itself not with static entities called organizations, but with an active process of organizing which is, at root, a cognitive enterprise. Individual members are continually engaged in attempting to know the organization, and to know themselves in the context of the organization. At the same time, their continuing efforts to know and to test their knowledge represent the object of their inquiry. Organizing is reflexive inquiry.... [Members] require external references. There must be public representations of organizational theory-in-use to which individuals can refer. This is the function of organizational maps. These are the shared descriptions of the organization which individuals jointly construct and use to guide their own inquiry....

Organizational theory-in-use, continually constructed through individual inquiry, is encoded in private images and in public maps. These are the media of organizational learning. With this set of moves we can see how Chris Argyris and Donald Schön connect up the individual world of the worker and practitioner with the world of organization. Their focus is much more strongly on individual and group interactions and defenses than upon systems and structures (we could contrast their position with that of Peter Senge 1990, for example). By looking at the way that people jointly construct maps it is then possible to talk about organizational learning (involving the detection and correction of error) and organizational theory-in-use. For organizational learning to occur, 'learning agents', discoveries, inventions, and evaluations must be embedded in organizational memory' (Argyris and Schön 1978: 19). If it is not encoded in the images that individuals have, and the maps they construct with others, then 'the individual will have learned but the organization will not have done so' (*op. cit.*).

In this organizational schema single-loop learning is characterized as when, 'members of the organization respond to changes in the internal and external environment of the organization by detecting errors which they then correct so as to maintain the central features of theory-in-use' (*ibid.*: 18). Double-loop learning then becomes: ... those sorts of organizational inquiry which resolve incompatible organizational norms by setting new priorities and weightings of norms, or by restructuring the norms themselves together with associated strategies and assumptions.

The next step is to argue that individuals using Model I create Organizational I (O-I) learning systems. These are characterized by 'defensiveness, self-fulfilling prophecies, self-fuelling processes, and escalating error' (Argyris 1982: 8). O-I systems involve a web of feedback loops that 'make organizational assumptions and behavioural routines self-reinforcing – inhibiting "detection and correction of error" and giving rise to mistrust, defensiveness and self-fulfilling prophecy'. In other words, if individuals in an organization make use of Model I learning the organization itself can begin to function in ways that act against its long-term interests. Indeed, in a very real sense systems can begin to malfunction. As Argyris and Schön (1996: 28) put it, 'The actions we take to promote productive organizational learning actually inhibit deeper learning'. The challenge is, then, to create a rare phenomenon – an Organizational II (O-II) learning system.

Here we come to the focus of organizational effort – the formulation and implementation of an intervention strategy. This, according to Argyris and Schön (1978: 220-1) involves the 'interventionist' in moving through six phases of work:

***Phase 1:*** Mapping the problem as clients see it. This includes the factors and relationships that define the problem, and the relationship with the living systems of the organization.

***Phase 2:*** The internalization of the map by clients. Through inquiry and confrontation the interventionists work with clients to develop a map for which clients can accept responsibility. However, it also needs to be comprehensive.

***Phase 3:*** Test the model. This involves looking at what 'testable predictions' can be derived from the map – and looking to practice and history to see if the predictions stand up. If they do not, the map has to be modified.

***Phase 4:*** Invent solutions to the problem and simulate them to explore their possible impact.

***Phase 5:*** Produce the intervention.

***Phase 6:*** Study the impact. This allows for the correction of errors as well as generating knowledge for future designs. If things work well under the conditions specified by the model, then the map is not disconfirmed.

By running through this sequence and attending to key criteria suggested by Model II, it is argued, organizational development is possible. The process entails looking for the maximum participation of clients, minimizing the risks of candid participation, starting where people want to begin (often with instrumental problems), and designing methods so that they value rationality and honesty.

### Conclusion

How are we to evaluate these models and line of argument? First, we can say that while there has been a growing research base concerning the models and interventionist strategy, it is still limited – and people sympathetic to the approach have largely undertaken it. However, as Peter Senge's experience (recounted at the top of the page) demonstrates, the process and the focus on reflection-in-action does appear to bear fruit in terms of people's connection with the exercise and their readiness to explore personal and organizational questions.

Second, it is assumed that 'good' learning 'takes place in a climate of openness where political behaviour is minimized'. This is an assumption that can be questioned. It could be argued that organizations are inherently political – and that it is important to recognize this. Organizations can be seen as coalitions of various individuals and interest groups. 'Organizational goals, structure and policies emerge from an ongoing process of bargaining and negotiation among major interest groups' Bolman and Deal 1997: 175). Thus, perhaps we need to develop theory that looks to the political nature of structures, knowledge and information. Here we might profitably look to games theory, the contribution of partisan and political institutions (Beem 1999) and an exploration of how managers can make explicit, and work with, political processes (Coopey 1998). Perhaps the aim should be 'to incorporate politics into organizational learning, rather than to eradicate it'.

Third, and this might be my prejudice, I think we need to be distrustful of bipolar models like Model I and Model II. They tend to set up an 'either-or' orientation. They are useful as teaching or sensitizing devices, alerting us to different and important aspects of organizational life, but the area between the models (and beyond them) might well yield interesting alternatives.

Fourth, the interventionist strategy is staged or phased – and this does bring with it some problems. Why should things operate in this order. Significantly, this does highlight a tension between Argyris's orientation and that of Schön (1983). Schön in his later work on reflection-in-action draws on his pragmatist heritage (and especially the work of Dewey) and presents the making of theory-in-action and the expression of professional artistry in a far less linear fashion. Rather than there being phases, we could argue that intervention of this kind involves a number of elements or dimensions working at once.

This said, the theorizing of theory-in-action, the educative power of the models, and the conceptualization of organizational learning have been, and continue to be, significant contributions to our appreciation of processes in organizations. The notion of 'double-loop learning' does help us to approach some of the more taken-for-granted aspects of organizations and experiences. It provides us with a way of naming a phenomenon (and problem), and a possible way of 'learning our way out' (Finger and Asún 2000). Argyris and Schön have made a significant contribution to pragmatic learning theory. First, by introducing the term 'theory' or 'theory in action', 'they provide the function of abstract conceptualization 'more structure and more coherence'. Abstract conceptualization 'becomes something one can analyse and work from' (*op. cit.*). Second, through the notion of 'learning-in-action' Argyris and Schön rework the experiential learning cycle.

Unlike Dewey's, Lewin's or Kolb's learning cycle, where one had, so to speak, to make a mistake and reflect upon it – that is, learn by trial and error – it is now possible thanks to Argyris and Schön's conceptualization, to learn by simply reflecting critically upon the theory-in-action. In other words, it is no longer necessary to go through the entire learning circle in order to develop the theory further. It is sufficient to readjust the theory through double-loop learning.

This is a very significant development and has important implications for educators. In the experiential learning model of Kolb (1984) the educator is in essence a facilitator of a person's learning cycle. To this role can be added that of teacher, coach or mentor, the person who 'helps individuals (managers, professionals, workers) to reflect upon their theories-in-action'. It is a significant development – but it has gone largely unnoticed in the adult education and lifelong learning fields. This is a result, in part, of rather blinkered reading by professionals and academics within that area, and because Argyris and Schön did not address, to any significant degree, the arena directly (Argyris's continued to focus on organization and management, and Schön's on professional thinking).

# 5

# Douglas McGregor

Douglas McGregor (1906 – 1964) was a Management professor at the MIT Sloan School of Management and president of Antioch College from 1948 to 1954. He also taught at the Indian Institute of Management Calcutta. His 1960 book *The Human Side of Enterprise* had a profound influence on education practices. In the book he identified an approach of creating an environment within which employees are motivated via authoritative, direction and control or integration and self-control, which he called theory X and theory Y, respectively. Theory Y is the practical application of Dr. Abraham Maslow's Humanistic School of Psychology, or Third Force psychology, applied to scientific management.

He is commonly thought of as being a *proponent* of Theory Y, but, as Edgar Schein tells in his introduction to McGregor's subsequent, posthumous (1967), book *The Professional Manager* : "In my own contacts with Doug, I often found him to be discouraged by the degree to which theory Y had become as monolithic a set of principles as those of Theory X, the over-generalization which Doug was fighting....Yet few readers were willing to acknowledge that the content of Doug's book made such a neutral point or that Doug's own presentation of his point of view was that coldly scientific".

Graham Cleverley in *Managers & Magic* (Longman's, 1971) comments: "...he coined the two terms Theory X and theory Y and used them to label two sets of beliefs a manager might hold about the origins of human behaviour. He pointed out that the manager's own behaviour would be largely determined by the particular beliefs that he subscribed to....McGregor hoped that his book would lead managers to investigate the two sets of beliefs, invent others, test out the assumptions underlying them, and develop managerial strategies that made sense in terms of those tested views of reality. "But that isn't what happened. Instead McGregor was interpreted as advocating Theory Y as a new and superior ethic-a set of moral values that *ought* to replace the values managers usually accept."

He earned a B.E. Mechanical from Rangoon Institute of Technology, an A.B. from Wayne State University in 1932, then earned an M.A. and Ph.D. in psychology from Harvard University in 1933 and 1935 respectively. In the 1970's, the McGregor school, a graduate level business school, was founded by Antioch College in his honour.

## Human Relations Contributors

### *Douglas McGregor*

*Theory X and Theory Y*

Douglas McGregor in his book, "The Human Side of Enterprise" published in 1960 has examined theories on behaviour of individuals at work, and he has formulated two models which he calls Theory X and Theory Y.

#### *Theory X Assumptions*

The average human being has an inherent dislike of work and will avoid it if he can.

- Because of their dislike for work, most people must be controlled and threatened before they will work hard enough.
- The average human prefers to be directed, dislikes responsibility, is unambiguous, and desires security above everything.
- These assumptions lie behind most organizational principles today, and give rise both to "tough" management with punishments and tight controls, and "soft" management which aims at harmony at work.
- Both these are "wrong" because man needs more than financial rewards at work, he also needs some deeper higher order motivation-the opportunity to fulfil himself.

- Theory X managers do not give their staff this opportunity so that the employees behave in the expected fashion.

*Theory Y Assumptions*

- The expenditure of physical and mental effort in work is as natural as play or rest.
- Control and punishment are not the only ways to make people work, man will direct himself if he is committed to the aims of the organization.
- If a job is satisfying, then the result will be commitment to the organization.
- The average man learns, under proper conditions, not only to accept but to seek responsibility.
- Imagination, creativity, and ingenuity can be used to solve work problems by a large number of employees.
- Under the conditions of modern industrial life, the intellectual potentialities of the average man are only partially utilized.

## Comments on Theory X and Theory Y Assumptions

These assumptions are based on social science research which has been carried out, and demonstrate the potential which is present in man and which organizations should recognize in order to become more effective. McGregor sees these two theories as two quite separate attitudes. Theory Y is difficult to put into practice on the shop floor in large mass production operations, but it can be used initially in the managing of managers and professionals.

In "The Human Side of Enterprise" McGregor shows how Theory Y affects the management of promotions and salaries and the development of effective managers. McGregor also sees Theory Y as conducive to participative problem solving. It is part of the manager's job to exercise authority, and there are cases in which this is the only method of achieving the desired results because subordinates do not agree that the ends are desirable.

However, in situations where it is possible to obtain commitment to objectives, it is better to explain the matter fully so that employees grasp the purpose of an action. They will then exert self-direction and control to do better work-quite possibly by better methods-than if they had simply been carrying out an order which the y did not fully understand.

The situation in which employees can be consulted is one where the individuals are emotionally mature, and positively motivated towards their work; where the work is sufficiently responsible to allow for flexibility and where the employee can see her or his own position in the management hierarchy. If these conditions are present, managers will find that the participative approach to problem solving leads to much improved results compared with the alternative approach of handing out authoritarian orders. Once management becomes persuaded that it is under estimating the potential of its human resources, and accepts the knowledge given by social science researchers and displayed in Theory Y assumptions, then it can invest time, money and effort in developing improved applications of the theory.

McGregor realizes that some of the theories he has put forward are unrealizable in practice, but wants managers to put into operation the basic assumption that:

## Theory X and theory Y

Theory X and Theory Y are theories of human motivation created and developed by Douglas McGregor at the MIT Sloan School of Management in the 1960s that have been used in human resource management, organizational behaviour, organizational communication and organizational development. They describe two very different attitudes toward workforce motivation. McGregor felt that companies followed either one or the other approach. He also thought that the key to connecting self-actualization with work is determined by the managerial trust of subordinates.

### *Theory X*

In this theory, which has been proven counter-effective in most modern practice, management assumes employees are inherently lazy and will avoid work if they can and that they inherently dislike work. As a result of this, management believes that workers need to be closely supervised and comprehensive systems of controls developed. A hierarchical structure is needed with narrow span of control at each and every level. According to this theory, employees will show little ambition without an enticing incentive program and will avoid responsibility whenever they can. According to Michael J. Papa, if the organizational goals are to be met, theory X managers rely heavily on threat and coercion to gain their employee's compliance. Beliefs of this theory lead to mistrust, highly restrictive supervision, and a punitive atmosphere. The Theory X manager tends to believe that everything must end in blaming someone. He or she thinks all prospective employees are only out for themselves. Usually these managers feel the sole purpose of the employee's interest in the job is money. They will blame the person first in most situations, without questioning whether it may be the system, policy, or lack of training that deserves the blame. A Theory X manager believes that his or her employees do not really want to work, that they would rather avoid responsibility and that it is the manager's job to structure the work and energize the employee. One major flaw of this management style is it is much more likely to cause Diseconomies of Scale in large businesses.

### *Theory Y*

In this theory, management assumes employees *may be* ambitious and self-motivated and exercise self-control. It is believed that employees enjoy their mental and physical work duties. According to Papa, to them work is as natural as play. They possess the ability for creative problem solving, but their talents are underused in most organizations. Given the proper conditions, theory Y managers believe that employees will learn to seek out and accept responsibility and to exercise self-control and self-direction in accomplishing objectives to which they are committed. A Theory Y manager believes that, given the right conditions, most people will want to do well at work. They believe that the satisfaction of doing a good job is a strong motivation. Many people interpret Theory Y as a positive set of beliefs about workers. A close reading of The Human Side of Enterprise reveals that McGregor simply argues for managers to be open to a more positive view of workers and the possibilities that this creates. He thinks that Theory Y managers are more likely than Theory X managers to develop the climate of trust with employees that is required for human resource development. It's here through human resource development that is a crucial aspect of any organization. This would include managers communicating openly with subordinates, minimizing the difference between superior-subordinate relationships, creating a comfortable environment in which subordinates can develop and use their abilities. This climate would include the sharing of decision making so that subordinates have say in decisions that influence them. This theory is a positive view to the employees.

### *Theory X and Theory Y combined*

For McGregor, Theory X and Y are not different ends of the same continuum. Rather they are two different continua in themselves. Thus, if a manager needs to apply Theory Y principles, that does not preclude him from being a part of Theory X & Y.

### *McGregor and Maslow's hierarchy*

McGregor's work was based on Maslow's hierarchy of needs. He grouped Maslow's hierarchy into "lower order" (Theory X) needs and "higher order" (Theory Y) needs. He suggested that management could use either set of needs to motivate employees. As management theorists became familiar with Maslow's work, they soon realized the possibility of connecting higher level needs to worker motivation. If organizational goals and individual needs could be integrated so that people would acquire self-esteem and, ultimately, self-actualization through work, then motivation would be self-sustaining. Today, his Theory Y principle influences the design of personnel policies, affects the way companies conduct performance reviews, and shapes the idea of pay for performance. According to the *Douglas McGregor: Theory X and Theory Y* article, "He is the reason we use the term 'human resources' instead of personnel department" says Brzezinski. "The idea that people are assets was unheard of before McGregor."

### *Criticisms*

Today the theories are seldom used explicitly, largely because the insights they provided have influenced and been incorporated by further generations of management theorists and practitioners. More commonly, workplaces are described as "hard" versus "soft." Taken too literally any such dichotomy including Theory X and Y seem to represent unrealistic extremes. Most employees (and managers) fall somewhere in between these poles. Naturally, McGregor was well aware of the heuristic as opposed to literal way in which such distinctions are useful. Theory X and Theory Y are still important terms in the field of management and motivation. Recent studies have questioned the rigidity of the model, but McGregor's X-Y Theory remains a guiding principle of positive approaches to management, to organizational development, and to improving organizational culture.

Douglas McGregor, an American social psychologist, proposed his famous X-Y theory in his 1960 book 'The Human Side Of Enterprise'. Theory x and theory y are still referred to commonly in the field of management and motivation, and whilst more recent studies have questioned the rigidity of the model, Mcgregor's X-Y Theory remains a valid basic principle from which to develop positive management style and techniques. McGregor's XY Theory remains central to organizational development, and to improving organizational culture. McGregor's X-Y theory is a salutary and simple reminder of the natural rules for managing people, which under the pressure of day-to-day business are all too easily forgotten. McGregor maintained that there are two fundamental approaches to managing people. Many managers tend towards theory x, and generally get poor results. Enlightened managers use theory y, which produces better performance and results, and allows people to grow and develop.

***Theory x ('Authoritarian Management' Style)***

- The average person dislikes work and will avoid it he/ she can.
- Therefore most people must be forced with the threat of punishment to work towards organisational objectives.
- The average person prefers to be directed; to avoid responsibility; is relatively unambitious, and wants security above all else.

***Theory y ('Participative Management' Style)***

- Effort in work is as natural as work and play.
- People will apply self-control and self-direction in the pursuit of organisational objectives, without external control or the threat of punishment.

- Commitment to objectives is a function of rewards associated with their achievement.
- People usually accept and often seek responsibility.
- The capacity to use a high degree of imagination, ingenuity and creativity in solving organisational problems is widely, not narrowly, distributed in the population.
- In industry the intellectual potential of the average person is only partly utilised.

## Tools for Teaching

The XY Theory diagram and measurement tool below are adaptations of McGregor's ideas for modern organizations, management and work. They were not created by McGregor. I developed them to help understanding and application of McGregor's XY Theory concept. The test is a simple reflective tool, not a scientifically validated instrument; it's a learning aid and broad indicator. Please use it as such.

### *Characteristics of the x Theory Manager*

Perhaps the most noticeable aspects of McGregor's XY Theory-and the easiest to illustrate-are found in the behaviours of autocratic managers and organizations which use autocratic management styles.

What are the characteristics of a Theory X manager? Typically some, most or all of these:

- results-driven and deadline-driven, to the exclusion of everything else
- intolerant
- issues deadlines and ultimatums
- distant and detached
- aloof and arrogant
- elitist
- short temper
- shouts
- issues instructions, directions, edicts
- issues threats to make people follow instructions
- demands, never asks

- does not participate
- does not team-build
- unconcerned about staff welfare, or morale
- proud, sometimes to the point of self-destruction
- one-way communicator
- poor listener
- fundamentally insecure and possibly neurotic
- anti-social
- vengeful and recriminatory
- does not thank or praise
- withholds rewards, and suppresses pay and remunerations levels
- scrutinises expenditure to the point of false economy
- seeks culprits for failures or shortfalls
- seeks to apportion blame instead of focusing on learning from the experience and preventing recurrence
- does not invite or welcome suggestions
- takes criticism badly and likely to retaliate if from below or peer group
- poor at proper delegating-but believes they delegate well
- thinks giving orders is delegating
- holds on to responsibility but shifts accountability to subordinates
- relatively unconcerned with investing in anything to gain future improvements
- unhappy

### *Managing your X Theory Boss*

Working for an X theory boss isn't easy-some extreme X theory managers make extremely unpleasant managers, but there are ways of managing these people upwards. Avoiding confrontation (unless you are genuinely being bullied, which is a different matter) and delivering results are the key tactics.

- Theory X managers (or indeed theory Y managers displaying theory X behaviour) are primarily results oriented-so orientate your own discussions and dealings with them around results-ie what you can deliver and when.

- Theory X managers are facts and figures oriented-so cut out the incidentals, be able to measure and substantiate anything you say and do for them, especially reporting on results and activities.
- Theory X managers generally don't understand or have an interest in the human issues, so don't try to appeal to their sense of humanity or morality. Set your own objectives to meet their organisational aims and agree these with the managers; be seen to be self-starting, self-motivating, self-disciplined and well-organised-the more the X theory manager sees you are managing yourself and producing results, the less they'll feel the need to do it for you.
- Always deliver your commitments and promises. If you are given an unrealistic task and/or deadline state the reasons why it's not realistic, but be very sure of your ground, don't be negative; be constructive as to how the overall aim can be achieved in a way that you know you can deliver.
- Stand up for yourself, but constructively-avoid confrontation. Never threaten or go over their heads if you are dissatisfied or you'll be in big trouble afterwards and life will be a lot more difficult.
- If an X theory boss tells you how to do things in ways that are not comfortable or right for you, then don't questioning the process, simply confirm the end-result that is required, and check that it's okay to 'streamline the process' or 'get things done more efficiently' if the chance arises-they'll normally agree to this, which effectively gives you control over the 'how', provided you deliver the 'what' and 'when'.

And this is really the essence of managing upwards X theory managers-focus and get agreement on the results and deadlines-if you consistently deliver, you'll increasingly be given more leeway on how you go about the tasks, which amounts to more freedom. Be aware also that many X theory managers are forced to be X theory by the short-term demands of the organisation and their own superiors-an X theory manager is usually someone with their own problems, so try not to give them any more.

### *Theory z-William Ouchi*

First things first-Theory Z is not a Mcgregor idea and as such is not Mcgregor's extension of his XY theory. Theory Z was developed by not by Mcgregor, but by William Ouchi, in his book 1981 'Theory Z: How American management can Meet the Japanese Challenge'. William Ouchi is professor of management at UCLA, Los Angeles, and a board member of several large US organisations.

Theory Z is often referred to as the 'Japanese' management style, which is essentially what it is. It's interesting that Ouchi chose to name his model 'Theory Z', which apart from anything else tends to give the impression that it's a Mcgregor idea. One wonders if the idea was not considered strong enough to stand alone with a completely new name... Nevertheless, Theory Z essentially advocates a combination of all that's best about theory Y and modern Japanese management, which places a large amount of freedom and trust with workers, and assumes that workers have a strong loyalty and interest in team-working and the organisation.

Theory Z also places more reliance on the attitude and responsibilities of the workers, whereas Mcgregor's XY theory is mainly focused on management and motivation from the manager's and organisation's perspective. There is no doubt that Ouchi's Theory Z model offers excellent ideas, albeit it lacking the simple elegance of Mcgregor's model, which let's face it, thousands of organisations and managers around the world have still yet to embrace. For this reason, Theory Z may for some be like trying to manage the kitchen at the Ritz before mastering the ability to cook a decent fried breakfast.

# 6

# Frederick Herzberg

Frederick Irving Herzberg (17 April 1923 – 19 January 2000) was an American psychologist who became one of the most influential names in business management. He is most famous for introducing job enrichment and the Motivator-Hygiene theory. His 1968 publication "One More Time, How Do You Motivate Employees?" had sold 1.2 million reprints by 1987 and was the most requested article from the Harvard Business Review. Herzberg attended City College of New York, but left part way through his studies to enlist in the army. As a patrol sergeant, he was a firsthand witness of the Dachau concentration camp. He believed that this experience, as well as the talks he had with other Germans living in the area was what triggered his interest in motivation. Herzberg graduated from City College in 1946 and moved to the University of Pittsburgh to undertake postgraduate workplace while teaching as a professor of psychology at Case Western Reserve University in Cleveland and later moved to the University of Utah where he held the position of professor of management in the college of business.

## Two Factor Theory "The Dual Structure Theory"

Herzberg proposed the Motivation-Hygiene Theory, also known as the *Two factor theory* (1959) of job satisfaction. According to his theory, people are influenced by two sets of factors:

***Motivator Factors***

- Achievement
- Recognition
- Work Itself

- Responsibility
- Promotion
- Growth

*Hygiene Factors*

- Pay and Benefits
- Company Policy and Administration
- Relationships with co-workers
- Supervision
- Status
- Job Security
- Working Conditions
- Personal life

He proposed several key findings as a result of this identification.

1. People are made dissatisfied by a bad environment, but they are seldom made satisfied by a good environment.
2. The prevention of dissatisfaction is just as important as encouragement of motivator satisfaction.
3. Hygiene factors operate independently of motivation factors. An individual can be highly motivated in his work and be dissatisfied with his work environment.
4. All hygiene factors are equally important, although their frequency of occurrence differs considerably.
5. Hygiene improvements have short-term effects. Any improvements result in a short-term removal of, or prevention of, dissatisfaction.
6. Hygiene needs are cyclical in nature and come back to a starting point. This leads to the "What have you done for me lately?" syndrome.
7. Hygiene needs have an escalating zero point and no final answer.

Frederick Herzberg, a German psychologist, theorized that an employee's productivity is tied to two distinct factors: motivation and hygiene. On the one hand, motivation factors such as achievement, recognition, responsibility, interest, and growth, if met, can lead to enhanced job satisfaction. On the other hand, hygiene factors such as salary, security, work conditions, quality of supervision, and interpersonal relations, if neglected, will lead to increased job dissatisfaction. Herzberg posits that the removal of hygiene issues such as poor work conditions will not necessarily lead to increased satisfaction. To improve job satisfaction, motivation factors must also be addressed.

Although Herzberg's theory is appealing given that its intuitive nature, it is at the same time highly problematic. First, Herzberg's theory implies that enhancing job satisfaction will lead to increased productivity; however, this is not always the case. A highly satisfied worker may become complacent and his performance may level or even tail off. Second, his assertions were developed from interviewing two hundred accountants and engineers in Pittsburgh in the 1950s. This is an extremely limited sample size in terms of number, profession, and location. What causes dissatisfaction for one accountant in Pittsburgh may not necessarily be seen as an irritant for another accountant in New York. Likewise, what motivates an architect may be completely different from what motivates an investment banker. Although his theory suffers from its simplistic assumption that the workforce is a homogenous mass, it nevertheless provides a useful framework that can be adapted to address variegated industries, firms, and individuals. The pertinent question for design professionals becomes: how can Herzberg's two-factor theory be translated into a series of actionable step to advance managerial practices in architecture?

## Hygiene Factors

Herzberg claims that although a generous salary has limited effects on motivation, the lack of money will most likely lead to dissatisfaction. However, an athletes' performance in the last year of their contract frequently exceeds their performance in their non-contract years. Known as 'contract year phenomenon', this occurrence contradicts Herzberg's assertion and implies that the potential for a larger salary can be an important motivator (although it may not lead to greater satisfaction). Again, the question becomes: does this apply to the design profession? And if so, how can one translate this into a successful remuneration strategy. The answer, of course, is: it depends.

Since architecture is composed of a wide range of firms (from large corporate office like SOM to small offices like Glenn Murcutt who runs a one-man practice), the type of architect who feels predisposed to work for SOM will invariably differ from one who wants to work for Frank Gehry. Also, a recent graduate may work for a corporate office initially in search for a higher wage to pay off their student loan before moving on to a smaller office. Thus, for a large corporate office, they must pay more than a smaller firm to induce graduates to join. For a partner at a corporate firm, it is sensible to provide the same base salary for the same level of architects, as this will help offset jealousy, which is likely to cause performance to suffer. To enhance productivity, a large firm can include a performance-related bonus (although this would admittedly be difficult to measure given the subjectivity of the design field). However, performance can be assessed through periodic reviews to let the employee know where they stand. This system assures that a person who places a greater value on money will be induced to perform more productively as they are provided with the opportunity to earn more.

On the other side of the spectrum, a smaller firm will unlikely be able to pay as much as large corporate firms, given their comparatively limited resources. However, this does not necessarily mean that smaller firms like Glen Murcutt Architect cannot attract the same quality of designer as SOM, nor does it mean that employees are more likely to be dissatisfied. Instead, graduates who gravitate towards these offices tend to do so because they are attracted by an office's design methodology, or by the work the office has done in the past, rather than a high salary. Students may form positive interpersonal relations with an architect, teaching at their school, and become convinced that the office can provide a great working environment (a friendly staff and good working conditions). Thus, smaller firms who cannot provide the same remuneration packages can nevertheless attract bright talents and motivate them to work. Like their corporate counterpart, however, it is wise to provide the same base salary for workers at the same level to prevent jealousy. Performance-related bonuses can diffuse dissatisfaction from employees who feel they have worked harder than others but are paid the same.

In addition to salary, Herzberg argues that 'company policy

and administration' is the single most important factor determining bad feelings about a job'. He identifies poorly defined jobs leading to duplication of effort, inefficiency, waste, and internal politics as potential detriments to an employee's level of satisfaction. In his book, 'The Motivation to Work', Herzberg uses an accounting supervisor to illustrator his point. In his anecdote, the supervisor's superior constantly bypasses him when assigning new projects to lower level employees. Not knowing why he was bypassed, he felt embarrassed and frustrated, and his performance consequently suffered. Again, how can this knowledge inform design principals seeking to limit dissatisfaction?

For large corporate offices, this can be translated to simplifying the hierarchy of a firm as much as possible to prevent duplication and communication mishaps. Thus, if a single partner was solely responsible for a project, the junior or senior architect will know who to go to for directions. Moreover, this prevents awkward situations like a partner being bypassed since a subordinate is unsure who to talk to.

In addition to a company's administrative structure, personnel policies can adversely affect an employee's attitude. During his interviews with accountants, Herzberg found that there was a growing dissatisfaction amongst the older generation of accountants who viewed preferential treatments (in terms of higher pay) given to younger employees with university degrees as unfair. For a design firm to avert such a pitfall, it is will be better if the company adopts a meritocratic system (giving recognition, rises, and promotion to those who perform) as this will more likely limit job dissatisfaction.

## Motivation Factors

Recognition, defined by Herzberg as 'some act of notice, praise, or blame' is a contentious issue within the field of architecture. One of the most common ways of recognizing someone within the design discipline is crediting him or her with authorship. However, this is problematic for two reasons. The first is that architecture is rarely designed by an individual, despite the romantic notion that equates an architect to a solitary genius. Rather, architecture is more commonly realized by the collective efforts of an interdisciplinary team. The second problem with the auteur theory is that often, principals at a firm take credit for a work which they may have had limited input; this is sometimes done as a marketing tool to lure potential clients who may be drawn to a certain brand (i.e. a 'Gehry' building). This conflict (over authorship) led Ken Shuttleworth, a former partner at Foster + Partners, to leave and start his own firm after disputes with Foster over the lack of recognition for the leading role he played over the design of the Gherkin. "Irked by his (Shuttleworth's) sudden departure, Norman Foster gained revenge last year, when he digitally altered a 'team' photo celebrating the Gherkin, moving Shuttleworth to a less prominent position."

To prevent the potential of losing a gifted designer and to improve employee fulfilment, design principles can adopt two related strategies. The first relates to how one can name his or her practice. Instead of using a personal name, the firm can adopt a name that reflects their design philosophy instead, like Make Architects (Shuttleworth's new firm). This allows individual efforts to be recognized in public without creating confusion (i.e. the Foster building was not designed by Foster?). Shuttleworth explains Make's business model, 'Our company structure engenders a strong sense of ownership and entitlement amongst staff, creating a vibrant and egalitarian studio environment with a united sense of purpose and drive.' The second strategy a firm can adopt is to shift the focus away from the architect as individual artist model to that of a team-driven, problem solving approach (an example would be The Architect's Collaborative). With this approach, instead of recognizing an individual by crediting them with authorship, verbal praise, which can also be accompanied by pay increases or promotional opportunities, can serve as an alternate form of recognition.

Apart from recognition, Herzberg identifies growth as another essential motivation factor. He defines growth as 'the possibility that one is able to advance in his or her skills and in his profession'.

Additionally, he offers three potential strategies to not only provide an expanded opportunity for growth, but also to enhance interest; they include: job enlargement, job rotation, and job enrichment. These strategies may have a larger impact on blue-collar workers doing monotonous jobs, as architects often confound projects, which range in scope, type, and location. Moreover, tasks architects perform day to day are quite diverse. Regardless, the factor is still applicable to the design field despite is relatively diminished impact. An architect, who specializes in a certain building typology, can be transferred to another team that specializes in another typology to expand his knowledge. Likewise, an employee working in an Asian branch of an office, can be transferred to an American or European branch of the same office to stimulate interest and broaden the employee's exposure to different environments. Thus, by adopting these strategies, design principals can ensure that their employee's job fulfilment remains optimized. Although Frederick Herzberg's two-factor theory suffers from a number of weaknesses, it nevertheless provides a useful general framework, which can be adapted to a variety of industries, firms, and individuals. For design principals leading a design project, the question of how to adapt Herzberg's theory depends on the size of a firm, and its culture. Thus, a design firm can customize each motivation and hygiene factors such as salary, company policies and administration, recognition, and growth to either enhance or rethink their existing strategy in how to motivate their workers.

## Two-factor Theory

The two-factor theory (also known as Herzberg's motivation-hygiene theory) states that there are certain factors in the workplace that cause job satisfaction, while a separate set of factors cause dissatisfaction. It was developed by Frederick Herzberg, a psychologist, who theorized that job satisfaction and job dissatisfaction act independently of each other.

### *Two-factor Theory Fundamentals*

Attitudes and their connection with industrial mental health are related to Maslow's theory of motivation. His findings have had a considerable theoretical, as well as a practical, influence on attitudes toward administration. According to Herzberg, individuals are not content with the satisfaction of lower-order needs at work, for example, those associated with minimum salary levels or safe and pleasant working conditions. Rather, individuals look for the gratification of higher-level psychological needs having to do with achievement, recognition, responsibility, advancement, and the nature of the work itself. So far, this appears to parallel

Maslow's theory of a need hierarchy. However, Herzberg added a new dimension to this theory by proposing a two-factor model of motivation, based on the notion that the presence of one set of job characteristics or incentives lead to worker *satisfaction* at work, while another and separate set of job characteristics lead to *dissatisfaction* at work. Thus, satisfaction and dissatisfaction are not on a continuum with one increasing as the other diminishes, but are independent phenomena. This theory suggests that to improve job attitudes and productivity, administrators must recognize and attend to both sets of characteristics and not assume that an increase in satisfaction leads to decrease in unpleasurable dissatisfaction.

The two-factor, or *motivation-hygiene theory*, developed from data collected by Herzberg from interviews with a large number of engineers and accountants in the Pittsburgh area. From analyzing these interviews, he found that job characteristics related to what an individual *does* — that is, to the nature of the work he performs — apparently have the capacity to gratify such needs as achievement, competency, status, personal worth, and self-realization, thus making him happy and satisfied. However, the *absence* of such gratifying job characteristics does not appear to lead to unhappiness and dissatisfaction. Instead, dissatisfaction results from unfavorable assessments of such job-related factors as company policies, supervision, technical problems, salary, interpersonal relations on the job, and working conditions. Thus, if management wishes to increase satisfaction on the job, it should be concerned with the nature of the work itself — the opportunities it presents for gaining status, assuming responsibility, and for achieving self-realization. If, on the other hand, management wishes to reduce dissatisfaction, then it must focus on the job environment — policies, procedures, supervision, and working conditions. If management is equally concerned with both (as is usually the case), then managers must give attention to both sets of job factors.

The theory was based around interviews with 203 American accountants & engineers in Pittsburgh, chosen because of their professions' growing importance in the business world. The subjects were asked to relate times when they felt exceptionally good or bad about their present job or any previous job, and to provide reasons, and a description of the sequence of events giving rise to that positive or negative feeling.

Here is the description of this interview analysis: Briefly, we asked our respondents to describe periods in their lives when they were exceedingly happy and unhappy with their jobs. Each respondent gave as many "sequences of events" as he could that met certain criteria—including a marked change in feeling, a beginning and an end, and contained some substantive description other than feelings and interpretations…

The proposed hypothesis appears verified. The factors on the right that led to satisfaction (achievement, intrinsic interest in the work, responsibility, and advancement) are mostly unipolar; that is, they contribute very little to job dissatisfaction. Conversely, the dis-satisfiers (company policy and administrative practices, supervision, interpersonal relationships, working conditions, and salary) contribute very little to job satisfaction.

Two-factor theory distinguishes between:

- Motivators (e.g., challenging work, recognition, responsibility) that give positive satisfaction, arising from intrinsic conditions of the job itself, such as recognition, achievement, or personal growth, *and*
- Hygiene factors (e.g. status, job security, salary and fringe benefits) that do not give positive satisfaction, though dissatisfaction results from their absence. These are extrinsic to the work itself, and include aspects such as company policies, supervisory practices, or wages/salary.

Essentially, hygiene factors are needed to ensure an employee is not dissatisfied. Motivation factors are needed to motivate an employee to higher performance, Herzberg also further classified our actions and how and why we do them, for example, if you perform a work related action because you *have* to then that is classed as movement, but if you perform a work related action because you *want* to then that is classed as motivation.

Unlike Maslow, who offered little data to support his ideas, Herzberg and others have presented considerable empirical evidence to confirm the motivation-hygiene theory. Their work, however, has been criticized on methodological grounds. Nevertheless, Herzberg and his associates have rendered a valuable service to science and to management through their efforts to apply scientific methods to understanding complex motivational problems at work and have stimulated others to continue the search.

### *Validity and Criticisms*

In 1968 Herzberg stated that his two-factor theory study had already been replicated 16 times in a wide variety of populations including some in Communist countries, and corroborated with studies using different procedures that agreed with his original findings regarding intrinsic employee motivation making it one of the most widely replicated studies on job attitudes. While the Motivator-Hygiene concept is still well regarded, satisfaction and dissatisfaction are generally no longer considered to exist on separate scales. The separation of satisfaction and dissatisfaction has been shown to be an artifact of the Critical Incident Technique (CIT) used by Herzberg to record events. Furthermore, it has been noted the theory does not allow for individual differences, such as a particular personality traits, which would affect individuals' unique responses to motivating or hygiene factors.

A number of behavioral scientists have pointed to inadequacies in the need hierarchy and motivation-hygiene theories. The most basic is the criticism that both of these theories contain the relatively explicit assumption that happy and satisfied workers produce more. Another problem is that these and other statistical theories are concerned with explaining "average" behaviour and, on the other hand, if playing a better game of golf is the means he chooses to satisfy his need for recognition, then he will find ways to play and think about golf more often, perhaps resulting in an accompanying lower output on the job. Finally, in his pursuit of status he might take a balanced view and strive to pursue several behavioral paths in an effort to achieve a combination of personal status objectives.

In other words, this individual's expectation or estimated probability that a given behaviour will bring a valued outcome determines his choice of means and the effort he will devote to these means. In effect, this diagram of expectancy depicts an employee asking himself the question posed by one investigator, *"How much payoff is there for me toward attaining a personal goal while expending so much effort toward the achievement of an assigned organizational objective?"* The Expectancy theory by Victor Vroom also provides a framework for motivation based on expectations.

This approach to the study and understanding of motivation would appear to have certain conceptual advantages over other theories: First, unlike Maslow's and Herzberg's theories, it is capable of handling individual differences. Second, its focus is toward the present and the future, in contrast to drive theory, which emphasizes past learning. Third, it specifically correlates with behaviour to a goal and thus eliminates the problem of assumed relationships, such as between motivation and performance. Fourth, it relates motivation to ability: Performance = Motivation*Ability.

That said, a study by the Gallup Organization, as detailed in the book "First, Break All the Rules: What the World's Greatest Managers Do" by Marcus Buckingham and Curt Coffman, appears to provide strong support for Herzberg's division of satisfaction and dissatisfaction onto two separate scales. In this book, the authors discuss how the study identified twelve questions that provide a framework for determining high-performing individuals and organizations. These twelve questions align squarely with Herzberg's motivation factors, while hygiene factors were determined to have little effect on motivating high performance. To better understand employee attitudes and motivation, Frederick Herzberg performed studies to determine which factors in an employee's work environment caused satisfaction or dissatisfaction. He published his findings in the 1959 book The Motivation to Work. The studies included interviews in which employees where asked what pleased and displeased them about their work. Herzberg found that the factors causing job satisfaction (and presumably motivation) were different from those causing job dissatisfaction. He developed the motivation-hygiene theory to explain these results. He called the satisfiers motivators and the dissatisfiers hygiene factors, using the term "hygiene" in the sense that they are considered maintenance factors that are necessary to avoid dissatisfaction but that by themselves do not provide satisfaction. The following table presents the top six factors causing dissatisfaction and the top six factors causing satisfaction, listed in the order of higher to lower importance.

Leading to satisfaction

- Achievement
- Recognition
- Work itself
- Responsibility
- Advancement

Growth:

- Leading to dissatisfaction
- Company policy
- Supervision
- Relationship with boss
- Work conditions
- Salary
- Relationship with peers
- Security

Herzberg reasoned that because the factors causing satisfaction are different from those causing dissatisfaction, the two feelings cannot simply be treated as opposites of one another. The opposite of satisfaction is not dissatisfaction, but rather, no satisfaction. Similarly, the opposite of dissatisfaction is no dissatisfaction. While at first glance this distinction between the two opposites may sound like a play on words, Herzberg argued that there are two distinct human needs portrayed. First, there are physiological needs that can be fulfilled by money, for example, to purchase food and shelter. Second, there is the psychological need to achieve and grow, and this need is fulfilled by activities that cause one to grow.

From the above table of results, one observes that the factors that determine whether there is dissatisfaction or no dissatisfaction are not part of the work itself, but rather, are external factors. Herzberg often referred to these hygiene factors as "KITA" factors, where KITA is an acronym for Kick In The Ass, the process of providing incentives or a threat of punishment to cause someone to do something. Herzberg argues that these provide only short-run success because the motivator factors that determine whether there is satisfaction or no satisfaction are intrinsic to the job itself, and do not result from carrot and stick incentives. In a survey of

80 teaching staff at Egyptian private universities, Mohamed Hossam El-Din Khalifa and Quang Truong (2009), has found out that Perception of Equity was directly related to job satisfaction when the outcome in the equity comparison was one of Herzberg's Motivators. On the contrary, perception of equity and job satisfaction were not related when the outcome in the equity comparison was one of Herzberg's Hygiene Factors. The findings of this study provide a kind of an indirect support to Herzberg's findings that improving Hygiene Factors would not lead to improvement in an employee's job satisfaction.

### *Implications for Management*

If the motivation-hygiene theory holds, management not only must provide hygiene factors to avoid employee dissatisfaction, but also must factors intrinsic to the work itself for employees to be satisfied with their jobs. Herzberg argued that job enrichment is required for intrinsic motivation, and that it is a continuous management process. According to Herzberg:

- The job should have sufficient challenge to utilize the full ability of the employee.
- Employees who demonstrate increasing levels of ability should be given increasing levels of responsibility.
- If a job cannot be designed to use an employee's full abilities, then the firm should consider automating the task or replacing the employee with one who has a lower level of skill. If a person cannot be fully utilized, then there will be a motivation problem.

Critics of Herzberg's theory argue that the two-factor result is observed because it is natural for people to take credit for satisfaction and to blame dissatisfaction on external factors. Furthermore, job satisfaction does not necessarily imply a high level of motivation or productivity. Herzberg's theory has been broadly read and despite its weaknesses its enduring value is that it recognizes that true motivation comes from within a person and not from KITA factors.(French, 2008)

## Factor Hygiene and Motivation Theory

Frederick Herzberg, contributed to human relations and motivation two theories of motivation as follows:

- Hygiene Theory
- Motivation.

Herzbergs' first component in his approach to motivation theory involves what are known as the hygiene factors and includes the work and organizational environment. These hygiene factors include:

- The organization
- Its policies and its administration
- The kind of supervision (leadership and management, including perceptions) which people receive while on the job
- Working conditions (including ergonomics)
- Interpersonal relations
- Salary
- Status
- Job security.

These factors do not lead to higher levels of motivation but without them there is dissatisfaction. The second component in Herzbergs' motivation theory involves what people actually do on the job and should be engineered into the jobs employees do in order to develop intrinsic motivation with the workforce. The motivators are

- Achievement
- Recognition
- Growth / advancement
- Interest in the job.

These factors result from internal instincts in employees, yielding motivation rather than movement. Both these approaches (hygiene and motivation) must be done simultaneously. Treat people as best you can so they have a minimum of dissatisfaction. Use people so they get achievement, recognition for achievement, interest, and responsibility and they can grow and advance in their work. Therefore, the hygiene and motivation factors can be listed as follows:

Hygiene:

- Company policies and administration

- Supervision
- Working conditions and interpersonal relations
- Salary, status and security.

Motivators:

- Achievement
- Recognition for achievement
- Interest in the task
- Responsibility for enlarged task
- Growth and advancement to higher level tasks.

### *Effects on Individuals of Working Environment*

The working environment has an effect on individuals as follows:

- It will provide at least sufficient for his basic needs and often much more. For example, 50 years ago in the United Kingdom, food and shelter were a person's basic needs. Today, most families will consider that the basic needs also include a car, television, overseas holiday, etc.
- It may or may not provide adequate security. Again, most individuals seek a secure job, there are others including some men on oil rigs, who seek high pay for a limited period but with limited security.
- It provides an individual with an identity. As a member of an organization, he carries out a specific function.
- It also gives the worker comradeship, freedom from boredom, and an interest during his working life.
- It also provides self-fulfilment for individual where consideration has been given to ensure that the job is creative and gives job satisfaction.
- It provides the individual with status. There is a status in all jobs providing the job content is investigated to make the work more interesting.

### *Work Groups of Working Environment*

Rensis Likert has already described how the various management styles in an organization can effect the groups in an organization. Whilst the working environment will affect individuals, it will undoubtedly have a greater effect on working groups, since whilst an individual may have certain needs, he will not obtain those needs if the working environment does not provide the needs of the working group.

The working group is the instrument of society through which in large measure the individual acquires his attitudes, opinions, goals and ideals, it is also one of the fundamental sources of discipline and social controls. Therefore, the working environment has an effect on groups as follows:

- It will affect the morale of the group.
- It will determine whether the group achieves the objectives set by the organization.
- It will determine whether the degree of cooperation provided by the group
- It will motivate the group to give of their best.
- It will determine whether the human relations within an organization are good or bad.
- It will also affect the relations between management and trade unions.

## Motivation Frederick Herzberg

Frederick Herzberg was born in Lynn, Massachusetts on April 18, 1923 and died on January 18, 2000 in Salt Lake City. He had been in Utah since 1972 when he was asked to join the University of Utah's College of Business. He gained a graduate degree at the University of Pittsburg. Before his move to Utah, he was professor of management at Case Western Reserve University where he established the Department of Industrial Mental Health.

He put forward the idea that certain factors in the workplace cause job satisfaction, while others lead to dissatisfaction. He became known as 'The Father of Job Enrichment' and the originator of the 'Motivation-Hygiene Theory' he was a big influence on post-war visionaries such as Abraham Maslow, Peter Drucker and Douglas McGregor. His book 'The work and the nature of man' was voted in the top 10, in 1995, in terms of impacting management theory and practice in the 20th century. His book 'The Motivation to Work', written with research colleagues B Mausner and B Snyderman in 1959, first established his theories about motivation in the workplace. This work was based upon the a study using 200 Pittsburgh engineers and accountants.

In 1959 he proposed the 'Two Factor theory' of human motivation in the workplace. According to his theory people are influenced by two factors:

- Satisfaction and psychological growth are a result of 'motivation factors'.
- Dissatisfaction is a result of a lack of 'hygiene factors'.

Most managers realise that a happy workforce leads to improved performance which holds equally well for leadership and training. Exactly what those factors are has lead to considerable debate. He suggested two basic needs one as an animal to avoid pain, and the second as a human being to grow psychologically. Frederick Herzberg, through observational research identified particular areas.

### *Hygiene Factors*

During his research, he established that particular factors often caused a worker to feel unsatisfied with his or her job. These factors seemed directly related to the person's environment, for example, the physical surroundings, other personnel such as supervisors and even the company itself. He called this his 'Hygiene Theory'. For the worker to remain happy these 'hygiene factors' should not cause any discomfort. If so performance is likely to become affected.

If you make sure the environmental factors are in place the worker will be more efficient in terms of performance. However, the independent drive associated with motivation may still be lacking. Hygiene might include:

- Policy.
- Relationship with supervisor and other managers.
- Work conditions.
- Physical environment.
- Salary.
- Company car.
- Status.
- Security.

- Relationship with subordinates.
- Personal life.

### *Motivation Factors*

Herzberg believed that workers responded to feelings of connection with their work. This happens by encouraging them to accept more authority as well as promoting feedback a useful technique in leadership and training. Motivators might include.

- Achievement.
- Recognition.
- Work itself.
- Responsibility.
- Advancement.
- Personal growth.
- Autonomy
- Intrinsic interests
- Creative opportunities.

### *Money as a Motivator*

Initially, many people would say that they only work because of the money, 'if you pay me more I will work harder' etc. etc. In fact, money is quite low on the list for most people that are unhappy about their jobs. If you paid someone money to literally just sit on a stool all day you could pretty much bet there would be plenty of resignations after day one. People need to have an interest in the job that makes it worthwhile. Many people who change jobs do so because of better promotion prospects, more challenging and varied work, or just a more exciting place of work. People who win large amounts of money in lotteries etc are never truly happy just spending money unless it is used for personal fulfilment.

# 7

# Frederick Winslow Taylor

Frederick Winslow Taylor (March 20, 1856–March 21, 1915), widely known as F. W. Taylor, was an American mechanical engineer who sought to improve industrial efficiency. He is regarded as the father of scientific management and was one of the first management consultants. Taylor was one of the intellectual leaders of the Efficiency Movement and his ideas, broadly conceived, were highly influential in the Progressive Era.

***Biography***

Taylor was born in 1856 to a wealthy Quaker family in Germantown, Philadelphia, Pennsylvania. Taylor's ancestor, Samuel Taylor, settled in Burlington, New Jersey, in 1677. Taylor's father, Franklin Taylor, a Princeton-educated lawyer, built his wealth on mortgages. Taylor's mother, Emily Annette Taylor (née Winslow), was an ardent abolitionist and a coworker with Lucretia Mott. Educated early by his mother, Taylor studied for two years in France and Germany and traveled Europe for 18 months. In 1872, he entered Phillips Exeter Academy in Exeter, New Hampshire.

Upon graduation, Taylor was accepted at Harvard Law. However, due to rapidly deteriorating eyesight, Taylor had to consider an alternative career. After the depression of 1873, Taylor became an industrial apprentice patternmaker, gaining shop-floor experience at a pump-manufacturing company, Enterprise Hydraulic Works, in Philadelphia. Taylor's career progressed in 1878 when he became a machine shop labourer at Midvale Steel Works. At Midvale, Taylor was promoted to gang-boss, foreman, research director, and finally chief engineer of the works. Taylor became a student of Stevens Institute of Technology, studying via correspondence and obtaining a degree in mechanical engineering in 1883. On May 3, 1884, he married Louise M. Spooner of Philadelphia.

From 1890 until 1893 Taylor worked as a general manager and a consulting engineer to management for the Manufacturing Investment Company of Philadelphia, a company that operated large paper mills in Maine and Wisconsin. He spent time as a plant manager in Maine. In 1893, Taylor opened an independent consulting practice in Philadelphia. His business card read "Systematizing Shop Management and Manufacturing Costs a Specialty". In 1898, Taylor joined Bethlehem Steel, where he, Maunsel White, and a team of assistants developed high speed steel. For his process of treating high speed tool steels he received a personal gold medal at the Paris exposition in 1900, and was awarded the Elliott Cresson Medal that same year by the Franklin Institute, Philadelphia. Taylor was forced to leave Bethlehem Steel in 1901 after antagonisms with other managers. In 1901, Frederick and Louise Taylor adopted three orphans Kempton, Robert and Elizabeth.

On October 19, 1906, Taylor was awarded an honorary degree of Doctor of Science by the University of Pennsylvania. Taylor eventually became a professor at the Tuck School of Business at Dartmouth College. Late winter of 1915 Taylor caught pneumonia and one day after his fifty-ninth birthday, on March 21, he died. He was buried in West Laurel Hill Cemetery, in Bala Cynwyd, Pennsylvania.

### *Work*

Taylor was a mechanical engineer who sought to improve industrial efficiency. Taylor is regarded as the father of scientific management, and was one of the first management consultants and director of a famous firm. In Peter Drucker's description,

Frederick W. Taylor was the first man in recorded history who deemed work deserving of systematic observation and study. On Taylor's 'scientific management' rests, above all, the tremendous surge of affluence in the last seventy-five years which has lifted the working masses in the developed countries well above any level recorded before, even for the well-to-do. Taylor, though the Isaac Newton (or perhaps the Archimedes) of the science of work, laid only first foundations, however. Not much has been added to them since-even though he has been dead all of sixty years.

Taylor was also an accomplished tennis player, who won the first doubles tournament in the 1881 U.S. National Championships, the precursor of the U.S. Open, with Clarence Clark.

### *Scientific Management*

Taylor believed that the industrial management of his day was amateurish, that management could be formulated as an academic discipline, and that the best results would come from the partnership between a trained and qualified management and a cooperative and innovative workforce. Each side needed the other, and there was no need for trade unions. Future U.S. Supreme Court justice Louis Brandeis coined the term *scientific management* in the course of his argument for the Eastern Rate Case before the Interstate Commerce Commission in 1910. Brandeis debated that railroads, when governed according to the principles of Taylor, did not need to raise rates to increase wages. Taylor used Brandeis's term in the title of his monograph *The Principles of Scientific Management*, published in 1911. The Eastern Rate Case propelled Taylor's ideas to the forefront of the management agenda. Taylor wrote to Brandeis "I have rarely seen a new movement started with such great momentum as you have given this one." Taylor's approach is also often referred to, as *Taylor's Principles*, or frequently disparagingly, as *Taylorism*. Taylor's scientific management consisted of four principles:

1. Replace rule-of-thumb work methods with methods based on a scientific study of the tasks.
2. Scientifically select, train, and develop each employee rather than passively leaving them to train themselves.
3. Provide "Detailed instruction and supervision of each worker in the performance of that worker's discrete task" (Montgomery 1997: 250).
4. Divide work nearly equally between managers and workers, so that the managers apply scientific management principles to planning the work and the workers actually perform the tasks.

## Managers and Workers

Taylor had very precise ideas about how to introduce his system: It is only through *enforced* standardization of methods, *enforced* adoption of the best implements and working conditions, and *enforced* cooperation that this faster work can be assured. And the duty of enforcing the adoption of standards and enforcing this cooperation rests with *management* alone.

Workers were supposed to be incapable of understanding what they were doing. According to Taylor this was true even for rather simple tasks. 'I can say, without the slightest hesitation,' Taylor told a congressional committee, 'that the science of handling pig-iron is so great that the man who is... physically able to handle pig-iron and is sufficiently phlegmatic and stupid to choose this for his occupation is rarely able to comprehend the science of handling pig-iron.

The introduction of his system was often resented by workers and provoked numerous strikes. The strike at Watertown Arsenal led to the congressional investigation in 1912. Taylor believed the labourer was worthy of his hire, and pay was linked to productivity. His workers were able to earn substantially more than those in similar industries and this earned him enemies among the owners of factories where scientific management was not in use.

### *Propaganda Techniques*

With the triumph of scientific management, unions would have nothing left to do, and they would have been cleansed of their most evil feature: the restriction of output. To underscore this idea, Taylor fashioned the myth that 'there has never been a strike of men working under scientific management', trying to give it credibility by constant repetition. In similar fashion he incessantly linked his proposals to shorter hours of work, without bothering to produce evidence of "Taylorized" firms that reduced working hours, and he revised his famous tale of Schmidt carrying pig iron at Bethlehem Steel at least three times, obscuring some aspects of his study and stressing others, so that each successive version made Schmidt's exertions more impressive, more voluntary and more rewarding to him than the last. Unlike [Harrington] Emerson, Taylor was not a charlatan, but his ideological message required the suppression of all evidence of worker's dissent, of coercion, or of any human motives or aspirations other than those his vision of progress could encompass.

### *Management Theory*

Taylor thought that by analyzing work, the "One Best Way" to do it would be found. He is most remembered for developing the time and motion study. He would break a job into its component parts and measure each to the hundredth of a minute. One of his most famous studies involved shovels.

He noticed that workers used the same shovel for all materials. He determined that the most effective load was 21½ lb, and found or designed shovels that for each material would scoop up that amount. He was generally unsuccessful in getting his concepts applied and was dismissed from Bethlehem Steel. It was largely through the efforts of his disciples (most notably H.L. Gantt) that industry came to implement his ideas. Nevertheless, the book he wrote after parting company with Bethlehem Steel, *Shop Management*, sold well.

### *Relations with ASME*

Taylor was president of the American Society of Mechanical Engineers (ASME) from 1906 to 1907. While president, he tried to implement his system into the management of the ASME but was met with much resistance. He was only able to reorganize the publications department and then only partially. He also forced out the ASME's long-time secretary, Morris L. Cooke, and replaced him with Calvin W. Rice. His tenure as president was trouble-ridden and marked the beginning of a period of internal dissension within the ASME during the Progressive Age.

In 1912, Taylor collected a number of his articles into a book-length manuscript which he submitted to the ASME for publication. The ASME formed an ad hoc committee to review the text. The committee included Taylor allies such as James Mapes Dodge and Henry R. Towne. The committee delegated the report to the editor of the *American Machinist*, Leon P. Alford. Alford was a critic of the Taylor system and the report was negative. The committee modified the report slightly, but accepted Alford's recommendation not to publish Taylor's book. Taylor angrily withdrew the book and published *Principles* without ASME approval.

### *Patents*

Taylor authored 42 patents.

## Taylor's Influence

### *United States*

- Carl Barth helped Taylor to develop speed-and-feed-calculating slide rules to a previously unknown level of usefulness. Similar aids are still used in machine shops today. Barth became an early consultant on scientific management and later taught at Harvard.
- H. L. Gantt developed the Gantt chart, a visual aid for scheduling tasks and displaying the flow of work.
- Harrington Emerson introduced scientific management to the railroad industry, and proposed the dichotomy of *staff* versus *line* employees, with the former advising the latter.
- Morris Cooke adapted scientific management to educational and municipal organizations.
- Hugo Münsterberg created industrial psychology.
- Lillian Gilbreth introduced psychology to management studies.
- Frank Gilbreth (husband of Lillian) discovered scientific management while working in the construction industry, eventually developing motion studies independently of Taylor. These logically complemented Taylor's time studies, as time and motion are two sides of the efficiency improvement coin. The two fields eventually became time and motion study.
- Harvard University, one of the first American universities to offer a graduate degree in business management in 1908, based its first-year curriculum on Taylor's scientific management.
- Harlow S. Person, as dean of Dartmouth's Amos Tuck School of Administration and Finance, promoted the teaching of scientific management.
- James O. McKinsey, professor of accounting at the University of Chicago and founder of the consulting firm bearing his name, advocated budgets as a means of assuring accountability and of measuring performance.

### *France*

In France, Le Chatelier translated Taylor's work and introduced scientific management throughout government owned plants during World War I. This influenced the French theorist Henri Fayol, whose 1916 *Administration Industrielle et Générale* emphasized organizational structure in management. In the classic General and Industrial Management Fayol wrote that "Taylor's approach differs from the one we have outlined in that he examines the firm from the "bottom up." he starts with the most elemental units of activity – the workers' actions – then studies the effects of their actions on productivity, devises new methods for making them more efficient, and applies what he learns at lower levels to the hierarchy..." He suggests that Taylor has staff analysts and advisors working with individuals at lower levels of the organization to identify the ways to improve efficiency. According to Fayol, the approach results in a "negation of the principle of unity of command." Fayol criticized Taylor's functional management in this way: In *Shop Management*, Taylor said « ... the most marked outward characteristics of functional management lies in the fact that each workman, instead of coming in direct contact with the management at one point only,... receives his daily orders and help from eight different bosses... these eight were (1) route clerks, (2) instruction card men, (3) cost and time clerks, (4) gang bosses, (5) speed bosses, (6) inspectors, (7) repair bosses, and the (8) shop disciplinarian. » This, Fayol said, was an unworkable situation, and that Taylor must have somehow reconciled the dichotomy in some way not described in Taylor's works.

### *Switzerland*

In Switzerland, the American Edward Albert Filene established the International Management Institute to spread information about management techniques.

### *USSR*

In the USSR, Lenin was very impressed by Taylorism, which he and Stalin sought to incorporate into Soviet manufacturing. Taylorism and the mass production methods of Henry Ford thus became highly influential during the early years of the Soviet Union. Nevertheless "[...] Frederick Taylor's methods have never really taken root in the Soviet Union.". The voluntaristic approach of the Stakhanovite movement in the 1930s of setting individual records was diametrically opposed to Taylor's systematic approach and proved to be counter-productive. The stop-and-go of the production process-workers having nothing to do at the beginning of a month and 'storming' during illegal extra shifts at the end of the month-which prevailed even in the 1980s had nothing to do with the successfully taylorized plants e.g. of Toyota which are characterized by *continuous* production processes (heijunka) which are *continuously* improved (kaizen).

"The easy availability of replacement labor, which allowed Taylor to choose only 'first-class men,' was an important condition for his system's success." The situation in the Soviet Union was very different. "Because work is so unrhythmic, the rational manager will hire more workers than he would need if supplies were even in order to have enough for storming. Because of the continuing labor shortage, managers are happy to pay needed workers more than the norm, either by issuing false job orders, assigning them to higher skill grades than they deserve on merit criteria, giving them 'loose' piece rates, or making what is supposed to be 'incentive' pay, premia for good work, effectively part of the normal wage. As Mary Mc Auley has suggested under these circumstances piece rates are not an incentive wage, but a way of justifying giving workers whatever they 'should' be getting, no matter what their pay is supposed to be according to the official norms."

Taylor and his theories are also referenced (and put to practice) in the 1921 dystopian novel *We* by Yevgeny Zamyatin.

### *Criticism of Taylor*

Management theorist Henry Mintzberg is highly critical of Taylor's methods. Mintzberg states that an obsession with efficiency allows measureable benefits to overshadow less quantifiable social benefits completely, and social values get left behind

### *Publications*

Taylor published many articles and short monographs. A selection:

- 1894. *Notes on Belting*

- 1895. *A Piece-rate System*
- 1896. *The adjustment of wages to efficiency; three papers....* New York, For the American economic association by the Macmillan company; London, S. Sonnenschein & co..
- 1903. *Shop management; a paper read before the American society of mechanical engineers.* New York.
- 1906. *On the art of cutting metals, by Mr. F. W. Taylor; an address made at the opening of the annual meeting in New York, December 1906.* New York, The American society of mechanical engineers.
- 1911. *Principles of Scientific Management.* New York and London, Harper & brothers.
- 1911. *Shop management, by Frederick Winslow Taylor... with an introduction by Henry R. Towne....* New York, London, Harper & Brothers.
- 1911. *A treatise on concrete, plain and reinforced: materials, construction, and design of concrete and reinforced concrete.* (2d ed). New York, J. Wiley & sons.
- 1912. *Concrete costs.* New York, J. Wiley & sons.

## Fundamentals of Scientific Management

The principal object of management should be to secure the maximum prosperity for the employer, coupled with the maximum prosperity for each employé. The words "maximum prosperity" are used, in their broad sense, to mean not only large dividends for the company or owner, but the development of every branch of the business to its highest state of excellence, so that the prosperity may be permanent.

In the same way maximum prosperity for each employé means not only higher wages than are usually received by men of his class, but, of more importance still, it also means the development of each man to his state of maximum efficiency, so that he may be able to do, generally speaking, the highest grade of work for which his natural abilities fit him, and it further means giving him, when possible, this class of work to do.

It would seem to be so self-evident that maximum prosperity for the employer, coupled with maximum prosperity for the employé, ought to be the two leading objects of management, that even to state this fact should be unnecessary. And yet there is no question that, throughout the industrial world, a large part of the organization of employers, as well as employés, is for war rather than for peace, and that perhaps the majority on either side do not believe that it is possible so to arrange their mutual relations that their interests become identical.

The majority of these men believe that the fundamental interests of employés and employers are necessarily antagonistic Scientific management, on the contrary, has for its very foundation the firm conviction that the true interests of the two are one and the same; that prosperity for the employer cannot exist through a long term of years unless it is accompanied by prosperity for the employeé, and *vice versa;* and that it is possible to give the workman what he most wants high wages and the employer what he wants a low labor cost—for his manufactures.

It is hoped that some at least of those who do not sympathize with each of these objects may be led to modify their views; that some employers, whose attitude toward their workmen has been that of trying to get the largest amount of work out of them for the smallest possible wages, may be led to see that a more liberal policy toward their men will pay them better; and that some of those workmen who begrudge a fair and even a large profit to their employers, and who feel that all of the fruits of their labor should belong to them, and that those for whom they work and the capital invested in the business are entitled to little or nothing, may be led to modify these views.

No one can be found who will deny that in the case of any single individual the greatest prosperity can exist only when that individual has reached his highest state of efficiency; that is, when he is turning out his largest daily output. The truth of this fact is also perfectly clear in the case of two men working together. To illustrate: if you and your workman have become so skilful that you and he together are making two pairs of shoes in a day, while your competitor and his work-nian are making only one pair, it is clear that after selling your two pairs of shoes you can pay your workman much higher wages than your competitor who produces only one pair of shoes is able to pay his man, and that there will still be enough money left over for you to have a larger profit than your competitor.

In the case of a more complicated manufacturing establishment, it should also be perfectly clear that the greatest permanent prosperity for the workman, coupled with the greatest prosperity for the employer, can be brought about only when the work of the establishment is done with the smallest combined expenditure of human effort, plus nature's resources, plus the cost for the use of capital in the shape of machines, buildings, etc. Or, to state the same thing in a different way: that the greatest prosperity can exist only as the result of the greatest possible productivity of the men and machines of the establishment that is, when each man and each machine are turning out the largest possible output; because unless your men and your machines are daily turning out more work than others around you, it is clear that competition will prevent your paying higher wages to your workmen than are paid to those of your competitor. And what is true as to the possibility of paying high wages in the case of two companies competing close beside one another is also true as to whole districts of the country and even as to nations which are in competition. In a word, that maximum prosperity can exist only as the result of maximum productivity. Later in this chapter illustrations will be given of several companies which are earning large dividends and at the same time paying from 30 per cent to 100 per cent higher wages to their men than are paid to similar men immediately around them, and with whose employers they are in competition. These illustrations will cover different types of work, from the most elementary to the most complicated.

If the above reasoning is correct, it follows that the most important object of both the workmen and the management should be the training and development of each individual in the establishment, so that he can do (at his fastest pace and with the maximum of efficiency) the highest class of work for which his natural abilities fit him. These principles appear to be so self-evident that many men may think it almost childish to state them. Let us, however, turn to the facts, as they actually exist in this country and in England. The English and American peoples are the greatest sportsmen in the world. Whenever an American workman plays baseball, or an English workman plays cricket, it is safe to say that he strains every nerve to secure victory for his side. He does his very best to make the largest possible number of runs. The universal sentiment is so strong that any man who fails to give out all there is in him in sport is branded as a "quitter," and treated with contempt by those who are around him.

When the same workman returns to work on the following day, instead of using every effort to turn out the largest possible amount of work, in a majority of the cases this man deliberately plans to do as little as he safely can—to turn out far less work than he is well able to do—in many instances to do not more than one-third to one-half of a proper day's work. And in fact if he were to do his best to turn out his largest possible day's work, he would be abused by his fellow-workers for so doing, even more than if he had proved himself a "quitter" in sport. Underworking, that is, deliberately working slowly so as to avoid doing a full day's work, "soldiering," as it is called in this country, "hanging it out," as it is called in England, "ca canae," as it is called in Scotland, is almost universal in industrial establishments, and prevails also to a large extent in the building trades; and the writer asserts without fear of contradiction that this constitutes tbe greatest evil with which the working-people of both England and America are now afflicted.

It will be shown later in this chapter that doing away with slow working and "soldiering" in all its forms and so arranging the relations between employer and employé that each workman will work to his very best advantage and at his best speed, accompanied by the intimate cooperation with the management and the help (which the workman should receive) from the management, would result on the average in nearly doubling the output of each man and each machine. What other reforms, among those which are being discussed by these two nations, could do as much toward promoting prosperity, toward the diminution of poverty, and the alleviation of suffering? America and England have been recently agitated over such subjects as the tariff, the control of the large corporations on the one hand, and of hereditary power on the other hand, and over various more or less socialistic proposals for taxation, etc. On these subjects both peoples have been profoundly stirred, and yet hardly a voice has been raised to call attention to this vastly greater and more important subject of "soldiering," which directly and powerfully affects the wages, the prosperity, and the life of almost every working-man, and also quite as much the prosperity of every industrial establishment in the nation.

The elimination of "soldiering" and of the several causes of slow working would so lower the cost of production that both our home and foreign markets would be greatly enlarged, and we could compete on more than e en terms with our rivals. It would remove one of the fundamental causes for dull times, for lack of employment, and for poverty, and therefore would have a more permanent and far-reaching effect upon these misfortunes than any of the curative remedies that are now being used to soften their consequences. It would insure higher wages and make shorter working hours and better working and home conditions possible.

Why is it, then, in the face of the self-evident fact that maximum prosperity can exist only as the result of the determined effort of each workman to turn out each day his largest possible day's work, that the great majority of our men are deliberately doing just the opposite, and that even when the men have the best of intentions their work is in most cases far from efficient? There are three causes for this condition, which may be briefly summarized as:

*First.* The fallacy, which has from time immemorial been almost universal among workmen, that a material increase in the output of each man or each machine in the trade would result in the end in throwing a large number of men out of work.

*Second.* The defective systems of management which are in common use, and which make it necessary for each workman to soldier, or work slowly, in order that he may protect his own best interests.

*Third.* The inefficient rule-of-thumb methods, which are still almost universal in all trades, and in practising which our workmen waste a large part of their effort.

This chapter will attempt to show the enormous gains which would result from the substitution by our workmen of scientific for rule-of-thumb methods.

To explain a little more fully these three causes:

*First.* The great majority of workmen still believe that if they were to work at their best speed they would be doing a great injustice to the whole trade by throwing a lot of men out of work, and yet the history of the development of each trade shows that each improvement, whether it be the invention of a new machine or the introduction of a better method, which results in increasing the productive capacity of the men in the trade and cheapening the costs, instead of throwing men out of work make in the end work for more men.

The cheapening of any article in common use almost immediately results in a largely increased demand for that article. Take the case of shoes, for instance. The introduction of machinery for doing every element of the work which was formerly done by hand has resulted in making shoes at a fraction of their former labor cost, and in selling them so cheap that now almost every man, woman, and child in the working-classes buys one or two pairs of shoes per year, and wears shoes all the time, whereas formerly each workman bought perhaps one pair of shoes every five years, and went barefoot most of the time, wearing shoes only as a luxury or as a matter of the sternest necessity. In spite of the enormously increased output of shoes per workman, which has come with shoe machinery, the demand for shoes has so increased that there are relatively more men working in the shoe industry now than ever before.

The workmen in almost every trade have before them an object lesson of this kind, and yet, because they are ignorant of the history of their own trade even, they still firmly believe, as their fathers did before them, that it is against their best interests for each man to turn out each day as much work as possible. Under this fallacious idea a large proportion of the workmen of both countries each day deliberately work slowly so as to curtail the output. Almost every labor union has made, or is contemplating making, rules which have for their object curtailing the output of their members, and those men who have the greatest influence with the working-people, the labor leaders as well as many people with philanthropic feelings who are helping them, are daily spreading this fallacy and at the same time telling them that they are overworked.

A great deal has been and is being constantly said about "sweat-shop" work and conditions. The writer has great sympathy with those who are overworked, but on the whole a greater sympathy for those who are *under paid.* For every individual, however, who is overworked, there are a hundred who intentionally underwork—greatly underwork—every day of their lives, and who for this reason deliberately aid in establishing those conditions which in the end inevitably result in low wages. And yet hardly a single voice is being raised in an endeavour to correct this evil.

As engineers and managers, we are more intimately acquainted with these facts than any other class in the community, and are therefore best fitted to lead in a movement to combat this fallacious idea by educating not only the workmen but the whole of the country as to the true facts. And yet we are practically doing nothing in this direction, and are leaving this field entirely in the hands of the labor agitators (many of whom are misinformed and misguided), and of sentimentalists who are ignorant as to actual working conditions.

*Second.* As to the second cause for soldiering—the relations which exist between employers and employés under almost all of the systems of management which are in common use—it is impossible in a few words to make it clear to one not familiar with this problem why it is that the *ignorance of employers* as to the proper time in which work of various kinds should be done makes it for the interest of the workman to "soldier."

The writer therefore quotes herewith from a paper read before The American Society of Mechanical Engineers in June, 1903, entitled "Shop Management," which it is hoped will explain fully this cause for soldiering: "This loafing or soldiering proceeds from two causes. First, from the natural instinct and tendency of men to take it easy, which may be called natural soldiering. Second, from more intricate second thought and reasoning caused by their relations with other men, which may be called systematic soldiering.

"There is no question that the tendency of the average man (in all walks of life) is toward working at a slow, easy gait, and that it is only after a good deal of thought and observation on his part or as a result of example, conscience, or external pressure that he takes a more rapid pace.

"There are, of course, men of unusual energy, vitality, and ambition who naturally choose the fastest gait, who set up their own standards, and who work hard, even though it may be against their best interests. But these few uncommon men only serve by forming a contrast to emphasize the tendency of the average.

"This common tendency to 'take it easy' is greatly increased by bringing a number of men together on similar work and at a uniform standard rate of pay by the day.

"Under this plan the better men gradually but surely slow down their gait to that of the poorest and least efficient. When a naturally energetic man works for a few days beside a lazy one, the logic of the situation is unanswerable. 'Why should I work hard when that lazy fellow gets the same pay that I do and does only half as much work?'

"A careful time study of men working under these conditions will disclose facts which are ludicrous as well as pitiable.

"To illustrate: The writer has timed a naturally energetic workman who, while going and coming from work, would walk at a speed of from three to four miles per hour, and not infrequently trot home after a day's work. On arriving at his work he would immediately slow down to a speed of about one mile an hour. When, for example, wheeling a loaded wheelbarrow, he would go at a good fast pace even up hill in order to be as short a time as possible under load, and immediately on the return walk slow down to a mile an hour, improving every opportunity for delay short of actually sitting down. In order to be sure not to do more than his lazy neighbour, he would actually tire himself in his effort to go slow.

"These men were working under a foreman of good reputation and highly thought of by his employer, who, when his attention was called to this state of things, answered: 'Well, I can keep them from sitting down, but the devil can't make them get a move on while they are at work.'

"The natural laziness of men is serious, but by far the greatest evil from which both workmen and employers are suffering is the *systematic soldiering* which is almost universal under all of the ordinary schemes of management and which results from a careful study on the part of the workmen of what will promote their best interests.

"The writer was much interested recently in hearing one small but experienced golf caddy boy of twelve explaining to a green caddy, who had shown special energy and interest, the necessity of going slow and lagging behind his man when he came up to the ball, showing him that since they were paid by the hour, the faster they went the less money they got, and finally telling him that if he went too fast the other boys would give him a licking.

"This represents a type of *systematic soldiering* which is not, however, very serious, since it is done with the knowledge of the employer, who can quite easily break it up if he wishes.

"The greater part of the *systematic soldiering*, however, is done by the men with the deliberate object of keeping their employers ignorant of how fast work can be done.

"So universal is soldiering for this purpose that hardly a competent workman can be found in a large establishment, whether he works by the day or on piece work, contract work, or under any of the ordinary systems, who does not devote a considerable part of his time to studying just how slow he can work and still convince his employer that he is going at a good pace.

"The causes for this are, briefly, that practically all employers determine upon a maximum sum which they feel it is right for each of their classes of employees to earn per day, whether their men work by the day or piece.

"Each workman soon finds out about what this figure is for his particular case, and he also realizes that when his employer is convinced that a man is capable of doing more work than he has done, he will find sooner or later some way of compelling him to do it with little or no increase of pay.

"Employers derive their knowledge of how much of a given class of work can be done in a day from either their own experience, which has frequently grown hazy with age, from casual and unsystematic observation of their men, or at best from records which are kept, showing the quickest time in which each job has been done. In many cases the employer will feel almost certain that a given job can be done faster than it has been, but he rarely cares to take the drastic measures necessary to force men to do it in the quickest time, unless he has an actual record proving conclusively how fast the work can be done. "It evidently becomes for each man's interest, then, to see that no job is done faster than it has been in the past. The younger and less experienced men are taught this by their elders, and all possible persuasion and social pressure is brought to bear upon the greedy and selfish men to keep them from making new records which result in temporarily increasing their wages, while all those who come after them are made to work harder for the same old pay.

"Under the best day work of the ordinary type, when accurate records are kept of the amount of work done by each man and of his efficiency, and when each man's wages are raised as he improves, and those who fail to rise to a certain standard are discharged and a fresh supply of carefully selected men are given work in their places, both the natural loafing and systematic soldiering can be largely broken up. This can only be done, however, when the men are thoroughly convinced that there is no intention of establishing piece work even in the remote future, and it is next to impossible to make men believe this when the work is of such a nature that they believe piece work to be practicable. In most cases their fear of making a record which will be used as a basis for piece work will cause them to soldier as much as they dare.

"It is, however, under piece work that the art of systematic soldiering is thoroughly developed; after a workman has had the price per piece of the work he is doing lowered two or three times as a result of his having worked harder and increased his output, he is likely entirely to lose sight of his employer's side of the case and become imbued with a grim determination to have no more cuts if soldiering can prevent it. Unfortunately for the character of the workman, soldiering involves a deliberate attempt to mislead and deceive his employer, and thus upright and straightforward workmen are compelled to become more or less hypocritical. The employer is soon looked upon as an antagonist, if not an enemy, and the mutual confidence which should exist between a leader and his men, the enthusiasm, the feeling that they are all working for the same end and will share in the results is entirely lacking.

"The feeling of antagonism under the ordinary piecework system becomes in many cases so marked on the part of the men that any proposition made by their employers, however reasonable, is looked upon with suspicion, and soldiering becomes such a fixed habit that men will frequently take pains to restrict the product of machines which they are running when even a large increase in output would involve no more work on their part."

*Third.* As to the third cause for slow work, considerable space will later in this chapter be devoted to illustrating the great gain, both to employers and employés, which results from the substitution of scientific for rule-of-thumb methods in even the smallest details of the work of every trade. The enormous saving of time and therefore increase in the output which it is possible to effect through eliminating unnecessary motions and substituting fast for slow and inefficient motions for the men working in any of our trades can be fully realized only after one has personally seen the improvement which results from a thorough motion and time study, made by a competent man.

To explain briefly: owing to the fact that the workmen in all of our trades have been taught the details of their work by observation of those immediately around them, there are many different ways in common use for doing the same thing, perhaps forty, fifty, or a hundred ways of doing each act in each trade, and for the same reason there is a great variety in the implements used for each class of work. Now, among the various methods and implements used in each element of each trade there is always one method and one implement which is quicker and better than any of the rest. And this one best method and best implement can only be discovered or developed through a scientific study and analysis of all of the methods and implements in use, together with accurate, minute, motion and time study. This involves the gradual substitution of science for rule of thumb throughout the mechanic arts.

This chapter will show that the underlying philosophy of all of the old systems of management in common use makes it imperative that each workman shall be left with the final responsibility for doing his job practically as he thinks best, with comparatively little help and advice from the management. And it will also show that because of this isolation of workmen, it is in most cases impossible for the men working under these systems to do their work in accordance with the rules and laws of a science or art, even where one exists.

The writer asserts as a general principle (and he proposes to give illustrations tending to prove the fact later in this chapter) that in almost all of the mechanic arts the science which underlies each act of each workman is so great and amounts to so much that the workman who is best suited to actually doing the work is incapable of fully understanding this science, without the guidance and help of those who are working with him or over him, either through lack of education or through insufficient mental capacity. In order that the work may be done in accordance with scientific laws, it is necessary that there shall be a far more equal division of the responsibility between the management and the workmen than exists under any of the ordinary types of management. Those in the management whose duty it is to develop this science should also guide and help the workman in working under it, and should assume a much larger share of the responsibility for results than under usual conditions is assumed by the management.

The body of this chapter will make it clear that, to work according to scientific laws, the management must take over and perform much of the work which is now left to the men; almost every act of the workman should be preceded by one or more preparatory acts of the management which enable him to do his work better and quicker than he otherwise could. And each man should daily be taught by and receive the most friendly help from those who are over him, instead of being, at the one extreme, driven or coerced by his bosses, and at the other left to his own unaided devices.

This close, intimate, personal cooperation between the management and the men is of the essence of modern scientific or task management.

It will be shown by a series of practical illustrations that, through this friendly cooperation, namely, through sharing equally in every day's burden, all of the great obstacles (above described) to obtaining the maximum output for each man and each machine in the establishment are swept away. The 30 per cent to 100 per cent increase in wages which the workmen are able to earn beyond what they receive under the old type of management, coupled with the daily intimate shoulder to shoulder contact with the management, entirely removes all cause for soldiering. And in a few years, under this system, the workmen have before them the object lesson of seeing that a great increase in the output per man results in giving employment to more men, instead of throwing men out of work, thus completely eradicating the fallacy that a larger output for each man will throw other men out of work.

It is the writer's judgment, then, that while much can be done and should be done by writing and talking toward educating not only workmen, but all classes in the community, as to the importance of obtaining the maximum output of each man and each machine, it is only through the adoption of modern scientific management that this great problem can be finally solved. Probably most of the readers of this chapter will say that all of this is mere theory. On the contrary, the theory, or philosophy, of scientific management is just beginning to be understood, whereas the management itself has been a gradual evolution, extending over a period of nearly thirty years. And during this time the employés of one company after another, including a large range and diversity of industries, have gradually changed from the ordinary to the scientific type of management. At least 50,000 workmen in the United States are now employed under this system; and they are receiving from 30 per cent to 100 per cent higher wages daily than are paid to men of similar calibre with whom they are surrounded, while the companies employing them are more prosperous than ever before. In these companies the output, per man and per machine, has on an average been doubled. During all these years there has never been a single strike among the men working under this system. In place of the suspicious watchfulness and the more or less open warfare which characterizes the ordinary types of management, there is universally friendly cooperation between the management and the men.

Several chapters have been written, describing the expedients which have been adopted and the details which have been developed under scientific management and the steps to be taken in changing from the ordinary to the scientific type. But unfortunately most of the readers of these papers have mistaken the mechanism for the true essence. Scientific management fundamentally consists of certain broad general principles, a certain philosophy, which can be applied in many ways, and a description of what any one man or men may believe to be the best mechanism for applying these general principles should in no way be confused with the principles themselves.

It is not here claimed that any single panacea exists for all of the troubles of the working-people or of employers. As long as some people are born lazy or inefficient, and others are born greedy and brutal, as long as vice and crime are with us, just so long will a certain amount of poverty, misery, and unhappiness be with us also. No system of management, no single expedient within the control of any man or any set of men can insure continuous prosperity to either workmen or employers. Prosperity depends upon so many factors entirely beyond the control of any one set of men, any state, or even any one country, that certain periods will inevitably come when both sides must suffer, more or less. It is claimed, however, that under scientific management the intermediate periods will be far more prosperous, far happier, and more free from discord and dissension. And also, that the periods will be fewer, shorter and the suffering less. And this will be particularly true in any one town, any one section of the country, or any one state which first substitutes the principles of scientific management for the rule of thumb.

That these principles are certain to come into general use practically throughout the civilized world, sooner or later, the writer is profoundly convinced, and the sooner they come the better for all the people.

## Frederick Taylor and Scientific Management

In 1911, Frederick Winslow Taylor published his work, *The Principles of Scientific Management*, in which he described how the application of the scientific method to the management of workers greatly could improve productivity. Scientific management methods called for optimizing the way that tasks were performed and simplifying the jobs enough so that workers could be trained to perform their specialized sequence of motions in the one "best" way. Prior to scientific management, work was performed by skilled craftsmen who had learned their jobs in lengthy apprenticeships. They made their own decisions about how their job was to be performed. Scientific management took away much of this autonomy and converted skilled crafts into a series of simplified jobs that could be performed by unskilled workers who easily could be trained for the tasks. Taylor became interested in improving worker productivity early in his career when he observed gross inefficiencies during his contact with steel workers.

### Soldiering

Working in the steel industry, Taylor had observed the phenomenon of workers' purposely operating well below their capacity, that is, *soldiering*. He attributed soldiering to three causes:

1. The almost universally held belief among workers that if they became more productive, fewer of them would be needed and jobs would be eliminated.
2. Non-incentive wage systems encourage low productivity if the employee will receive the same pay regardless of how much is produced, assuming the employee can convince the employer that the slow pace really is a good pace for the job. Employees take great care never to work at a good pace for fear that this faster pace would become the new standard. If employees are paid by the quantity they produce, they fear that management will decrease their per-unit pay if the quantity increases.
3. Workers waste much of their effort by relying on rule-of-thumb methods rather than on optimal work methods that can be determined by scientific study of the task.

To counter soldiering and to improve efficiency, Taylor began to conduct experiments to determine the best level of performance for certain jobs, and what was necessary to achieve this performance.

### Time Studies

Taylor argued that even the most basic, mindless tasks could be planned in a way that dramatically would increase productivity, and that scientific management of the work was more effective than the "initiative and incentive" method of motivating workers. The initiative and incentive method offered an incentive to increase productivity but placed the responsibility on the worker to figure out how to do it. To scientifically determine the optimal way to perform a job, Taylor performed experiments that he called *time studies,* (also known as *time and motion studies*). These studies were characterized by the use of a stopwatch to time a worker's sequence of motions, with the goal of determining the one best way to perform a job. The following are examples of some of the time-and-motion studies that were performed by Taylor and others in the era of scientific management.

### *Pig Iron*

If workers were moving 12 1/2 tons of pig iron per day and they could be incentivized to try to move 47 1/2 tons per day, left to their own wits they probably would become exhausted after a few hours and fail to reach their goal. However, by first conducting experiments to determine the amount of resting that was necessary, the worker's manager could determine the optimal timing of lifting and resting so that the worker could move the 47 1/2 tons per day without tiring. Not all workers were physically capable of moving 47 1/2 tons per day; perhaps only 1/8 of the pig iron handlers were capable of doing so. While these 1/8 were not extraordinary people who were highly prized by society, their physical capabilities were well-suited to moving pig iron. This example suggests that workers should be selected according to how well they are suited for a particular job.

### *The Science of Shoveling*

In another study of the "science of shoveling", Taylor ran time studies to determine that the optimal weight that a worker should lift in a shovel was 21 pounds. Since there is a wide range of densities of materials, the shovel should be sized so that it would hold 21 pounds of the substance being shovelled. The firm provided the workers with optimal shovels. The result was a three to four fold increase in productivity and workers were rewarded with pay increases. Prior to scientific management, workers used their own shovels and rarely had the optimal one for the job.

### *Bricklaying*

Others performed experiments that focused on specific motions, such as Gilbreth's bricklaying experiments that resulted in a dramatic decrease in the number of motions required to lay bricks. The husband and wife Gilbreth team used motion picture technology to study the motions of the workers in some of their experiments.

### *Taylor's 4 Principles of Scientific Management*

After years of various experiments to determine optimal work methods, Taylor proposed the following four principles of scientific management:

1. Replace rule-of-thumb work methods with methods based on a scientific study of the tasks.
2. Scientifically select, train, and develop each worker rather than passively leaving them to train themselves.
3. Cooperate with the workers to ensure that the scientifically developed methods are being followed.
4. Divide work nearly equally between managers and workers, so that the managers apply scientific management principles to planning the work and the workers actually perform the tasks.

These principles were implemented in many factories, often increasing productivity by a factor of three or more. Henry Ford applied Taylor's principles in his automobile factories, and families even began to perform their household tasks based on the results of time and motion studies.

### *Drawbacks of Scientific Management*

While scientific management principles improved productivity and had a substantial impact on industry, they also increased the monotony of work. The core job dimensions of skill variety, task identity, task significance, autonomy, and feedback all were missing from the picture of scientific management.

While in many cases the new ways of working were accepted by the workers, in some cases they were not. The use of stopwatches often was a protested issue and led to a strike at one factory where "Taylorism" was being tested. Complaints that Taylorism was dehumanizing led to an investigation by the United States Congress. Despite its controversy, scientific management changed the way that work was done, and forms of it continue to be used today.

# 8

# Henri Fayol

Henri Fayol (Istanbul, 29 July 1841–Paris, 19 November 1925) was a French mining engineer, director of mines, and management theorist, who developed independent of the theory of Scientific Management, a general theory of business administration also known as Fayolism. He was one of the most influential contributors to modern concepts of management.

### *Biography*

Fayol was born in 1841 in a suburb of Istanbul, Turkey, where his father, an engineer, was appointed superintendent of works to build a bridge over the Golden Horn (Galata Bridge). They returned to France in 1847. Fayol studied at the mining school "École Nationale Supérieure des Mines" in Saint-Étienne.

When 19 years old he started as an engineer at a mining company "Compagnie de Commentry-Fourchambeau-Decazeville" in Commentry. He became director in 1888, when the mine company employed over 1,000 people, and held that position over 30 years until 1918. By 1900 the company was one of the largest producers of iron and steel in France and was regarded as a vital industry. In 1916 he published his experience in the book "Administration Industrielle et Générale", only a few years after Frederick Winslow Taylor had published his theory of Scientific Management.

## Work

### *Fayolism*

Fayolism is one of the first comprehensive statements of a general theory of management, developed by Fayol. He has proposed that there are six primary functions of management and 14 principles of management

1. forecasting
2. planning
3. organizing
4. commanding
5. coordinating
6. controlling

Controlling is described in the sense that a manager must receive feedback about a process in order to make necessary adjustments. Principles of Management:

1. Division of work. This principle is the same as Adam Smith's 'division of labour'. Specialisation increases output by making employees more efficient.
2. Authority. Managers must be able to give orders. Authority gives them this right. Note that responsibility arises wherever authority is exercised.
3. Discipline. Employees must obey and respect the rules that govern the organisation. Good discipline is the result of effective leadership, a clear understanding between management and workers regarding the organisation's rules, and the judicious use of penalties for infractions of the rules.
4. Unity of command. Every employee should receive orders from only one superior.
5. Unity of direction. Each group of organisational activities that have the same objective should be directed by one manager using one plan.
6. Subordination of individual interests to the general interest. The interests of any one employee or group of employees should not take precedence over the interests of the organisation as a whole.
7. Remuneration. Workers must be paid a fair wage for their services.
8. Centralisation. Centralisation refers to the degree to which subordinates are involved in decision making. Whether decision making is centralised (to management) or

decentralised (to subordinates) is a question of proper proportion. The task is to find the optimum degree of centralisation for each situation.

9. Scalar chain. The line of authority from top management to the lowest ranks represents the scalar chain. Communications should follow this chain. However, if following the chain creates delays, cross-communications can be allowed if agreed to by all parties and superiors are kept informed.
10. Order. People and materials should be in the right place at the right time.
11. Equity. Managers should be kind and fair to their subordinates.
12. Stability of tenure of personnel. High employee turnover is inefficient. Management should provide orderly personnel planning and ensure that replacements are available to fill vacancies.
13. Initiative. Employees who are allowed to originate and carry out plans will exert high levels of effort.
14. Esprit de corps. Promoting team spirit will build harmony and unity within the organisation.

Fayol's work has stood the test of time and has been shown to be relevant and appropriate to contemporary management. Many of today's management texts including Daft have reduced the six functions to four: (1) planning; (2) organizing; (3) leading; and (4) controlling. Daft's text is organized around Fayol's four functions.

## Functions and Principles of Management

Henri Fayol, a French engineer and director of mines, was little unknown outside France until the late 40s when Constance Storrs published her translation of Fayol's 1916 " Administration Industrielle et Generale ".

Fayol's career began as a mining engineer. He then moved into research geology and in 1888 joined, Comambault as Director. Comambault was in difficulty but Fayol turned the operation round. On retirement he published his work-a comprehensive theory of administration-described and classified administrative management roles and processes then became recognised and referenced by others in the growing discourse about management. He is frequently seen as a key, early contributor to a classical or administrative management school of thought (even though he himself would never have recognised such a "school"). His theorising about administration was built on personal observation and experience of what worked well in terms of organisation. His aspiration for an "administrative science" sought a consistent set of principles that all organizations must apply in order to run properly.

F. W. Taylor published "The Principles of Scientific Management" in the USA in 1911, and Fayol in 1916 examined the nature of management and administration on the basis of his French mining organisation experiences..

Fayol synthesised various tenets or principles of organisation and management and Taylor on work methods, measurement and simplification to secure efficiencies. Both referenced functional specialisation. Both Fayol and Taylor were arguing that principles existed which all organisations-in order to operate and be administered efficiently-could implement. This type of assertion typifies a "one best way" approach to management thinking. Fayol's five functions are still relevant to discussion today about management roles and action.

1. to forecast and plan-prevoyance examine the future and draw up plans of action
2. to organise build up the structure, material and human of the undertaking
3. to command maintain activity among the personnel
4. to co-ordinate bind together, unify and harmonise activity and effort
5. to control see that everything occurs in conformity with policy and practise

Fayol also synthesised 14 principles for organisational design and effective administration. It is worthwhile reflecting on these are comparing the conclusions to contemporary utterances by Peters, Kanter and Handy to name but three management gurus. Fayol's 14 principles are:

- specialisation/division of labour: A principle of work

allocation and specialisation in order to concentrate activities to enable specialisation of skills and understandings, more work focus and efficiency.

- authority with corresponding responsibility : If responsibilities are allocated then the post holder needs the requisite authority to carry these out including the right to require others in the area of responsibility to undertake duties. Authority stems from:
- that ascribed from the delegation process (the job holder is assigned to act as the agent of the high authority to whom they report-hierarchy)
- allocation and permission to use the necessary resources needed (budgets, assets, staff) to carry out the responsibilities.
- selection-the person has the expertise to carry out the responsibilities and the personal qualities to win the support and confidence of others.

The R = A correspondence is important to understand. R = A enables accountability in the delegation process. Who do we cope with situations where R > A? Are there work situations where our R< A? "judgement demands high moral character, therefore, a good leader should possess and infuse into those around him courage to accept responsibility. The best safeguard against abuse of authority and weakness on the part of a higher manager is personal integrity and particularly high moral character of such a manager..... this integrity, is conferred neither by election nor ownership. " 1916

A manager should never be given authority without responsibility—and also should never be given responsibility without the associated authority to get the work done.

- discipline : The generalisation about discipline is that discipline is essential for the smooth running of a business and without it-standards, consistency of action, adherence to rules and values-no enterprise could prosper. "in an essence-obedience, application, energy, behaviour and outward marks of respect observed in accordance with standing agreements between firms and its employees " 1916

- unity of command : The idea is that an employee should receive instructions from one superior only. This generalisation still holds-even where we are involved with team and matrix structures which involve reporting to more than one boss-or being accountable to several clients. The basic concern is that tensions and dilemmas arise where we report to two or more bosses. One boss may want X, the other Y and the subordinate is caught between the devil and the deep blue sea.
- unity of direction : The unity of command idea of having one head (chief executive, cabinet consensus) with agree purposes and objectives and one plan for a group of activities) is clear.
- subordination of individual interest to the general interest : Fayol's line was that one employee's interests or those of one group should not prevail over the organisation as a whole. This would spark a lively debate about who decides that the interests of the organisation as a whole are. Ethical dilemmas and matters of corporate risk and the behaviour of individual "chancers" are involved here. Fayol's work-assumes a shared set of values by people in the organisation-a unitarism where the reasons for organisational activities and decisions are in some way neutral and reasonable.
- remuneration of staff : " the price of services rendered. " 1916.

The general principle is that levels of compensation should be "fair" and as far as possible afford satisfaction both to the staff and the firm (in terms of its cost structures and desire for profitability/surplus).

- centralisation : Centralisation for HF is essential to the organisation and a natural consequence of organising. This issue does not go away even where flatter, devolved organisations occur. Decentralisation-is frequently centralisaed-decentralisation !!! The modes of control over the actions and results of devolved organisations are still matters requiring considerable attention.
- scalar chain/line of authority : The scalar chain of command

of reporting relationships from top executive to the ordinary shop operative or driver needs to be sensible, clear and understood.

- order : The level of generalisation becomes difficult with this principle. Basically an organisation "should" provide an orderly place for each individual member-who needs to see how their role fits into the organisation and be confident, able to predict the organisations behaviour towards them. Thus policies, rules, instructions and actions should be understandable and understood. Orderliness implies steady evolutionary movement rather than wild, anxiety provoking, unpredictable movement.
- equity : Equity, fairness and a sense of justice "should"pervade the organisation-in principle and practice.
- stability of tenure : Time is needed for the employee to adapt to his/her work and perform it effectively. Stability of tenure promotes loyalty to the organisation, its purposes and values.
- initiative : At all levels of the organisational structure, zeal, enthusiasm and energy are enabled by people having the scope for personal initiative. (Note: Tom Peters recommendations in respect of employee empowerment)
- esprit de corps : Here Fayol emphasises the need for building and maintaining of harmony among the work force, team work and sound interpersonal relationships.

In the same way that Alfred P Sloan, the executive head of General Motors reorganised the company into semi-autonomous divisions in the 1920s, corporations undergoing reorganisation still apply "classical organisation" principles-very much in line with Fayol's recommendations.

## Fayolism

Fayolism is one of the first comprehensive statement of a general theory of management, developed by the French management theorist Henri Fayol (1841–1925): one of the most influential contributors to modern concepts of management,

Fayol has proposed that there are five primary functions of management: (1) planning, (2) organizing, (3) commanding,

(4) coordinating, and (5) controlling (Fayol, 1949, 1987). Controlling is described in the sense that a manager must receive feedback on a process in order to make necessary adjustments.

Fayol's work has stood the test of time and has been shown to be relevant and appropriate to contemporary management. Many of today's management texts including Daft (2005) have reduced the five functions to four: (1) planning, (2) organizing, (3) leading, and (4) controlling. Daft's text is organized around Fayol's four functions.

### *The 6 types of Operations*

For Fayol any Organisation can be subdivided into six types of *Operations*. Each *Operation* being fulfilled by its corresponding *Essential Function*:

1. Technical Operations (production, manufacturing, transformation)
2. Commercial Operations (purchases, sales, exchanges)
3. Financial Operations (seek for capital and finance management)
4. Security Operations (protection of goods and people)
5. Accounting Operations (balance, P&L, cost control, statistics, etc)
6. Administrative' *Operations (Management)*.

In 1925 six month before Henri Fayol's death Verney helped Fayol redefine The function of administration (Administration Industrielle et Generale).

### *The 9 Levels*

Fayol was representing an organisation like a living body (« corps social », i.e. "social body") with main organs hierarchically structured as follow:

1. Shareholders,
2. Board of Administration,
3. General Direction and its General staff (advisors),
4. Regional/local Directions,
5. Main Engineers,
6. Services Managers,

7. Workshops Managers,
8. Foremen,
9. Workers.

### *The 5 Elements of Administration*

Popularized by Fayol with the acronym of POCCC:

1. *Planning'* (to foresee/anticipate and make plans)
2. Organisation (to provide the *Function* with all is needed for its smooth running: Supplies, Tools, Funding, Employees)
3. Commandment (to lead the people employed by the organisation)
4. Coordination (to harmonise all actions of an Organisation in order to facilitate its smooth running and *success*)
5. Control (to verify if everything happens in accordance with defined plans, orders given, and accepted principles).

The word *Control* clearly provoked some misunderstanding by English-readers because its 1st meaning in French is "to check" and its 2nd meaning is "to have a grip over". And it is the other way round in English. So for the French-reader Fayol clearly meant "Check everything!".

For Fayol, "*The Art of Commanding* relies upon certain personal qualities and upon the knowledge of management general principles. (...) It has, like all other arts, its degrees. (...) The manager in charge of a commandment must:

1. have a deep knowledge of his staff;
2. cull the incapables;
3. well know the conventions binding the organisation and its members;
4. give the good example (by his attitude);
5. conduct regular inspections of the corps social;
6. get together his main partners in conferences (meetings) where are prepared the Unity of Direction and the Focus of Efforts;
7. not be distracted by details;
8. aim to make prevalent among his staff, energy, initiative and dévouement."

***The 14 Principles of Administration***

1. Division of work: *Reduces the span of attention or effort for any one person or group. Develops practice or routine and familiarity.*
2. Authority: *"The right to give orders. Should not be considered without reference to responsibility."*
3. Discipline: *"Outward marks of respect in accordance with formal or informal agreements between a firm and it's employees."*
4. Unity of command: *"One man one superior!"*
5. Unity of direction: *"One head and One plan for a group of activities with the same objective."*
6. Subordination of Individual Interests to the Common Interest: *"The interests of one individual or group should not prevail over the general or common good."*
7. Remuneration of personnel: *"Pay should be fair to both the worker as well as the organization."*
8. Centralisation: *"Is always present to a greater or lesser extent, depending on the size of the company and the quality of its managers."*
9. Scalar chain: *"The line of authority from top to bottom of the organization."*
10. Order: *"A place for everything and everything in its right place; ie. the right man in the right place."*
11. Equity: *"A combination of kindness and justice towards employees."*
12. Stability of personnel tenure: *"Employees need to be given time to settle in to their jobs, even though this may be a lengthy period in the case of some managers."*
13. Initiative: *"Within the limits of authority and discipline, all levels of staff should be encouraged to show initiative."*
14. Esprit de corps (Union is strength): *"Harmony is a great strength to an organization; teamwork should be encouraged."*

Fayol suggested that it is important to have unity of command: a concept that suggests there should be only one supervisor for each person in an organization. Like Socrates, Fayol suggested that management is a universal human activity that applies equally well to the family as it does to the corporation.

### *The 16 Management Duties of the Organisation*

1. To aim at giving serious thoughts to activity plans and having them firmly executed.
2. To aim at having employed people and used equipment being relevant to the goal, the resources and the needs of the organisation.
3. To set up a unique Direction (top management), skilled and vigorous.
4. To consult others for actions, to coordinate efforts.
5. To formulate decisions in a clear, clean and precise way.
6. To aim to an efficient recruitment, each department needing to be lead by a skilled and active man, each employee being at the place where he can provide the most services.
7. To define clearly the attributions (i.e. job description).
8. To encourage people to take initiatives and responsibilities.
9. To pay fairly and expertly for the services provided to the Organisation.
10. to sanction faults and errors.
11. To enforce discipline.
12. To aim at having individual interests subordinated to the Organisation's interest.
13. To give a special attention to the Unity of Command.
14. To supervise the material order and social order (i.e. to keep the place tidy and to avoid strikes).
15. To verify everything (i.e. to apply quality control on every operation).
16. To fight against the red tape attitude.

### *The 7 Qualities*

The 7 qualities he was expecting from managers were:

1. Health and vigour;
2. Cleverness;
3. Moral qualities;
4. General knowledge (culture);
5. Management capacity;
6. Notions about other functions (activities);

7. The strongest skills in the function managed.

For the Top Managing Director, the 7th quality was "the broadest skills in the dedicated activity of the organisation". For example, if the organisation was a car manufacturer, the top Director must have the largest possible knowledge about the manufacturing of cars. This was suggesting that this Director would have to be probably a former car manufacturing engineer.

Managers need the ability to perform the elements of Management but they also need abilities in the Technical, commercial, financial, security, and Accounting areas of the enterprise. Managerial Ability became more important as he moves up to upper level management. Fayol's ideas inspired a number of individuals to teach and Write about management(Wren).

### *Research & Teaching of Management*

Fayol believed management theories could be developed, then taught (to students of Grandes écoles). His theories were published in a monograph titled *General and Industrial Management* (1916). In doing so, he stated,"...starting a general discussion-that is what I am trying to do by publishing this survey, and I hope that a theory will emanate from it."

His theories and ideas were ideally a result of his environment; that of a post revolutionized France in which a republic bourgeois was emerging. A bourgeois himself, He believed in the controlling of workers in order to achieve a greater productivity over all other managerial considerations. However, through reading *General and Industrial Management,* it is apparent that Fayol advocated a flexible approach to management, one which he believed could be applied to any circumstance whether in the home, the workplace, or within the state. He stressed the importance and the practice of forecasting and planning in order to apply these ideas and techniques which demonstrated his ability and his emphasis in being able to adapt to any sort of situation. In *General and Industrial Management* he outlines an agenda whereby, under an accepted theory of management, every citizen is exposed and taught some form of management education and allowed to exercise management abilities first at school and later on in the workplace.

*"Everyone needs some concepts of management; in the home, in affairs of state, the need for managerial ability is in keeping with the*

*importance of the undertaking, and for individual people the need is everywhere in greater accordance with the position occupied.* '-excerpt from *General and Industrial Management*

***Discussion***

Fayol has been described as the father of modern operational management theory (George, p. 146). Although his ideas have become a universal part of the modern management concepts, some writers continue to associate him with Frederick Winslow Taylor. Taylor's scientific management deals with the efficient organisation of production in the context of a competitive enterprise that has to control its production costs. That was only one of the many areas that Fayol addressed. Perhaps the connection with Taylor is more one of time, than of perspective. According to Claude George (1968), a primary difference between Fayol and Taylor was that Taylor viewed management processes from the bottom up, while Fayol viewed it from the top down. George's comment may have originated from Fayol himself. In the classic *General and Industrial Management* Fayol wrote that "Taylor's approach differs from the one we have outlined in that he examines the firm from the "bottom up."

He starts with the most elemental units of activity—the workers' actions—then studies the effects of their actions on productivity, devises new methods for making them more efficient, and applies what he learns at lower levels to the hierarchy...." He suggests that Taylor has staff analysts and advisors working with individuals at lower levels of the organization to identify the ways to improve efficiency. According to Fayol, the approach results in a "negation of the principle of unity of command". Fayol criticized Taylor's functional management in this way. "... the most marked outward characteristics of functional management lies in the fact that each workman, instead of coming in direct contact with the management at one point only, ... receives his daily orders and help from eight different bosses...". Those eight, Taylor said, were (1) route clerks, (2) instruction card men, (3) cost and time clerks, (4) gang bosses, (5) speed bosses, (6) inspectors, (7) repair bosses, and the (8) shop disciplinarian.--This, Fayol said, was an unworkable situation, and that Taylor must have somehow reconciled the dichotomy in some way not described in Taylor's works.

Fayol's desire for teaching a generalized theory of management stemmed from the belief that each individual of an organization at one point or another takes on duties that involve managerial decisions. Unlike Taylor, however, who believed management activity was the exclusive duty of an organizations dominant class. Fayol's approach was more in sync with his idea of Authority which stated that the right to give orders should not be considered without the acceptance and understanding of responsibility.

Noted as one of the early fathers of the *Human Relations* movements, Fayol expressed ideas and theories with practices which differed from Taylor in that they showed flexibility and adaptation as well as stressed the importance of Interpersonal Interaction among employees.

Fayol believed that animosity and unease within the workplace occurred among employees in different departments often due to communication in writing; i.e. letters, (or in current times) e-mails. Among scholars of organizational communication and psychology, e-mails and letters as a form of communication in work are said to induce or solidify the idea of importance of an individual within the workplace and furthermore give way to selfish thinking which leads to arguments and conflict among employees.

Fayol expressed this idea in his book by stating," in some firms... employees in neighbouring departments with numerous points of contact, or even employees within a department, who could quite easily meet, communicate with each other in writing... there is to be observed a certain amount of animosity prevailing between different departments or different employees within a department. The system of written communication usually brings this result. There is a way of putting an end to this deplorable system and that is to forbid all communication in writing which could easily and advantageously be replaced by verbal ones."

While Fayol's theories are typically refereed to as rigid and inflexible, it is practices and theories such as these which show flexibility in his theories of management. He developed and used theses ideas in order to diagnose a problem and eventually find solutions which provided methods to work around and fix these situations. This all led to his general idea of controlling employees in order to achieve increased productivity.

Fayol also expressed ideas which would later on lead to influence Systems and Contingency theories. The two are said to have emerged as a result of management theorists' desire to integrate ideas of the human relation theories within management which is what Fayol's General theory of Management relied upon.

Systems theory, first introduced in 1958 by Ludwig von Bertalanffy and later on published in 1968 attempts to understand organizations by comparing them to living organisms. Systems Theory is broken down into four distinct characteristics which reflect the biological resemblance between living organisms and organizations.

First, *Wholeness* expresses the idea that an organization is a set of individual elements which are interdependent in the sense that the actions of one individual or group will affect the rest of the system or organization.

The second is described as *Hierarchy* or the division of individuals into subsystems. This can be illustrated by groups within an organization. With regards to organisms, this could be called the organs of the body.

Third, the organization may be regarded as, *"Open or closed,"* in that systems can be characterized by their level of active exchange with the outside environment; successful organizations must be actively open.

Lastly, open systems are characterized by two processes; maintenance and adaptation. Both of these processes act on *Feedback* to actions taken by the groups in order to maintain stability and adapt to environmental changes.

Fayol illustrated all of these ideas in his theories on general management. First, he believed in the division of labor among organizations (subsystems) by relating them to living organisms. He states that, *"...it is observable in the animal world where the more highly developed the creature the more highly differentiated it's organs."* He continues to describe the same scenario replicating that of an individual within a group and of a group within an organization. This is described in his 14 principles as the principle of *Order* System Theory relies heavily on interdependence which Fayol also suggests is a vital part of management as he states, *""Man... plays a role like that of a cell in the animal... As the development of the organism is effected the grouping together of elemental units the organs appear, they are differentiated and perfected in proportion as the number of combined elements increase. In the social organism, as in the animal, a small number of functional elements accounts for an infinite variety of activities."*

*Contingency Leadership Theory* which was produced around the same time as *Systems Theory,* roughly states that no one leadership or management style is ideal and that the best leadership is that which reflects the internal and external environment of the organization. This is perhaps the most important concept that Fayol based his ideas around as well as the area where he and Taylor differ the most.

*"Seldom do we have to apply the same principle twice in identical conditions; allowance must be made for different changing circumstances... Therefore principles...[must be]... flexible and capable of adaptation to every need; it is a matter of knowing how to make use of them which is a difficult art requiring intelligence, experience, decision, and proportion.*-excerpt from *General and Industrial Management*

***Rodrigues***

Early last century, Fayol offered 14 principles of management aimed to help managers manage more effectively. Many organizations in technologically advanced countrys interpret the principles quite differently from the way they were interpreted in Fayol's time. These differences and the cultural challenges managers face when implementing this new framework are presented. The fourteen principles are: (1) Division of work, (2) Authority and responsibility, (3) Discipline, (4) Unity of command, (5) Unity of direction, (6) Subordination of individual interests to the common good, (7) Remuneration of personnel, (8) Centralization, (9) Scaler chain (10) Order, (11) Equity, (12) Stability of personnel tenure, (13) Initiative, (14) Esprit de corps.

**Wren & Bluedorn**

Daniel A. Wren wrote on a study Bluedorn critical review of the study. The study had said that traditional management occupies only a small portion of managerial activities and this review by Bluedorn shows that Fayol was a real manager and his Administrative theory should still be studied today. Real Managers did not "explode the myths" of traditional management but rather confirmed, classical BY Fayol. The problem resides in the assumption made that Fayol limited managerial activities to planning, decision making, and controlling. There is a misunderstanding of Fayol and classical theory in the development of management thought. Bluedorn introduced a review of the work of Fayol and other theorists of his day. Bluedorn said that "most of the content that was examined is surprisingly valid. Before his review managers and others criticize Fayol and others work because they forget, ignoring, misunderstand, and re-label their ideas. This makes it more difficult to develop a body of knowledge that can be translated into action-practice in skill development. This research shows that managers need to actually be trained using Fayol's administrative theory and other theorists theory's because they are still relevant today.

# 9

# Herbert Simon

Herbert Alexander Simon (June 15, 1916– February 9, 2001) was an American political scientist, economist, and psychologist, and professor—most notably at Carnegie Mellon University—whose research ranged across the fields of cognitive psychology, computer science, public administration, economics, management, philosophy of science, sociology, and political science. With almost a thousand very highly cited publications, he is one of the most influential social scientists of the 20th century.

Simon was a polymath, among the founding fathers of several of today's important scientific domains, including artificial intelligence, information processing, decision-making, problem-solving, attention economics, organization theory, complex systems, and computer simulation of scientific discovery. He coined the terms *bounded rationality* and *satisficing*, and was the first to analyse the architecture of complexity and to propose a preferential attachment mechanism to explain power law distributions.

He also received many top-level honours later in life. These include: the ACM's Turing Award for making "basic contributions to artificial intelligence, the psychology of human cognition, and list processing" (1975); the Nobel Memorial Prize in Economics "for his pioneering research into the decision-making process within economic organizations" (1978); the National Medal of Science (1986); and the APA's Award for Outstanding Lifetime Contributions to Psychology (1993). As a testament to his interdisciplinary approach, Simon was affiliated with such varied Carnegie Mellon departments as the School of Computer Science, Tepper School of Business, Departments of Philosophy, Social and Decision Sciences, and Psychology.

### *Life*

Herbert Alexander Simon was born into a Jewish family in Milwaukee, Wisconsin on June 15, 1916. His father, Arthur Simon (1881–1948) was an electrical engineer who had come to the United States from Germany in 1903 after earning his engineering degree from the Technische Hochschule of Darmstadt. Arthur, an inventor who was granted "several dozen patents", was also an independent patent attorney. Herbert's mother, Edna Marguerite Merkel, was an accomplished pianist whose ancestors had come from Prague and Cologne. Herbert's European ancestors had been piano makers, goldsmiths, and vintners.

Herbert Simon was educated as a child in the public school system in Milwaukee where he developed an interest in science. He found schoolwork to be interesting but rather easy. Unlike many children, Simon was exposed to the idea that human behaviour could be studied scientifically at a relatively young age due to the influence of his mother's younger brother, Harold Merkel, who had studied economics at the University of Wisconsin–Madison under John R. Commons. Through his uncle's books on economics and psychology, Simon discovered the social sciences. Simon received both his B.A. (1936) and his Ph.D. (1943) in political science, from the University of Chicago, where he studied under Harold Lasswell and Charles Edward Merriam.

Among his earliest influences, Simon has cited Richard Ely's economics textbook, Norman Angell's *The Great Illusion*, and Henry George's *Progress and Poverty*. In 1933, Simon entered the University of Chicago, and following those early influences, he studied the social sciences and mathematics. He was interested in biology, but chose not to study it because of his "color-blindness and awkwardness in the laboratory" He chose instead to focus on political science and economics.

His most important mentor at the University was Henry Schultz who was an econometrician and mathematical economist. After enrolling in a course on "Measuring Municipal Governments," Simon was invited to be a research assistant for Clarence Ridley, with whom he coauthored the book *Measuring Municipal Activities* in 1948. Eventually his studies led him to the field of organizational decision-making, which would become the subject of his doctoral dissertation.

From 1939 to 1942, Simon acted as director of a research group at the University of California, Berkeley. When the group's grant was exhausted, he took a position in political science at the Illinois Institute of Technology. Back in Chicago, he began participating in the seminars held by the staff of the Cowles Commission who at that time included Trygve Haavelmo, Jacob Marschak, and Tjalling Koopmans. He thus began a more in-depth study of economics in the area of institutionalism. Marschak brought Simon in to assist in the study he was currently undertaking with Sam Schurr of the "prospective economic effects of atomic energy".

In 1949, Simon became a professor of administrations and chairman of the Department of Industrial Management at Carnegie Tech (later to become Carnegie Mellon University). He continued to teach in various departments at Carnegie Mellon, including psychology and computer science, until his death in 2001.

From 1950 to 1955, Simon studied mathematical economics and during this time, together with David Hawkins, discovered and proved the Hawkins-Simon theorem on the "conditions for the existence of positive solution vectors for input-output matrices." He also developed theorems on near-decomposability and aggregation. Having begun to apply these theorems to organizations, Simon determined around 1954 that the best way to study problem-solving was to simulate it with computer programs, which led to his interest in computer simulation of human cognition. End 1950s he was among the first members of the Society for General Systems Research.

Simon was a member of the First Unitarian Church of Pittsburgh. He had a keen interest in the arts. He was a friend of Robert Lepper and Richard Rappaport and he influenced Lepper's interest in the impact of machine on society. Rappaport also painted Simon's commissioned portrait at Carnegie Mellon University.

### *Contributions to Artificial Intelligence*

Simon was a pioneer in the field of artificial intelligence, creating with Allen Newell the Logic Theory Machine (1956) and the General Problem Solver (GPS) (1957) programs. GPS was possibly the first method of separating problem solving strategy from information about particular problems. Both programs were developed using the Information Processing Language (IPL) (1956) developed by Newell, Cliff Shaw and Simon. Donald Knuth mentions the development of list processing in IPL with the linked list originally called "NSS memory" for its inventors. In 1957, Simon predicted that computer chess would surpass human chess abilities within "10 years" when, in reality, that transition took about 40 years.

In the early 1960s Simon wrote a chapter responding to a claim by the psychologist Ulric Neisser that machines might be able to replicate 'cold cognition', e.g. processes like reasoning, planning, perceiving, and deciding, but could not replicate 'hot cognition', including desiring, feeling pain or pleasure, and having emotions. Simon's chapter was eventually published in 1967. It was ignored by the AI research community for some years, but later became very influential e.g. indirectly through the work of Sloman and Picard on emotions.

Simon also collaborated with James G. March on several works in organization theory. With Allen Newell, Simon developed a theory for the simulation of human problem solving behaviour using production rules. The study of human problem solving required new kinds of human measurements and, with Anders Ericsson, Simon developed the experimental technique of verbal protocol analysis. Simon was interested in the role of knowledge in expertise. He said that to become an expert required about 10 years of experience and he and colleagues estimated that expertise was the result of learning roughly 50,000 chunks of information. A chess expert was said to have learned about 50,000 chunks or chess position patterns.

Simon was also interested in how humans learn and, with Edward Feigenbaum, he developed the EPAM (Elementary Perceiver and Memorizer) theory, one of the first theories of learning to be implemented as a computer program. EPAM was able to explain a large number of phenomena in the field of verbal learning. Later versions of the model were applied to concept formation and the acquisition of expertise. He was awarded the ACM's A.M. Turing Award along with Allen Newell in 1975. "In joint scientific efforts extending over twenty years, initially in collaboration with J. C. (Cliff) Shaw at the RAND Corporation, and subsequentially with numerous faculty and student colleagues at Carnegie Mellon University, they have made basic contributions to artificial intelligence, the psychology of human cognition, and list processing."

## Contributions to Economics

Herbert Simon has been credited for revolutionary changes in microeconomics. He is responsible for the concept of organizational decision-making as it is known today. He was also the first to discuss this concept in terms of uncertainty; i.e. it is impossible to have perfect and complete information at any given time to make a decision. While this notion was not entirely new, Simon is best known for its origination. It was in this area that he was awarded the Nobel Prize in 1978.

At the Cowles Commission, Simon's main goal was to link economic theory to mathematics and statistics. His main contributions were to the fields of general equilibrium and econometrics. He was greatly influenced by the marginalist debate that began in the 1930s. The popular work of the time argued that it was not empirically apparent that entrepreneurs needed to follow the marginalist principles of profit-maximization/cost-minimization in running organizations. The argument went on to note that profit-maximization was not accomplished, in part, because of the lack of complete information. In decision-making, Simon believed that agents face uncertainty about the future and costs in acquiring information in the present. These factors limit the extent to which agents can make a fully rational decision, thus they possess only "bounded rationality" and must make decisions by "satisficing," or choosing that which might not be optimal but which will make them happy enough.

Simon was known for his research on industrial organization. He determined that the internal organization of firms and the external business decisions thereof did not conform to the Neoclassical theories of "rational" decision-making. Simon wrote many articles on the topic over the course of his life mainly focusing on the issue of decision-making within the behaviour of what he termed "bounded rationality". "Rational behaviour, in economics, means that individuals maximizes his utility function under the constraints they face (e.g., their budget constraint, limited choices,...) in pursuit of their self-interest. This is reflected in the theory of subjective expected utility. The term bounded rationality is used to designate rational choice that takes into account the cognitive limitations of both knowledge and cognitive capacity. Bounded rationality is a central theme in behavioral economics. It is concerned with the ways in which the actual decision-making process influences decisions. Theories of bounded rationality relax one or more assumptions of standard expected utility theory".

Simon determined that the best way to study these areas was through computer simulation modeling. As such, he developed an interest in computer science. Herbert Simon's main interests in computer science were in artificial intelligence, human-computer interaction, principles of the organization of humans and machines as information processing systems, the use of computers to study (by modeling) philosophical problems of the nature of intelligence and of epistemology, and the social implications of computer technology. Some of Simon's economic research was directed toward understanding technological change in general and the information processing revolution in particular. While living in Pittsburgh, PA, he advised the citizenry on various issues including the use of public funds to build stadiums and the method of raising tax revenue. Simon emphasized the usefulness of the land tax, reflecting the early influence of Henry George on his economic thought.

## Contribution to Library Science

Satisficing, as defined by Simon, can be applied to library and information science where researchers assess how much information is adequate to meet their information need. With the huge volume of information today, library researchers are forced to use Simon's model of satisficing when searching. The first satisfactory alternative is chosen over the best. Applying satisficing to research is a way for researchers to adjust to the vast amount of information today.

### *Studying Decision-making*

*Administrative Behaviour* was Herbert Simon's doctoral dissertation and his first book. It served as the foundation for his life's work. The centerpiece of this book is the behavioral and cognitive processes of making rational human choices, that is, decisions. An operational administrative decision should be correct and efficient, and it must be practical to implement with a set of coordinated means. Any decision involves a choice selected from a number of alternatives, directed toward an organizational goal or subgoal. Realistic options will have real consequences consisting of personnel actions or non-actions modified by environmental facts and values. In actual practice, some of the alternatives may be conscious or unconscious; some of the consequences may be unintended as well as intended; and some of the means and ends may be imperfectly differentiated, incompletely related, or poorly detailed.

The task of rational decision making is to select the alternative that results in the more preferred set of all the possible consequences. This task can be divided into three required steps: (1) the identification and listing of all the alternatives; (2) the determination of all the consequences resulting from each of the alternatives; and (3) the comparison of the accuracy and efficiency of each of these sets of consequences. Any given individual or organization attempting to implement this model in a real situation would be unable to comply with the three requirements. It is highly improbable that one could know all the alternatives, or all the consequences that follow each alternative. The question here is: given the inevitable limits on rational decision making, what other techniques or behavioral processes can a person or organization bring to bear to achieve approximately the best result? Simon writes:" The human being striving for rationality and restricted within the limits of his knowledge has developed some working procedures that partially overcome these difficulties. These procedures consist in assuming that he can isolate from the rest of the world a closed system containing a limited number of variables and a limited range of consequences."

Administrative Behaviour, as a text, addresses a wide range of human behaviors, cognitive abilities, management techniques, personnel policies, training goals and procedures, specialized roles, criteria for evaluation of accuracy and efficiency, and all of the ramifications of communication processes. Simon is particularly interested in how these factors directly and indirectly influence the making of decisions.

Authority is a well studied, primary mark of organizational behaviour, and is straightforwardly defined in the organizational context as the ability and right of an individual of higher rank to determine the decision of an individual of lower rank. The actions, attitudes, and relationships of the dominant and subordinate individuals constitute components of role behaviour that can vary widely in form, style, and content, but do not vary in the expectation of obedience by the one of superior status, and willingness to obey from the subordinate. Authority is highly influential on the formal structure of the organization, including patterns of communication, sanctions, and rewards, as well as on the establishment of goals, objectives, and values of the organization.

Decisions can be complex admixtures of facts and values. Information about facts, especially empirically proven facts or facts derived from specialized experience, are more easily transmitted in the exercise of authority than are the expressions of values. Simon is primarily interested in seeking identification of the individual employee with the organizational goals and values. Following Lasswell he states that "a person identifies himself with a group when, in making a decision, he evaluates the several alternatives of choice in terms of their consequences for the specified group". A person may identify himself with any number of social, geographic, economic, racial, religious, familial, educational, gender, political, and sports groups. Indeed, the number and variety are unlimited. The fundamental problem for organizations is to recognize that personal and group identifications can either facilitate or obstruct correct decision making for the organization. A specific organization has to deliberately determine and specify in appropriate detail and clear language its own goals, objectives, means, ends, and values.

Chester Barnard pointed out that "the decisions that an individual makes as a member of an organization are quite distinct from his personal decisions". Personal choices may determine whether an individual joins a particular organization, and continue to be made in his or her extra-organizational private life. But, as a member of an organization, that individual makes decisions not in relationship to personal needs and results, but in an impersonal sense as part of the organizational intent, purpose, and effect. Organizational inducements, rewards, and sanctions are all designed to form, strengthen, and maintain this identification.

The correctness of decisions is measured by two major criteria: (1) adequacy of achieving the desired objective; and (2) the efficiency with which the result was obtained. Many members of the organization may focus on adequacy, but the overall administrative management must pay particular attention to the efficiency with which the desired result was obtained. Simon's contributions to research in the area of decision-making have become increasingly mainstream in the business community thanks to the growth of management consulting.

## Herbert Simon's Intelligent Altruism

In a series of published and unpublished exchanges toward the end of the twentieth century, Herbert Simon and Oliver Williamson engaged in arguments about the relationship between TCE and behavioural economics. The exchange derived from personal biography as well as intellectual history and attested to differences not only of ideas but of worldviews. Augier and March (2001) provides one explanation for the disagreement in terms of a family quarrel about the degree to which one ought to assume unbounded rationality, opportunism, and conflict in the creation and sustenance of human organizations.

Another aspect to the quarrel consists in the fact that Simon was not merely or even primarily an economist or social scientist. He was a Renaissance man, a polymath – deeply interested in how the human mind works and how that coheres with how the universe works. Opportunism, like unbounded rationality and conflict, did not make sense to him as fundamentals of human behaviour either empirically or historically and certainly not in terms of what we know about biological evolution. These concepts also did not make sense to him normatively, as guides for future action, for creatures consciously engaged in 'designing' their own environments, nor for scientists studying such creatures – scientists of 'the artificial'.

Concepts such as bounded rationality, docility, and intelligent altruism were more interesting and fundamental to him, even if they were 'messier' because (a) they were empirically-based, and (b) they were necessary to hold together a larger, more general tapestry of what we know about human evolution and history within which organizations and markets play smaller roles. Simon explicitly stated that he was not in favour of sacrificing an empirical understanding of how actual humans behaved even if this meant sacrificing simplicity and elegance in the theories that ensued. His argument about Occam's razor is telling in this regard: The application of the principle of satisficing to theories is sometimes defended as an application of Occam's Razor. But Occam's Razor has a double edge. Succinctness of statement is not the only measure of a theory's simplicity. Occam understood his rule as recommending theories that make no more assumptions than necessary to account for the phenomena.

Throughout a career spanning over six decades, Simon inveighed against economists' penchant for ignoring facts on the ground and clinging to an edifice of economic 'laws' built on increasingly shaky behavioural foundations. In a full-scale argument on this topic in 1997, in a published version of the Raffaele Mattioli Lectures, Simon (1997b) emphasized the importance of getting the empirics right:

The [neoclassical] model itself is manipulated with great mathematical formality, and if it is tested with quantitative data, high standards of sophistication are imposed on the statistical methods employed. What is omitted is any serious testing of the validity of the assumptions of the model itself, even the kind of historical, experiential and anecdotal testing that we find in Smith and Marshall. This might be all right if the quantitative, econometric tests were generally sharp and decisive. Almost always, they are not. The literature of modern economics is full of examples of the sensitivity of models to small changes of assumptions – many, if not most of them beyond the limits of accuracy of statistical tests.
For the most part, Simon has won the argument with regard to bounded rationality, but his challenges continue with regard to other assumptions. One such assumption of particular importance to TCE is opportunism.

### *Opportunism in Transaction Cost Economics*

Just as Simon's early decades were focused on convincing economists and others that 'the major reason why we humans do not behave in a globally rational way was because we cannot,' in the latter decades, he began to focus on the fact that 'we are highly dependent on those around us' (Simon, 1997b). Both empirical findings and evolutionary arguments led Simon to conclude that pure self-interest, or its stronger cousin, opportunism, was an inappropriate assumption in models of transactions, not to mention inaccurate and even normatively dangerous for our understanding and design of organizations.

We can trace back TCE's behavioural assumptions about opportunism and ensuing lack of trust in concepts such as altruism, loyalty, and organizational identification, to a partial reading of Adam Smith. For example, economists often cite and build upon *The Wealth of Nations*, (Smith, 1776), in which Smith developed his ideas about the spontaneous benefits of selfishness, an idea he got from Mandeville (1714). The oft-quoted but mostly misunderstood passage from that book concerning the butcher and baker (Baumol, 2002) forms the basis for economists' generalization of the fundamental behavioural assumption about human self-interest. But his (arguably) most important work, *Theory of Moral Sentiments* (Smith, 1759) needs to be consulted if we are to have a complete picture of Smith's position on the matter. By ignoring this latter work, economists have set the stage for a continuing debate between their own normative theorizing and the observed empirical experience of human transactions, both within and outside organizations. The notion of opportunism, defined as 'self-interest seeking with guile' is rather recent and can be found in Williamson (1975). It is important to note here that Williamson is not saying that opportunism is always at work; he is only saying that contracts should be made on the assumption that it could be at work. In other words, contracts should be made with an eye to the opportunistic potential they offer (Williamson, 1985).

The work of Douglas North (1978) in economic history illustrates well both the potential for and limits to economic analysis built on assumptions of opportunism. In using opportunismdriven transaction costs as prime movers in economic history, North had to provide an explanation for the observed evidence of successful collective action such as the voting paradox, the absence of free riding in various human organizations, the pervasiveness of charity, and so on. In seeking to explain these manifest phenomena, North introduces the notion of 'ideology' as the missing factor in economic analyses. However, North does not have an underlying explanation why people should buy into 'ideology.' Similarly, scholars who argue in a more strictly neoclassical vein, such as Stigler and Becker (1977), Becker (1996), and Gauthier (1984) all have the problem of being unable to explain why rational actors would acquire beliefs and behaviours that are not in their narrow self-interest. While North's conclusions also cohere with those of Arrow (1974) and Sen (1985), others have posited other exogenous factors such as the Protestant ethic (Weber, 1905).

### *Docility and Intelligent Altruism*

Simon has a different explanation, a behavioural construct that brings together experimental evidence and formal evolutionary models to provide an alternative assumption for transactional and organizational economics. That construct is *docility*. Simon defined it as: *The tendency to* depend on suggestions, recommendation, persuasion, and information obtained through social *channels as a major basis of choice.* (1993) Docility follows directly from the limitations of human cognition. Through a series of articles, essays and lectures, Simon developed a notion of 'intelligent' altruism based on this notion of docility to argue that bounded rationality not only limits our ability to undertake the computational demands of highly opportunistic behaviour, but also selects such behaviour out (in an evolutionary sense) and selects in those who are willing and able to depend on others and help sustain others in a group – i.e. intelligent altruists.

More recently, Knudsen (2003) has argued for the role of docility in the emergence of altruism in biological populations. The case for the evolutionary dominance of intelligent altruists is also well-argued from perspectives other than those resting on docility. Hill (1990) for example shows that under the normal assumptions of neoclassical economics, the invisible hand of the market will tend to weed out persistently opportunistic behaviour. Interestingly enough, without resorting to evolutionary arguments, Adam Smith himself had made the case for the fundamental behavioural assumption of persuasion in all economic exchanges: Different genius is not the foundation of this disposition to barter which is the cause of the division of labour. The real foundation of it is that principle to perswade which so much prevails in human nature... We ought then to mainly cultivate the power to perswasion, and indeed we do so without intending it. Since the whole life is spent in the exercise of it, a ready method of bargaining with each other must undoubtedly be attained. (Smith, 1978).

Game-theoretic and behavioural-economic evidence of all kinds has been accumulating over the last two or more decades pressing us to rethink the assumption of pure opportunism. In fact, what we know about self-interest based on empirical evidence, both in the lab and in the field suggests that neither opportunism nor altruism or trust can possibly form clear bases for predictions about human behaviour. Both are confounded not only by heterogeneity in behavioural traits and choices, but are situated and change over time. Dawes and Thaler (1988) capture this in an eloquent passage:

In the rural areas around Ithaca it is common for farmers to put some fresh produce on the table by the road. There is a cash box on the table, and customers are expected to put money in the box in return for the vegetables they take. The box has just a small slit, so money can only be put in, not taken out. Also, the box is attached to the table, so no one can (easily?) make off with the money. We think that the farmers have just about the right model of human nature. They feel that enough people will volunteer to pay for the fresh corn to make it worthwhile to put it out there. The farmers also know that if it were easy enough to take the money, someone would do so.

Besides the negative evidence against any default propensity for opportunism, there is also direct positive evidence for the construct of docility — the fact that human beings are prone both to give and take advice. In a summary of findings on the subject, Schotter (2003) concludes:

(i) Laboratory subjects tend to follow the advice of naïve advisors (i.e. advisors who are hardly more expert in the task at hand than they are).

(ii) This advice changes their behaviour in the sense that subjects who play games or make decisions with naïve advice play differently than those who play identical games without such advice.

(iii) The decision made in games played with naïve advice are closer to the predictions of economic theory than those made without it.

(iv) If given a choice between getting advice or the information upon which that advice was based, subjects tend to opt for the advice, indicating a kind of underconfidence in their decision-making abilities that is counter to the usual egocentric bias or overconfidence observed by psychologists.

(v) The reason why advice increases efficiency or rationality is that the process of giving or receiving advice forces decision-makers to think about the problem they are facing in a way different from the way they would if no advice were offered.

For Simon the important point was that most of what we do we have learned from those around us because [b]ehaving in this fashion contributes heavily to our fitness because... the information on which this advice is based is far better than the information we could gather independently. As a result, *people exhibit a very large measure of docility*.. By fitness, Simon meant our biological fitness i.e. the effectiveness with which we produced progeny. Simon theorized that social information contributes so heavily to our fitness – it is such an adaptive trait-that docile human beings drove out non-docile human beings *in actual evolutionary competition*. He believed that [t]he farther the complexities of the real world extend beyond our capabilities for knowledge and calculation, the more valuable is docility, to enable us to benefit from the collective knowledge and skill of our society.

From a gene's-eye perspective, docility would be strongly selected for because it enhances the reproductive fitness of each human being. In other words, docility is the individual's way of leveraging the advantages of social living. As a result of being fitnessenhancing at the level of the gene, the population of human beings that now walks the planet exhibits a large degree of docility.

It is interesting to speculate what a TCE that took docility as its fundamental behavioural assumption would look like. Perhaps we would need to go beyond bargaining to negotiation – and not merely distributive negotiation (aimed at dividing the pie) but integrative negotiation to grow the pie under negotiation. In other words, TCE could be incorporated into growth models and in the economics of innovation in new ways – not only competition, but cooperation could also serve as a discovery procedure. In fact, the results summarized by Schotter (2003) suggest an explicit role for docility in coming up with creative solutions to problems. Similarly docility-based TCE might provide ways to move beyond static models of social networks to dynamic ones. In a worldview in which opportunism is not such a big hurdle and the ability and willingness to persuade and be persuaded is a dominant characteristic, humans will be able to build new relationships more easily and grow their networks faster. This could bring to the fore interesting challenges to current static models such as Burt's (1992) structural holes. Simon the man

It is perhaps appropriate to conclude a biographical sketch with the scholar's personal stance on the subject of behavioural assumptions at the heart of our choices in building a better society. In terms of personal political preference, Simon was a New Deal Democrat. In a characteristically profound yet simple way, he explained his choice as follows: The reason is depressingly simple, and has little to do with the wisdom or unwisdom of specific policies of either political party. Among the fundamental problems in every society, two stand out. People have to be motivated to contribute to the society, to produce. At the same time, they have to be protected if they are unable to take care of themselves adequately. You can think of it as the balance between incentives and distributive justice. Too much concern with the latter may weaken the former, and vice versa.

Using this simple-minded dichotomy, you can classify people (roughly) into two groups by their answers to the following question: Is it more important that (a) all chiselers be detected and removed from the welfare lists, or (b) no sparrow should fall from Heaven unseen and uncared for. If the answer is (a), the respondent is a Republican; if (b), a Democrat. Either answer is rationally defensible. I just happen to prefer the second one. In a world where 'liberal' has become a bad word that current American politics is striving to re-define, it is perhaps time for economists too to rethink the fundamental assumption about human behaviour that is used to explain and inform the design of our social and political institutions. It is cause for comfort to know that while Simon, the scientist, urged this from an empirical standpoint, Simon, the person, also believed it would be a good guiding principle for building a better society.

# 10

# Karl Marx

Karl Heinrich Marx (May 5, 1818 – March 14, 1883) was a German philosopher, political economist, historian, sociologist, humanist, political theorist and revolutionary credited as the founder of communism. Marx summarized his approach to history and politics in the opening line of the first chapter of *The Communist Manifesto* (1848): "The history of all hitherto existing society is the history of class struggles". Marx argued that capitalism, like previous socioeconomic systems, will produce internal tensions which will lead to its destruction. Just as capitalism replaced feudalism, capitalism itself will be displaced by communism, a stateless, classless society which emerges after a transitional period, the 'dictatorship of the proletariat'.

On the one hand, Marx argued for a systemic understanding of socioeconomic change. He argued that the structural contradictions within capitalism necessitate its end, giving way to communism: "The development of Modern Industry, therefore, cuts from under its feet the very foundation on which the bourgeoisie produces and appropriates products. What the bourgeoisie, therefore, produces, above all, are its own grave-diggers. Its fall and the victory of the proletariat are equally inevitable." — (The Communist Manifesto)

On the other hand, Marx argued that socioeconomic change occurred through organized revolutionary action. He argued that capitalism will end through the organized actions of an international working class, led by a Communist Party: "Communism is for us not a state of affairs which is to be established, an ideal to which reality [will] have to adjust itself. We call communism the real movement which abolishes the present state of things. The conditions of this movement result from the premises now in existence." (from *The German Ideology*)

While Marx remained a relatively obscure figure in his own lifetime, his ideas began to exert a major influence on workers' movements shortly after his death. This influence was given added impetus by the victory of the Marxist Bolsheviks in the Russian October Revolution, and there are few parts of the world which were not significantly touched by Marxian ideas in the course of the twentieth century.

## Biography

Karl Heinrich Marx was born in Trier, in the Kingdom of Prussia's Province of the Lower Rhine as the third of his parents' seven children. His father, Heinrich Marx (1777–1838), born Herschel Mordechai, the son of Levy Mordechai (1743-1804) and Eva Lwow (1753-1823), descended from a long line of rabbis but converted to Lutheran Christianity, despite his many deistic tendencies and his admiration of such Enlightenment figures as Voltaire and Rousseau, in order to be allowed to practice Law. Marx's mother was Henriette *nee* Pressburg (1788–1863). His siblings were Sophie (d. 1883) (m. Wilhelm Robert Schmalhausen), Hermann (1819-1842), Henriette (1820-1856), Louise (1821-1893) (m. Johann Carel Juta), Emilie, Caroline (1824-1847) and Eduard (1834-1837). His mother was the grand-aunt of industrialists Gerard Philips and Anton Philips and a maternal descendant of the Barent-Cohen family through her parents Isaac Heijmans Presburg (Presburg, c. 1747 – Nijmegen, May 3, 1832) and wife Nanette Salomon Barent-Cohen (Amsterdam, c. 1764 – Nijmegen, April 7, 1833), the daughter of Salomon David Barent-Cohen (d. 1807) and wife Sara Brandes, in turn the uncle and aunt by marriage of Nathan Mayer Rothschild's wife.

Soon after losing his job as editor of *Rheinische Zeitung*, a Cologne newspaper, Karl Marx married Jenny von Westphalen, the educated daughter of a Prussian baron, on June 19, 1843 in Kreuznacher Pauluskirche, Bad Kreuznach. Their engagement was kept secret at first, and for several years was opposed by both the Marxes and Westphalens. From 1844 to 1848, Marx enjoyed a very comfortable lifestyle, with income derived from the sale of his works, his salary, gifts from friends and allies; a large inheritance from his father's death, long delayed, also became available in March 1848.

During the first half of the 1850s the Marx family lived in poverty and constant fear of creditors in a three room flat on Dean Street in Soho, London. Marx and Jenny already had four children and three more were to follow. Of these only three survived to adulthood. Marx's major source of income at this time was Engels, who was drawing a steadily increasing income from the family business in Manchester. This was supplemented by weekly articles written as a foreign correspondent for the *New York Daily Tribune.* Inheritances from one of Jenny's uncles and her mother who died in 1856 allowed the family to move to somewhat more salubrious lodgings at 9 Grafton Terrace, Kentish Town a new suburb on the then-outskirts of London. Marx generally lived a hand-to-mouth existence, forever at the limits of his resources, although this did to some extent depend upon his spending on relatively bourgeois luxuries, which he felt were necessities for his wife and children given their social status and the mores of the time.

Marx had the following children by his wife: Jenny Caroline (m. Longuet; 1844–1883); Jenny Laura (m. Lafargue; 1845–1911); Edgar (1847–1855); Henry Edward Guy ("Guido"; 1849–1850); Jenny Eveline Frances ("Franziska"; 1851–1852); Jenny Julia Eleanor (1855–1898); and one more who died before being named (July 1857).

Following the death of his wife Jenny in December 1881, Marx developed a catarrh that kept him in ill health for the last fifteen months of his life. It eventually brought on the bronchitis and pleurisy that killed him in London on March 14, 1883. He died a stateless person and was buried in Highgate Cemetery, London, on March 17, 1883. The messages carved on Marx's tombstone are: "WORKERS OF ALL LANDS UNITE", the final line of *The Communist Manifesto*, and Engels' version of the 11th *Thesis on Feuerbach*: "The philosophers have only interpreted the world in various ways-the point however is to change it"

The Communist Party of Great Britain had the monumental tombstone built in 1954 with a portrait bust by Laurence Bradshaw; Marx's original tomb had been humbly adorned. In 1970, there was an unsuccessful attempt to destroy the monument, with a homemade bomb. Several of Marx's closest friends spoke at his funeral, including Wilhelm Liebknecht and Friedrich Engels. Engels' speech included the words: "On the 14th of March, at a quarter to three in the afternoon, the greatest living thinker ceased to think. He had been left alone for scarcely two minutes, and when we came back we found him in his armchair, peacefully gone to sleep — but forever."

In addition to Engels and Liebknecht, Marx's daughter Eleanor and Charles Longuet and Paul Lafargue, Marx's two French socialist sons-in-law, also attended his funeral. Liebknecht, a founder and leader of the German Social-Democratic Party, gave a speech in German, and Longuet, a prominent figure in the French working-class movement, gave a short statement in French. Two telegrams from workers' parties in France and Spain were also read out. Together with Engels' speech, this was the entire programme of the funeral. Those attending the funeral included Friedrich Lessner, who had been sentenced to three years in prison at the Cologne communist trial of 1852; G. Lochner, who was described by Engels as "an old member of the Communist League" and Carl Schorlemmer, a professor of chemistry in Manchester, a member of the Royal Society, but also an old communist associate of Marx and Engels. Three others attended the funeral — Ray Lankester, Sir John Noe and Leonard Church — making eleven in all.

Marx's daughter Eleanor became a socialist like her father and helped edit his works. Karl Marx was known to become the first major social theorist to form a series of concepts within the break between modern and premodern societies.

## Career in Education

Marx's parents had him educated at home until the age of thirteen. After graduating from the Trier Gymnasium, Marx enrolled in the University of Bonn in 1835 at the age of seventeen; he wished to study philosophy and literature, but his father insisted that it was more practical to study law. At Bonn he joined the Trier Tavern Club drinking society and at one point served as its president. Because of Marx's poor grades, his father forced him to transfer to the far more serious and academically oriented Humboldt-Universıtat in Berlin. During this period, Marx wrote many poems and essays concerning life, using the theological language acquired from his liberal, deistic father, such as "the Deity," but also absorbed the atheistic philosophy of the Young Hegelians who were prominent in Berlin at the time. Marx earned a doctorate in 1841 with a thesis titled *The Difference Between the Democritean and Epicurean Philosophy of Nature*, but he had to submit his dissertation to the University of Jena as he was warned that his reputation among the faculty as a Young Hegelian radical would lead to a poor reception in Berlin.

## Young Hegelians

The Left, or Young Hegelians, consisted of a group of philosophers and journalists circling around Ludwig Feuerbach and Bruno Bauer, and opposing their teacher Hegel. Despite their criticism of Hegel's metaphysical assumptions, they made use of Hegel's dialectical method as a powerful weapon for the critique of established religion and politics. One of them, Max Stirner, turned critically against both Feuerbach and Bauer in his book "Der Einzige und sein Eigenthum" (1845, *The Ego and Its Own*), calling these atheists "pious people" for their reification of abstract concepts. Marx, at that time a follower of Feuerbach, was deeply impressed by the work and abandoned Feuerbachian materialism and accomplished what recent authors have denoted as an "epistemological break." He developed the basic concept of historical materialism against Stirner in his book, "Die Deutsche Ideologie" (1846, The German Ideology), which he did not publish. Another link to the Young Hegelians was Moses Hess, with whom Marx eventually disagreed, yet to whom he owed many of his insights into the relationship between state, society and religion.

### *Paris and Brussels*

Towards the end of October 1843, Marx arrived in Paris, France. Paris at this time served as the home and headquarters of armies of German, British, Polish, and Italian revolutionaries. Marx, for his part, had come to Paris to work with Arnold Ruge, another revolutionary from Germany, on the *Deutsch-Franzosische Jahrbucher*. There, on August 28, 1844, at the Cafe de la Regence on the Place du Palais he met Friedrich Engels, who was to become his most important friend and life-long collaborator. Engels had met Marx only once before and briefly at the office of the *Rheinische Zeitung* in 1842; he went to Paris to show Marx his recently published book, *The Condition of the Working Class in England in 1844*. It was this book that convinced Marx that the working class would be the agent and instrument of the final revolution in history.

After the failure of the *Deutsch-Franzosische Jahrbucher*, Marx, living on the rue Vaneau, wrote for the most radical of all German newspapers in Paris, indeed in Europe, the *Vorwarts*, established and run by the secret society called *League of the Just*. When not writing, Marx studied the history of the French Revolution and read Proudhon. He also spent considerable time studying a side of life he had never been acquainted with before—a large urban proletariat. "[Hitherto exposed mainly to university towns...] Marx's sudden espousal of the proletarian cause can be directly attributed (as can that of other early German communists such as Weitling) to his first hand contacts with socialist intellectuals [and books] in France."

He re-evaluated his relationship with the Young Hegelians, and as a reply to Bauer's atheism wrote *On the Jewish Question*. This essay consisted mostly of a critique of current notions of civil and human rights and political emancipation; it also included several critical references to Judaism as well as Christianity from a standpoint of social emancipation. Engels, a committed communist, kindled Marx's interest in the situation of the working class and guided Marx's interest in economics. Marx became a communist and set down his views in a series of writings known as the Economic and Philosophical Manuscripts of 1844, which remained unpublished until the 1930s. In the Manuscripts, Marx outlined a humanist conception of communism, influenced by the philosophy of Ludwig Feuerbach and based on a contrast between the alienated nature of labour under capitalism and a communist society in which human beings freely developed their nature in cooperative production.

In January 1845, after *Vorwarts* expressed its hearty approval of the assassination attempt on Frederick William IV, King of Prussia, the French authorities ordered Marx, among many others, to leave Paris. He and Engels moved on to Brussels, Belgium.

Marx devoted himself to an intensive study of history, and in collaboration with Engels elaborated on his idea of historical materialism, particularly in a manuscript (published posthumously as *The German Ideology*), the basic thesis of which was that "the nature of individuals depends on the material conditions determining their production." Marx traced the history of the various modes of production and predicted the collapse of the present one—industrial capitalism—and its replacement by communism. This was the first major work of what scholars consider to be his later phase, abandoning the Feuerbach-influenced humanism of his earlier work.

Next, Marx wrote *The Poverty of Philosophy* (1847), a response to Pierre-Joseph Proudhon's *The Philosophy of Poverty* and a critique of French socialist thought. These works laid the foundation for Marx and Engels' most famous work, *The Communist Manifesto*, first published on February 21, 1848, as the manifesto of the Communist League, a small group of European communists who had come to be influenced by Marx and Engels. Later that year, Europe experienced a series of protests, rebellions, and often violent upheavals known as the Revolutions of 1848. Marx was arrested and expelled from Belgium.

In February 1848 a radical movement had seized power from King Louis-Philippe in France, and invited Marx to return to Paris, where he witnessed the revolutionary June Days Uprising first hand. When this collapsed in 1849, Marx moved back to Cologne and started the *Neue Rheinische Zeitung* ("New Rhenish Newspaper"). During its existence he was put on trial twice, on February 7, 1849 because of a press misdemeanor, and on the 8th charged with incitement to armed rebellion. Both times he was acquitted. The paper was soon suppressed and Marx returned to Paris, but was forced out again. This time he sought refuge in London.

### London

Marx moved to London in May 1849 and remained there for the rest of his life. For the first few years there, he and his family lived in extreme poverty, which is believed to have acutely damaged Marx's health and shortened his life. He briefly worked as correspondent for the New York Tribune in 1851. In London Marx devoted himself to two activities: revolutionary organizing, and an attempt to understand political economy and capitalism. Having read Engels' study of the working class, Marx turned away from philosophy and devoted himself to the First International, to whose General Council he was elected at its inception in 1864. He was particularly active in preparing for the annual Congresses of the International and leading the struggle against the anarchist wing led by Mikhail Bakunin (1814–1876).

Although Marx won this contest, the transfer of the seat of the General Council from London to New York in 1872, which Marx supported, led to the decline of the International. The most important political event during the existence of the International was the *Paris Commune of 1871* when the citizens of Paris rebelled against their government and held the city for two months. On the bloody suppression of this rebellion, Marx wrote one of his most famous pamphlets, *The Civil War in France*, an enthusiastic defence of the Commune.

Given the repeated failures and frustrations of worker's revolutions and movements, Marx also sought to understand capitalism, and spent a great deal of time in the British Library studying and reflecting on the works of political economists and on economic data. By 1857 he had accumulated over 800 pages of notes and short essays on capital, landed property, wage labour, the state, foreign trade and the world market; this work however did not appear in print until 1941, under the title *Grundrisse*. In 1859, Marx was able to publish *Contribution to the Critique of Political Economy*, his first serious economic work.

In the early 1860s he worked on composing three large volumes, the *Theories of Surplus Value*, which discussed the theoreticians of political economy, particularly Adam Smith and David Ricardo. This work, that was published posthumously under the editorship of Karl Kautsky is often seen as the Fourth book of *Capital*, and constitutes one of the first comprehensive treatises on the history of economic thought. In 1867, well behind schedule, the first volume of *Capital* was published, a work which analyzed the capitalist process of production. Here, Marx elaborated his labour theory of value and his conception of surplus value and exploitation which he argued would ultimately lead to a falling rate of profit and the collapse of industrial capitalism. Volumes II and III remained mere manuscripts upon which Marx continued to work for the rest of his life and were published posthumously by Engels.

During the last decade of his life, Marx's health declined and he became incapable of the sustained effort that had characterized his previous work. He did manage to comment substantially on contemporary politics, particularly in Germany and Russia. His *Critique of the Gotha Programme*, opposed the tendency of his followers Wilhelm Liebknecht (1826–1900) and August Bebel (1840–1913) to compromise with the state socialism of Ferdinand Lassalle in the interests of a united socialist party. In his correspondence with Vera Zasulich, Marx contemplated the possibility of Russia's bypassing the capitalist stage of development and building communism on the basis of the common ownership of land characteristic of the village *Mir*.

## Marx's Thought

A Karl Marx monument in the German city Chemnitz, formerly the East German city *Karl-Marx-Stadt* (Karl Marx City). The American Marx scholar Hal Draper once remarked, "there are few thinkers in modern history whose thought has been so badly misrepresented, by Marxists and anti-Marxists alike." The legacy of Marx's thought has become bitterly contested between numerous tendencies which each see themselves as Marx's most accurate interpreters, including but not exclusively Marxist-Leninism, Trotskyism, Maoism, and libertarian Marxism.

## Influences on Marx's thought

Marx's thought was strongly influenced by: Hegel's dialectical method and historical orientation; the classical political economy of Adam Smith and David Ricardo; French socialist and sociological thought, in particular the thought of Jean-Jacques Rousseau, Henri de Saint-Simon and Charles Fourier; earlier German philosophical materialism, particularly Ludwig Feuerbach the solidarity with the working class of Friedrich Engels

Marx's view of history, which came to be called historical materialism (controversially adapted as the philosophy of dialectical materialism by Engels and Lenin) certainly shows the influence of Hegel's claim that reality (and history) should be viewed dialectically. Hegel believed that human history is characterized by the movement from the fragmentary toward the complete and the real (which was also a movement towards greater and greater rationality). Sometimes, Hegel explained, this progressive unfolding of the Absolute involves gradual, evolutionary accretion but at other times requires discontinuous, revolutionary leaps — episodal upheavals against the existing status quo. For example, Hegel strongly opposed slavery in the United States during his lifetime, and he envisioned a time when Christian nations would eliminate it from their civilization.

Marx's critiques of German philosophical idealism, British political-economy, and French socialism depended heavily on the influence of Feuerbach and Engels. Hegel had thought in an idealist terms, and Marx sought to rewrite dialectics in materialist terms. He wrote that Hegelianism stood the movement of reality on its head, and that it was necessary to set it upon its feet. Marx's acceptance of this notion of *materialist* dialectics which rejected Hegel's idealism was greatly influenced by Ludwig Feuerbach. In *The Essence of Christianity*, Feuerbach argued that God is really a creation of man and that the qualities people attribute to God are really qualities of humanity. Accordingly, Marx argued that it is the material world that is real and that our ideas of it are consequences, not causes, of the world. Thus, like Hegel and other philosophers, Marx distinguished between appearances and reality. But he did not believe that the material world hides from us the "real" world of the ideal; on the contrary, he thought that historically and socially specific ideology prevented people from seeing the material conditions of their lives clearly.

The other important contribution to Marx's revision of Hegelianism came from Engels' book, *The Condition of the Working Class in England in 1844*, which led Marx to conceive of the historical dialectic in terms of class conflict and to see the modern working class as the most progressive force for revolution. Engels' article "Outlines of Political Economy" in *Deutsch-Franzosische Jahrbucher* also had a great influence in directing him towards the study of the workings of the capitalist economy.

Marx believed that he could study history and society scientifically and discern tendencies of history and the resulting outcome of social conflicts. Some followers of Marx concluded, therefore, that a communist revolution will inevitably occur. However, Marx famously asserted in the eleventh of his *Theses on Feuerbach* that "philosophers have only interpreted the world, in various ways; the point however is to change it", and he clearly dedicated himself to trying to alter the world. Consequently, most followers of Marx are not fatalists, but activists who believe that revolutionaries must organize social change.

### *Philosophy*

Marx's philosophy hinges on his view of human nature. Fundamentally, Marx assumed that it is human nature to transform nature, and he calls this process of transformation "labour" and the capacity to transform nature "labour power." For Marx, this is simultaneously a physical and a mental act: "A spider conducts operations that resemble those of a weaver, and a bee puts to shame many an architect in the construction of her cells. But what distinguishes the worst architect from the best of bees is this, that the architect raises his structure in imagination before he erects it in reality."

Marx did not believe that all people worked the same way, or that one works in an entirely personal and individual way. Instead, he argued that work is a social activity and that the conditions and forms under and through which people work are socially determined and change over time. Beyond these basic points, Marx made no claims about human nature.

Marx's analysis of history focuses on the organization of labour and is based on his distinction between the means / forces of production, literally those things such as land, natural resources, and technology, that are necessary for the production of material goods, and the relations of production, in other words, the social relationships people enter into as they acquire and use the means of production. Together these compose the mode of production, and Marx distinguished historical eras in terms of distinct modes of production. For example, Marx observed that European societies had progressed from a feudal mode of production to a capitalist mode of production. Marx believed that under capitalism, the means of production change more rapidly than the relations of production (for example, we develop a new technology, such as the Internet, and only later do we develop laws to regulate that technology). For Marx this mismatch between (economic) base and (social) superstructure is a major source of social disruption and conflict.

Marx understood the "social relations of production" to comprise not only relations among individuals, but between or among groups of people, or classes. As a scientist and materialist, Marx did not understand classes as purely subjective (in other words, groups of people who consciously identified with one another). He sought to define classes in terms of objective criteria, such as their access to resources. For Marx, different classes have divergent interests, which provides another source of social disruption and conflict. Conflict between social classes he regards as something inherent in all human history: "The history of all hitherto existing society is the history of class struggles."

Marx had a special concern with how people relate to that most fundamental resource of all, their own labour power. Marx wrote extensively about this in terms of the problem of alienation. As with the dialectic, Marx began with a Hegelian notion of alienation but developed a more materialist conception. Under capitalism, social relationships of production, such as among workers or between workers and capitalists, are mediated through commodities, including labour, that are bought and sold on the market. For Marx, the possibility that one may give up ownership of one's own labour— one's capacity to transform the world — is tantamount to being alienated from one's own nature; it is a spiritual loss. Marx described this loss in terms of commodity fetishism, in which the things that people produce, commodities, appear to have a life and movement of their own to which humans and their behaviour merely adapt. This disguises the fact that the exchange and circulation of commodities really are the product and reflection of social relationships among people. Marx called this reversal "commodity fetishism" (at the time Marx wrote, historians of religion used the word fetish to describe something made by people, which people believed had power over them).

Commodity fetishism provides an example of what Engels called false consciousness, which is closely related to the understanding of ideology. By ideology they meant ideas that reflect the interests of a particular class at a particular time in history, but which are presented as universal and eternal. Marx and Engels' point was not only that such beliefs are at best half-truths; they serve an important political function. Put another way, the control that one class exercises over the means of production includes not only the production of food or manufactured goods; it includes the production of ideas as well (this provides one possible explanation for why members of a subordinate class may hold ideas contrary to their own interests). Thus, while such ideas may be false, they also reveal in coded form some truth about political relations. For example, although the belief that the things people produce are actually more productive than the people who produce them is literally absurd, it does reflect (according to Marx and Engels) that people under capitalism are alienated from their own labour-power. Another example of this sort of analysis is Marx's understanding of religion, summed up in a passage from the preface to his 1843 *Contribution to the Critique of Hegel's Philosophy of Right*: "Religious suffering is, at one and the same time, the expression of real suffering and a protest against real suffering. Religion is the sigh of the oppressed creature, the heart of a heartless world, and the soul of soulless conditions. It is the opium of the people." — (Contribution to the Critique of Hegel's Philosophy of Right)

Whereas his Gymnasium senior thesis argued that the primary social function of religion was to promote solidarity, here Marx sees the social function in terms of political and economic inequality. Moreover, he provides an analysis of the ideological functions of religion: to reveal "an *inverted consciousness of the world.*" He continues: "It is the immediate *task of philosophy*, which is in the service of history, to unmask self-estrangement in its *unholy forms*, once [religion,] the *holy form* of human self-estrangement has been unmasked". For Marx, this unholy self-estrangement, the "loss of man," is complete for the sphere of the proletariat. His final conclusion is that for Germany, general human emancipation is only possible as a suspension of private property by the proletariat.

## Political Economy

Marx argued that this alienation of human work (and resulting commodity fetishism) functions precisely as the defining feature of capitalism. Prior to capitalism, markets existed in Europe where producers and merchants bought and sold commodities. According to Marx, a capitalist mode of production developed in Europe when labour itself became a commodity—when peasants became free to sell their own labour-power, and needed to do so because they no longer possessed their own land. People sell their labour-power when they accept compensation in return for whatever work they do in a given period of time (in other words, they are not selling the product of their labour, but their capacity to work). In return for selling their labour power they receive money, which allows them to survive. Those who must sell their labour power are "proletarians". The person who buys the labour power, generally someone who does own the land and technology to produce, is a "capitalist" or "bourgeois". The proletarians inevitably outnumber the capitalists.

Marx distinguished industrial capitalists from merchant capitalists. Merchants buy goods in one market and sell them in another. Since the laws of supply and demand operate within given markets, a difference often exists between the price of a commodity in one market and another. Merchants, then, practise arbitrage, and hope to capture the difference between these two markets. According to Marx, capitalists, on the other hand, take advantage of the difference between the labour market and the market for whatever commodity is produced by the capitalist. Marx observed that in practically every successful industry input unit-costs are lower than output unit-prices. Marx called the difference "surplus value" and argued that this surplus value had its source in surplus labour, the difference between what it costs to keep workers alive and what they can produce.

Capitalism is capable of tremendous growth because the capitalist can, and has an incentive to, reinvest profits in new technologies and capital equipment. Marx considered the capitalist class to be the most revolutionary in history, because it constantly improved the means of production. But Marx argued that capitalism was prone to periodic crises. He suggested that over time, capitalists would invest more and more in new technologies, and less and less in labour. Since Marx believed that surplus value appropriated from labour is the source of profits, he concluded that the rate of profit would fall even as the economy grew. When the rate of profit falls below a certain point, the result would be a recession or depression in which certain sectors of the economy would collapse. Marx thought that during such a crisis the price of labour would also fall, and eventually make possible the investment in new technologies and the growth of new sectors of the economy.

Marx believed that increasingly severe crises would punctuate this cycle of growth, collapse, and more growth. Moreover, he believed that the long-term consequence of this process was necessarily the enrichment and empowerment of the capitalist class and the impoverishment of the proletariat. He believed that were the proletariat to seize the means of production, they would encourage social relations that would benefit everyone equally, and a system of production less vulnerable to periodic crises. In general, Marx thought that peaceful negotiation of this problem was impracticable, and that a massive well-organized violent revolution would be required, because the ruling class would not give up power without struggle. He theorized that to establish the socialist system, a dictatorship of the proletariat-a period where the needs of the working-class, not of capital, will be the common deciding factor-must be created on a temporary basis. As he wrote in his "Critique of the Gotha Programme", "between capitalist and communist society there lies the period of the revolutionary transformation of the one into the other. Corresponding to this is also a political transition period in which the state can be nothing but the revolutionary dictatorship of the proletariat." While he allowed for the possibility of peaceful transition in some countries with strong democratic institutional structures (such as Britain, the US and the Netherlands), he suggested that in other countries with strong centralized state-oriented traditions, like France and Germany, the "lever of our revolution must be force."

### *Influence of Marx*

The work of Marx and Engels covers a wide range of topics and presents a complex analysis of history and society in terms of class relations. Followers of Marx and Engels have drawn on this work to propose a grand, cohesive theoretical outlook dubbed Marxism. Nevertheless, Marxists have frequently debated amongst themselves over how to interpret Marx's writings and how to apply his concepts to their contemporary events and conditions. Moreover, it is important to distinguish between "Marxism" and "what Marx believed"; for example, shortly before he died in 1883, Marx wrote a letter to the French workers' leader Jules

Guesde, and to his own son-in-law Paul Lafargue, accusing them of "revolutionary phrase-mongering" and of lack of faith in the working class. After the French party split into a reformist and revolutionary party, some accused Guesde (leader of the latter) of taking orders from Marx; Marx remarked to Lafargue, "if that is Marxism, then I am not a Marxist" (in a letter to Engels, Marx later accused Guesde of being a "Bakuninist").

Essentially, people use the word "Marxist" in one of two ways:

1. to describe those who rely on Marx's conceptual language (*e.g.* "mode of production", "class", "commodity fetishism") to understand capitalist and other societies; or:
2. to describe those who believe that a workers' revolution is the only means to a communist society.

Some, particularly in academic circles, who accept much of Marx's theory, but not all its implications, call themselves "Marxian" instead.

Six years after Marx's death, Engels and others founded the "Second International" as a base for continued political activism. This organization proved far more successful than the First International, containing mass workers' parties, particularly the large and successful Social Democratic Party of Germany, which was predominantly Marxist in outlook. This international collapsed in 1914, however, in part because some members turned to Edward Bernstein's "evolutionary socialism", and in part because of divisions precipitated by World War I.

World War I also led to the Russian Revolution of 1917, in which a left splinter of the Second International, the Bolsheviks, led by Vladimir Lenin, took power. The revolution dynamized workers around the world into setting up their own section of the Bolsheviks' "Third International". Lenin presented himself as both the philosophical and the political heir to Marx, and developed a political programme, called "Leninism" or "Bolshevism", which called for revolution organized and led by a centrally organized vanguard "Communist Party".

Marx believed that the communist revolution would take place in advanced industrial societies such as France, Germany and England, but Lenin argued that in the age of imperialism, and due to the "law of uneven development", where Russia had on the one hand, an antiquated agricultural society, but on the other hand, some of the most up-to-date industrial concerns, the "chain" might break at its weakest points, that is, in the so-called "backward" countries, and ignite revolution in the advanced industrial societies of Europe, where society is ready for socialism, and which could then come to the aid of the workers state in Russia.

Marx and Engels make a very significant comment in the preface to the Russian edition of the *Communist Manifesto*: "Now the question is: can the Russian obshchina, though greatly undermined, yet a form of primeval common ownership of land, pass directly to the higher form of Communist common ownership? Or, on the contrary, must it first pass through the same process of dissolution such as constitutes the historical evolution of the West? The only answer to that possible today is this: If the Russian Revolution becomes the signal for a proletarian revolution in the West, so that both complement each other, the present Russian common ownership of land may serve as the starting point for a communist development." — (Marx and Engels, Preface to the Russian edition of the Communist Manifesto)

Marx's words served as a starting point for Lenin, who, together with Trotsky, always believed that the Russian revolution must become a "signal for a proletarian revolution in the West". Supporters of Trotsky argue that the failure of revolution in the West (along the lines envisaged by Marx) to come to the aid of the Russian revolution after 1917 led to the rise of Stalinism and set the cast of human history for seventy years. This is termed the theory of the Permanent Revolution, which became official policy in Russia until Lenin's death in 1924 and the subsequent development of the concept of "Socialism in one country" by Stalin. 100 Mark der DDR note used in the German Democratic Republic. 100 Mark banknotes with Marx's portrait were current from 1964 until monetary union with West Germany in July 1990.

In China Mao Zedong also claimed to be an heir to Marx, but argued that peasants and not just workers could play leading roles in a Communist revolution, even in third world countries marked by peasant feudalism in the absence of industrial workers. Mao termed this the New Democratic Revolution. It was a departure from Marx, who had stated that the revolutionary transformation of society could take place only in countries that have achieved a capitalist stage of development with a proletarian majority. Marxism-Leninism as espoused by Mao came to be internationally known as Maoism.

Under Lenin, and particularly under Joseph Stalin, Soviet suppression of the rights of individuals in the name of the struggle against capitalism, as well as Stalinist purges themselves, came in the minds of many to be characteristic of Marxism. Capitalism-oriented western states encouraged this impression, as did the politics of the Cold War. There were, nonetheless, always dissenting Marxist voices — Marxists of the old school of the Second International, the left communists who split off from the Third International shortly after its formation, and later Leon Trotsky and his followers, who set up a "Fourth International" in 1938 to compete with that of Stalin, claiming to represent true Bolshevism.

Coming from the Second International milieu, in the 1920s and 1930s, a group of dissident Marxists founded the Institute for Social Research in Germany, among them Max Horkheimer, Theodor Adorno, Erich Fromm, and Herbert Marcuse. As a group, these authors often became known as the Frankfurt School. Their work is known as Critical Theory, a type of Marxist philosophy and cultural criticism heavily influenced by Hegel, Freud, Nietzsche, and Max Weber. The Frankfurt School broke with earlier Marxists, including Lenin and Bolshevism in several key ways. First, writing at the time of the ascendancy of Stalinism, they had grave doubts as to the traditional Marxist concept of proletarian class consciousness. Second, unlike earlier Marxists, especially Lenin, they rejected economic determinism. Though the Frankfurt School became highly influential, both orthodox Marxists and some Marxists involved in political practice have criticized their work for divorcing Marxist theory from practical struggle and turning Marxism into a purely academic enterprise.

Influential Marxists of the same period include the Third International's Georg Lukacs and Antonio Gramsci, who along with the Frankfurt School are often known by the term Western Marxism. Marx was an important influence as well on the German philosopher and literary critic Walter Benjamin, an occasional associate Adorno and the Frankfurt School. In 1949 Paul Sweezy and Leo Huberman founded *Monthly Review*, a journal and press, to provide an outlet for Marxist thought in the United States independent of the American Communist Party.

In 1978, G. A. Cohen attempted to defend Marx's thought as a coherent and scientific theory of history by restating its central tenets in the language of analytic philosophy. This gave birth to Analytical Marxism, an academic movement which also included Jon Elster, Adam Przeworski and John Roemer. Bertell Ollman is another Anglophone champion of Marx within the academy, as is the Israeli Shlomo Avineri.

In *Marx's 'Das Kapital'* (2006), biographer Francis Wheen reiterates David McLellan's observation that since Marxism had not triumphed in the West, "it had not been turned into an official ideology and is thus the object of serious study unimpeded by government controls."

The following countries had governments at some point in the twentieth century who at least nominally adhered to Marxism (those in bold still did as of 2008): Albania, Afghanistan, Angola, Bulgaria, China, Cuba, Czechoslovakia, East Germany, Ethiopia, Hungary, Laos, Moldova, Mongolia, Mozambique, Nicaragua, North Korea, Poland, Romania, Russia, Yugoslavia, Vietnam. In addition, the Indian states of Kerala, Tripura and West Bengal have had Marxist governments. Marxist political parties and movements have significantly declined since the fall of the Soviet Union, with some exceptions, perhaps most notably Nepal. Marx was ranked #27 on Michael H. Hart's list of the most influential figures in history. In July 2005 Marx was the surprise winner of the "Greatest Philosopher of All Time" poll by listeners of the BBC *Radio 4* series *In Our Time*.

## Criticisms

Many proponents of capitalism have argued that capitalism is a more effective means of generating and redistributing wealth than socialism or communism, or that the gulf between rich and poor that concerned Marx and Engels was a temporary phenomenon. Some suggest that self-interest and the need to acquire capital is an inherent component of human behaviour, and is not caused by the adoption of capitalism or any other specific economic system and that different economic systems reflect different social responses to this fact. The Austrian School of economics has criticized Marx's use of the labour theory of value. In addition, the political repression and economic problems of several historical Communist states have done much to destroy Marx's reputation in the Western world, particularly following the fall of the Berlin Wall and the collapse of the Soviet Union.

Some argue that while socioeconomic gaps between the bourgeoisie and proletariat remained, industrialization in countries such as the United States and Great Britain also saw the rise of a middle class not inclined to revolution, and of a welfare state that helped mitigate any revolutionary tendencies among the working class; although it can be argued that this apparent decrease in class disparity is simply due to the fact that the disparity has been shifted between so-called developed nations and developing nations. While the economic devastation of the Great Depression broadened the appeal of Marxism in the developed world, future government safeguards and economic recovery led to a decline in its influence. In contrast, Marxism remained extremely influential in feudal and industrially underdeveloped societies such as Tsarist Russia, where the Bolshevik Revolution was successful.

### *Systematic*

An intriguing critic of Marx, although he also paid tribute to many of Marx's basic ideas, was Louis Feuer, the late professor of philosophy at University of California, Berkeley. In his introduction to *Selected Works on Economics and Politics by Karl Marx*, published in 1960, Feuer argued strongly for the viewpoint, also expressed by others, that Marxism has many of the characteristics of a religion—in other words, that Marxism largely depends upon a fervent kind of faith, not provable scientifically, which is typical of religious believers. Just the same, Feuer in his introduction, and in other works, argued that Marx has had a very enduring and positive influence on the social and economic thinking of almost every modern country, particularly in Western Europe, but also in the United States. He made the interesting comment that Marxism largely depends upon the injection of ethical thinking into economic and political analysis—in contrast to modern trends which prefer to discuss these important areas in a totally "objective" manner without ethical values.

Still others criticize Marx from the perspective of philosophy of science. Karl Popper has criticized Marx's theories for not being falsifiable, which he believed rendered some aspects of Marx's historical and socio-political argument unscientific; Popper's falsifiability standard, though very influential, has itself proven controversial. Popper also criticized Marx for 'historicism'; that is, the assumption that the development of human societies follows a fixed and discernable set of rules.

While Marx and Engels focused almost exclusively on developments in the West following the prospective development of capitalism, this left the problems of the less developed nations, such as Russia, largely unaddressed. This perceived problem with Marxist theory—that revolutions nevertheless took place in less developed areas of the world, even rather more than within the most advanced capitalist ones—was known from the beginning of the 20th century, and much of the work of Vladimir Lenin and other Marxist and Marxian authors and theorists became dedicated to addressing it. Lenin's collected works contain dozens of examples of his insistence that the victory of socialism in Russia was dependent upon its spread to the heavily industrialized nations. Trotsky famously developed the theory of *Permanent Revolution* to show how revolutions in backward countries like Russia could succeed so long as they spread to the West.

After Lenin's death, this was opposed by Stalin, who argued that it was possible to establish "socialism in one country." In essence, Lenin argued, taking the theory from several other contemporary Marxist writers, that through imperialism the bourgeoisie of wealthy countries is using "superprofits" from the imperial colonies to effectively bribe the working class back home in order to appease it. Nevertheless, after the Russian Revolution of 1917, Western capitalist nations did experience (unsuccessful) revolutions more or less along the "proletarian" lines that Marx envisaged, notably in Germany (1918, 1919, 1923), Hungary (1919), Finland (1918), and Spain (leading to the Spanish Civil War) with upheavals in eastern China, France, Italy, and the UK (the general strike of 1926) and elsewhere. Others, like Shlomo Avineri, have argued that the pre-capitalist structure of 1917 Russia, as well as the strong authoritarian traditions of the Russian state and its weak civil society, pushed the Soviet revolution towards its repressive development. Critics have also claimed to have shown problems with the concept of historical materialism. At the base of historical materialism, they claim, is the view that the mode of production creates all historical events and changes. But critics have asked the question 'Where does the mode of production come from?'.

Murray Rothbard argues that "...Marx never attempts to provide an answer. Indeed he cannot, since if he attributes the state of technology or technological change to the actions of man, of individual men, his whole system falls apart. For human consciousness, and individual consciousness at that, would then be determining [the mode of production] rather than the other way round." However, Marx's famous *Preface to A Contribution to the Critique of Political Economy* states "In the social production of their existence, men inevitably enter into definite relations, which are independent of their will, namely relations of production appropriate to a given stage in the development of their material forces of production." Marx clearly attributes the productive forces and their development to the actions of human beings, but emphasises the social nature of this development, based on necessity, the need to maintain their existence, which thus develops "independent of their will", as individuals, and thus impacts back on the individual in ways which reflect the given social conditions.

### *From the Left*

Marx has also been criticized from the Left. Marx and Henry George were contemporaries, and George claimed that if Marx's ideas were ever tried, political repression would be the inevitable results. More recently, some have argued that class is not the most fundamental inequality in history and call attention to patriarchy or race, as not being, as Marxists argue, dependent on class. It could however be argued that Marx does not suggest that class divisions are more fundamental than patriarchy, since the division between men and women, as Engels pointed out, predates class divisions, but only that the movement of history can be best understood in terms of class, and that class struggle is the mechanism of change. Anarchists, on the other hand, have usually opposed Marxism, even its most libertarian forms, as being too authoritarian, and missing the basic necessity of rebellion against authority by concentrating on economic matters.

Some today question the theoretical and historical validity of "class" as an analytic construct or as a political actor. In this line, some question Marx's reliance on 19th century notions that linked science with the idea of "progress". Many observe that capitalism has changed much since Marx's time, and that class differences and relationships are much more complex — citing as one example the fact that much corporate stock in the United States is owned by workers through pension funds. Critics of this analysis retort that the top 1% of stock owners still own nearly 50% of the nation's publicly traded company stocks.

The Left Wing philosopher Peter Singer argues in the book A Darwinian Left that the Marxist view of human nature as highly flexible is incorrect. The Scientist Lionel Tiger has also argued against the Marxist view of Human nature. Lionel Tiger argues that Marxist states have failed to wither away and give power to the Proletariat because Marxist Socialism fails to realize that because humans have inherited competitive and despotic tendencies from their primate ancestors a system of "checks and balances" and restrictions on individuals gaining power and wealth are necessary to maintain an egalitarian Socialist society.

## Marx and Antisemitism

Some commentators, like Bernard Lewis, Edward H. Flannery and Hyam Maccoby, have seen Marx's *On The Jewish Question* as an antisemitic work, and identify antisemitic epithets in his published and private writings. According to them, Marx regarded Jews as the embodiment of capitalism and the creators of its evils. In their view, Marx's equation of Judaism with capitalism, together with his pronouncements on Jews, strongly influenced socialist movements and shaped their attitudes and policies toward the Jews. In these scholars' opinions, Marx's 'On the Jewish Question' influenced National Socialist, as well as Soviet and Arab anti-Semites. Hyam Maccoby has suggested that Marx was embarrassed by his Jewish background. The above authors often quote the following excerpt from *On The Jewish Question* to support their arguments: "What is the secular basis of Judaism? Practical need, selfishness. What is the secular cult of the Jew? Haggling. What is his secular god? Money. Well then, an emancipation from haggling and money, from practical, real Judaism would be the self emancipation of our age."

On the other hand, David McLellan and Francis Wheen argue that readers should interpret *On the Jewish Question* in the context of Marx's debates with Bruno Bauer, author of *The Jewish Question*, about the nature of political emancipation in Germany. Wheen says: *Those critics, who see this as a foretaste of 'Mein Kampf', overlook one, essential point: in spite of the clumsy phraseology and crude stereotyping, the essay was actually written as a defence of the Jews. It was a retort to Bruno Bauer, who had argued that Jews should not be granted full civic rights and freedoms unless they were baptised as Christians.*

According to McLellan, Marx used the word *Judentum* colloquially, as *commerce*, arguing that Germans suffer, and must be emancipated from, capitalism, concluding that the essay's second half should be read as *an extended pun at Bauer's expense.* According to Jonathan Sacks, Chief Rabbi of the United Kingdom, at the time Marx wrote *On the Jewish Question*, virtually all major philosophers were antisemitic, but the word "antisemitism" had not yet been coined or developed a racial component, and little awareness existed of the depths of European prejudice against Jews. Marx was thus simply expressing, in Sacks's view, the commonplace thinking of his era. In a letter to Engels, Marx referred to Ferdinand Lasalle as a "Jewish Nigger".

## Criticisms of Marxism

Various aspects of Marxist theory have been criticized. These criticisms concern both the theory itself, and its later interpretations and implementations. Criticisms of Marxism have come from the political left as well as the political right. Democratic socialists and social democrats reject the idea that socialism can be accomplished only through class conflict and a violent proletarian revolution. Many anarchists reject the need for a transitory state phase. Some thinkers have rejected the fundamentals of Marxist theory, such as historical materialism and the labor theory of value, and gone on to criticize capitalism-and advocate socialism-using other arguments. Racist attitudes have been identified in works by Marx and Engels including claims of certain nations being at a higher level of civilization than others, and claims that certain races, such as Slavs were uncivilized, traitors, and enemies of proletarian revolution.

Some contemporary supporters of Marxism argue that many aspects of Marxist thought are viable, but that the corpus also fails to deal effectively with certain aspects of economic, political or social theory. They may therefore combine some Marxist concepts with the ideas of other theorists such as Max Weber: the Frankfurt school is one example.

### *Marxian Class Theory*

Marxian Class Theory upholds that class structure is ultimately determined by the structure of the production process. One major thread of argument within Marxian Class theory holds that an individual's class position is then determined by his role in the production process, while his political and ideological consciousness is shaped by this structurally determined class position (Parkin). Other positions, such as that of E. P. Thompson or Mario Tronti, holds that class consciousness within production arguably precedes the formation of productive relationships, as part of pre-existing class struggle.

### *Origins of Marx's Theory*

Marx's class theory originates in the unique methodological mixture of left Hegelianism, Scottish Empiricism and Anglo-French political-economics. Marx's view of class combines his interest in alienation and the potential for human action in history, in that classes have a historical consciousness and project. Political-economy contributed to Marx's thought, in terms of the concept of "origin of income" present in the division of society into Rentier, Capitalist, and Worker in Ricardo's theory of capitalism. To this is added the empiricist interest in provable, verifiable relationships, which lead Marx to seek a definition of class embedded in productive relations rather than social status. As Marx's political economic thought developed towards an interest in production as opposed to distribution, production became central to his concept of class.

### *Class Structure*

Marx distinguishes one class from another on the basis of two criteria, ownership of the means of production and control of the labor power of others. He defines three classes in modern society. Capitalists, also known as bourgeoisie, own the means of production and purchase the labor power of others; workers, or proletariat, who neither own the means of production nor purchase the labor power of others, but rather they sell their own labor power; and the minor and transitional class of the petite bourgeoisie owns the means of production, but do not purchase labor power. In the Communist Manifesto, Marx fails to define the petite bourgeoisie as anything more than "smaller capitalists" (Marx and Engels, 1848, 25). Class thus is determined by property relations, not by income or status. These are determined by distribution and consumption, which itself ultimately reflects the production and power relations of classes.

### *Class Relations: Conflict*

"The history of all hitherto existing society is the history of class struggles... Freeman and slave, patrician and plebeian, lord and serf, guild-master and journeyman, in a word, oppressor and oppressed, stood in constant opposition to one another, carried on an uninterrupted, now hidden, now open fight, a fight that each time ended, either in a revolutionary reconstruction of society at large, or in the common ruin of the contending classes.... The modern bourgeois society that has sprouted from the ruins of feudal society has not done away with class antagonisms. It has but established new classes, new conditions of oppression, new forms of struggle in place of the old ones. Our epoch, the epoch of the bourgeoisie, possesses, however, this distinctive feature: it has simplified class antagonisms. Society as a whole is more and more splitting up into two great hostile camps, into two great classes directly facing each other: Bourgeoisie and Proletariat." – Communist Manifesto

Marx established conflict as the key driving force of history and the main determinant of social trajectories (Kingston). However in order to understand the nature of "class conflict," we must first understand that such conflict arises from a unified class interest, also known as class consciousness. Class consciousness is an aspect of Marxist theory, referring to the self-awareness of social classes, the capacity to act in its own rational interests, or measuring the extent to which an individual is conscious of the historical tasks their class (or class allegiance) sets for them. Moreover, by definition, the objective interests of classes are fundamentally in opposition; consequently, these opposing interests and consciousnesses eventually lead to class conflict. Marx first saw the development of class conflict confined to individual factories and capitalists. However, given the maturation of capitalism, the life conditions of bourgeoisie and proletariat began to grow more disparate. This increased the homogenization within classes to foster the environment for individual struggles to become more generalized. When increasing class conflict is manifested at the societal level, class consciousness and common interests are also increased. Consequently when class consciousness is augmented, policies are organized to ensure the duration of such interest for the ruling class. Here begins the use of the struggle for political power and classes become political forces.

Since the distribution of political power is determined by power over production, or power over capital, it is no surprise that the bourgeois class uses their wealth to legitimatize and protect their property and consequent social relations. Thus the ruling class is those who hold the economic power and make the decisions (Dahrendorf).

### *Socialist Revolution*

Marx assumes the inevitability of the revolution of capitalist society into socialist society because of eventual discontent. The socialization of labor, in the growth of large-scale production, capitalist interest groups and organizations, as well as in the enormous increase in the dimensions and power of finance capital provides the principal material foundation for the unavoidable arrival of socialism. The physical, intellectual and moral perpetrator of this transformation is the proletariat. The proletariat's struggle against the bourgeoisie inevitably becomes a political struggle with the goal of political conquest by the proletariat. With the domination of the proletariat, the socialization of production cannot help but lead to the means of production to become the property of society. The direct consequences of this transformation are a tremendous rise in labor productivity, a shorter working day, and the replacement of small-scale unified production by collective and improved labor. Capitalism breaks for all time the ties between producer and owner, once held by the bond of class conflict. Now a new union will be formed based on the conscious application of science and the concentration of collective labor.

He also extended this redistribution to the structure of power in families. Marx imagined that with socialism women's status would increase, leading to the break-up of the patriarchal family... "Modern industry, by assigning as it does, an important part in the socially organized process of production, outside the domestic sphere, to women, to young persons, and to children of both sexes, creates a new economic foundation for a higher form of the family and of the relations between the sexes... Moreover, it is obvious that the fact of the collective working group being composed of individuals of both sexes and all ages, must necessarily, under suitable conditions, become a source of human development; although in its spontaneously developed, brutal, capitalistic form, where the labourer exists for the process of production, and not the process of production for the labourer, that fact is a pestiferous source of corruption and slavery.".

# 11

# Luther Gulick

Luther Halsey Gulick (January 17, 1892 in Osaka – January 10, 1993 in Walden, Vermont) was an expert on public administration. He was the son of Congregationalist missionary, Sidney Lewis Gulick and his wife, Clara May (Fisher) Gulick. Luther Gulick graduated from Oberlin College in 1914 and received his Ph.D. from Columbia University in 1920. He taught at Columbia from 1931-1942. In 1921 he became president of the Institute of Public Administration and served as such until 1962. He then became its chairman and served until 1982.From 1936-1938 he served on a three member panel appointed by President Franklin D. Roosevelt to reorganize the executive branch of the federal government. From 1954 to 1956, he served as city administrator of New York City.

Among many other accomplishments in the field of public administration, Gulick is perhaps best known for the functions of the executive represented in the acronym PODSCORB (or POSDCORB depending on the source). Each letter stands for Planning, Organizing, Directing, Staffing, Coordinating, Reporting and Budgeting.

Gulick's advocacy (with Alvin Hansen) during World War II of Keynesian policies to promote full employment post-war helped to persuade John Maynard Keynes to help develop post-war plans for the international economy that included considerable emphasis on free trade.

In a time where the prevalent theme was the separation of politics and administration, Gulick advocated that it was impossible to separate the two.

## Key Ideas

According to John Gustav-Wrathall, Gulick appeared to embrace many contradictions. On the one hand, he occasionally seemed obsessed with rules and self-control; on the other, he frequently showed evidence of favoring spontaneity over order, principles over rules, and experimentation over legalism. At times he seemed to favour sexual repression; at other times, he displayed rational moderation in the realm of human sexual behaviour. He was an advocate of eugenics and a believer in social Darwinism who also upheld altruism, service, and self sacrifice as the highest form of religion (Gustav-Wrathall, 1998: 28-20). Notwithstanding, several major ideas can be identified.

The foundation of his thought was the so-called 'Recapitulation Theory'. According to Recapitulation Theory, each individual, just like each human race (and that included at the time what we now would refer to as ethnic groups), recapitulates human evolution.

Child study experts, such as G. Stanley Hall, president of Clark University and founding father of psychology in the United States, for example argued that each boy had a "little Indian" stage in his development. That is, on the way towards maturity each individual relives past stages of evolution. It was central, then, to shape behaviour towards civilized self-possession as each individual moves away from the more atavistic behavioral stages of human evolution. Luther Gulick believed that this could be achieved best through proper training and development of spirit, mind, and body and to overcome the mind-body dualism in social thought and to understand human beings as holistic entities instead.

This brought Gulick to create a new symbol for the YMCA- a triangle, inscribed with the words 'body,' 'mind,' and 'spirit,' adopted as YMCA logo in 1895 at the YMCA Convention in Springfield, Massachusetts. Gulick, then, promoted what was known at the time as a "Muscular Christianity."

At the time when social anthropology and social psychology slowly became established as recognized disciplines Luther Gulick believed and argued that the individual and its behaviour are established through interpersonal relations and that values are collective phenomenon to a large extent. This was the foundation of his belief in the necessity of building team spirit and team work. This guided his ideas for games. When Gulick handed James Naismith a set of rules for him to design a game around it, this is what he had in mind: a game that could be played in doors, that is year round; a game that promoted the unity and development of body, mind, and spirit; and a game that played on the individuals social instincts and promoted team work.

## Contributions to Education

Luther Halsey Gulick made numerous contributions to education. When he and Robert J. Roberts launched the first course for gymnasium instructors at the YMCA College at Springfield, the association did not see physical training as the integral part of its program, and of an education of its members to be well-rounded men, but merely as a bait to draw young men to what the YMCA considered its main mission-religious work. Physical directors tended to be former athletes, pugilists, ex-soldiers, and former circus performers who mostly lacked a serious commitment to the Christian mission of the YMCA.

Luther Gulick changed that by instituting a training program for physical directors, who would combine preparation in physical education with Christian commitment and the abilities of a good teacher. He contributed to a more rational approach to physical education and the professionalization of physical education instructors. Luther Halsey Gulick's goals for physical education were wide-ranging. He aimed at bodily symmetry, muscular strength and control, endurance, agility, grace, courage, self-possession, and expression. Physical education, he believed, would make better men and fathers. To convince the YMCA as a whole of the value of such an approach took time, though. It was only a the 1889 International Convention of the YMCA in Philadelphia that the association made Gulick's approach program. In addition to his contribution to physical education in the YMCA, Gulick also advocated boys work. He believed it would be more effective to approach boys at an impressionable age, rather than aim at young men who had already reached adulthood.

As director of physical education of the public schools of greater New York, Luther Halsey Gulick initiated several innovations. First, he created a Public School Athletic League for boys, funded not by the city but by the contributions of wealthy citizens. Second, in 1905, a number of prominent women approached Gulick to help form a Girls' Branch. This Girls' Branch instituted folk dancing for girls.

Gulick himself hoped that such a program would instill the girls with an appreciation for different ethnic traditions (although the majority of the dances used were Swedish) and create a sense of a larger, common sense of an American identity. The book that resulted from this work, *The Healthful Art of Dancing* (1910) was used into the mid-30s as reference work by dance teachers. Gulick also was crucial in promoting urban playgrounds. In 1907, 90 cities had such facilities. Due to the effort of Luther Gulick and the Playground and Recreation Society, by 1910, 531 cities had such playgrounds.

Luther Gulick also devoted his attention to school hygiene and health. Together with Leonard Ayres, Gulick conducted the "Backward Children's Investigation" for the Russell Sage Foundation. This investigation showed that signs of mental retardation were not a sign of physical defects but could be addressed by care and attention and that alleged defects can decrease with age. So-called "retardation" was recognized as a developmental and not a physical issue.. As a result of the investigation the New York Board of Education established a Department of Investigation that used *Medical Inspection of Schools,* the results of Gulick's and Ayres' study as manual. The findings of the Russell Sage Backward Children Investigation under the leadership of Luther Gulick and the auspices of the Russell Sage Foundation more and more cities began to create systems of medical inspection. Their number rose from 135 (1908) to over 700 (1912).

### *Conclusion*

Throughout his life time, Luther Halsey Gulick made numerous contributions to physical education and recreation. It is difficult to trace Gulick's influence on education in detail. He often changed his position; moved from one organization to another. Luther Gulick saw himself as a planner and initiator rather than an executor. Gulick's role as innovator was less grounded in truly original thought but more in his ability to pick up new ideas and currents of thought and blend them together and to promote the results through a range of offices and institutions, many of which he founded himself. In that sense, he was more of a social engineer than a generator of new ideas. Moreover, more research on Luther Gulick is needed. However, despite his short life, Gulick remains significant to physical education. Beginning in 1923 and continuing to this day, the American Alliance for Health, Physical Education, Recreation and Dance (AAHPERD) annually awards the Luther Halsey Gulick Medal, as its highest honour to a distinguished leader in any one of the alliance's fields of activity-a strong sign of Gulick's widespread influence on a number of fields in physical education and recreation.

# 12

# Lyndall Urwick

Lyndall Fownes Urwick (March 3, 1891-December 5, 1983) was an influential business consultant and thinker in the United Kingdom. He is recognized for integrating the ideas of earlier theorists like Henri Fayol into a comprehensive theory of administration. He wrote a book called *The Elements of Business Administration*, published in 1943. With Luther Gulick, he founded the academic journal *Administrative Science Quarterly*.

### *Early Life and Education*

Lyndall Urwick was born in Worcestershire, the son of a partner in Fownes Brothers, a long-established glove-making firm. He was educated at Boxgrove Primary School, Repton School and New College, Oxford, where he read History.

### *Military Service*

He saw active service in the trenches during the First World War, rising to the rank of Major, and being awarded the Military Cross. Though he did not himself attend the military Staff College at Camberley, his respect for military training would affect his outlook on management in later life.

### *Career*

After the war, he joined his father's business of Fownes Brothers. He was then recruited by Seebohm Rowntree, head of the York chocolate company and progressive philanthropist. Urwick's role involved assisting the modernisation of the company, bringing to bear his own thinking which had two main influences. One was the work of Frederick Winslow Taylor with its concept of scientific management, and the other, counterbalancing it in its emphasis on the humanity of management was Mary Parker Follett, for whom he had great admiration. Urwick's own prolific writings on management truly began in this period.

His growing reputation as a British thinker on management and administration won him appointment in 1928 as Director of the International Management Institute in Geneva. The Institute may have proven short-lived, closing in 1933, but it provided Urwick the opportunity not only to lecture widely but to produce his books *The Meaning of Rationalisation* and *The Management of Tomorrow*. It was also the time that he became particularly keen to promote the writings of Henri Fayol to an English audience.

When Urwick returned to Britain, he established a management consultancy, Urwick Orr and Partners which came to be one of the leading companies of its type in the 1940s and 1950s. At the same time, his intellectual interests continued. An increasing concern of his was the lack of management education in Britain. He was involved in the very earliest discussions for what would become, in 1948, the Administrative Staff College. His own view of the education required did not accord with the College as it was finally established, which concentrated on a three-month course for established executives. He would have preferred something much closer to the model of the American business school, involving a longer course and aimed at pre-experience students. It was a continuing frustration for Urwick that England's two ancient universities failed to promote management education.

In later years, Lyndall Urwick retired to Australia, where he died in 1983. His papers were donated to the Administrative Staff College, by then re-named Henley Management College.

## Urwick on the Business Academy

Lyndall Urwick was born in England in 1891. He attended Repton and New College, Oxford, and was awarded a B.A. degree in 1913 and an M.A. degree in 1919. He began his career in his family's glove manufacturing business, Fownes Brothers and Company. Following service in the First World War, he became organizing secretary for Rowntree and Company, a confectioner. He subsequently moved to the position of administrator of the Management Research Groups and then became Director of the

International Management Institute in Geneva in 1929. When the Great Depression cut short the life of the Institute, Urwick returned to England and established the management consultancy Urwick, Orr and Partners.

During World War I1 he was an advisor in organization to His Majesty's Treasury, and in 1942 he moved to the Petroleum Warfare Department. From 1945 until 1965 Urwick continued his work as a management consultant and served as a visiting faculty member at such universities as Toronto, New South Wales, California, and Minnesota. He retired to Australia, where he died in 1983 at the age of 92.

Urwick's books include: Factory Organization (1928), coauthored with C. Northcott, O. Sheldon, and J. Wardopper; The Meaning of Rationalization (1929); and with H. Metcalf, Dynamic Administration: The Collected Papers of Mark Parker Follett (1941). He also wrote a number of shorter works published by such groups as the British Institute of Management, the Institute of Labor Management, the Institute of Personnel Management, the American Management Association, and the Academy of Management.

In the late 1920s, Urwick became a vigorous advocate for a staff college for industry. He felt that such an institution was urgently needed and should be structured along the lines of the existing staff colleges of the various branches of the military. In 1942 he was joined in his efforts by others who provided planning support and came up with sufficient money and students to give the project a reasonable chance for success. In 1948, the Administrative Staff College was opened by Clement Artlee, Prime Minister of England. It served as a model for many other similar undertakings that followed, both in Great Britain and throughout the world. During his lifetime, Urwick's membership in professional associations included The British Institute of Management (fellow), the International Academy of Management (charter fellow), the Academy of Management (fellow), and the American Management Association (life member). Among the awards he received were the Order of the British Empire and Military Cross (British Army), Gantt Medal (American Management Society and the American Society of Mechanical Engineers), and Knight, First Class, Order of Saint Olaf (Norway).

Additional biographical details about Urwick can be found in the London Times (1983), the work of Trosky (1984), and the writing of Bedian (1984), from which the information presented here was extracted. Many early management texts, such as Mooney and Reiley (1939), Dennison (1931), and Sheldon (1923), can provide supporting background particulars as well.

### *The Operating Era*

Urwick can probably be grouped with those who first made a significant concerted effort to formulate a discrete body of management knowledge. These pioneers of management study are generally termed "classicists" and can normally be divided into two schools of thought: those with a micro focus who centred their attention on the incremental bits and pieces in the workplace for the purpose of improving efficiency ("scientific managers"), and those with more of a macro bent, who viewed the overall organization with the intent of enhancing effectiveness ("comprehensive managers"). Urwick can be placed in the latter group, with recognition that underlying much of his work was the inherent objective of the bettering productivity across the entire organization.

The classicists, as a group, were generally criticized by those who followed for their alleged failure to emphasize adequately the human variable in their work. Some who voiced such concerns felt that sociology and psychology rather than engineering and natural science should form the underpinnings of management. More specifically, they expressed apprehension that insufficient attention was given to some interpersonal areas, such as leadership, motivation, and communication. To those who held such reservations, the classicist's reply was short and simple, perhaps best exemplified in Urwick's reply to those who found fault with his organizational theory. In his short concise treatment of the principles of organization, he wrote that while there are those who believe that the manager cannot set down an organizational structure, complete with a distribution of duties, responsibilities, and relationships, and then expect people to conform, this in fact is exactly what the manager can and should do (1947).

The classicists, however, did freely acknowledge that follow-up modifications would have to be made in the mechanisms they created because human beings do form an integral part of the whole. To this end they prudently sought out and adopted the applicable findings of psychologists and sociologists. Whereas the goal was to achieve a strong, mechanically perfect organization, with accompanying objectively based standard operating practices that collectively would function more or less as a perfect bureaucracy, fine-tuning to account for the human element was recognized and implemented as needed. Overall, the contributions of the work of Urwick and others were generally accepted and put into place as the foundation on which the discipline of management was built. The classicists did not contend that people are to be taken as a passive given, regardless of the mission of the organization and the nature of the work. Neither did those who followed subscribe to the belief that the organization and its operation should be based completely on the needs of people. In reality, the difference between the two was more of emphasis than substance and, with the passage of time, a constructive blending of an interface, and mutual acceptance of it, was generally achieved.

A fuller understanding of this stage of management may be found in a number of basic texts, such as Certo (1980), Dale (1965), and Donnelly et al. (1975). It was a period that attempted to treat the frustration growing out of a lack of management principles, deal with a morass of administrative muddling and misunderstanding, and cope with a capricious waste of resources.

### *On People and Technology*

About ten years before his death, in private correspondence and personal conversation, Urwick expressed some thoughts related to schools of business. These opinions were purposely sought out in an informal and unstructured solicitation of his feelings. Whether these opinions persisted through the later years of his life is difficult to say, but one might dare answer "yes." As to whether Urwick would want these feelings publicized—for his remarks were more off than on the record— again, an affirmative determination might not be too wrong.

When Urwick retired, it was his intent to "get out of the boys' hair," spending his time reading and writing. However, he soon found it increasingly impossible to begin to keep up with what academics were publishing. He felt that even if he were to do nothing but read 12 hours a day, every day, keeping abreast of the literature would be out of the question. Management professors, he thought, were moving their writing at a pace much too fast for the practitioner. This was not because business people were slow or stupid. Rather, it was because managers had a very exacting week's worth of work to do on their jobs, whereas academics had little else to do but think and write. As a result, the two were tending to get more and more out of step with each other.

Urwick felt that this state of the world partly grew out of a situation in which it was common for the academy to expect its faculty to deliver, repeatedly, a new theory of management at a rate approximating that of the gestation period for a new child—nine months. The gestation period for even the simplest of new ideas, Urwick believed, was closer to that of an elephant than a human. He thought it extremely important for management professors to realize that the speed at which new ideas can effectively be absorbed and put into operation, in an organization of any size, is much slower than the speed at which they can be generated by individuals.

Along these lines he noted that although the history of management had its beginning about the year 1900, it had already passed through what many felt was about four or five eras. However, the current era was no longer being perceived as a couple of centuries, or even a generation, but rather was being measured in terms of decades. This telescoping of history he attributed to the rapidity with which academics were writing books and promulgating new thoughts. Although movement was certainly desirable, he believed it was essential that the speed be kept at a level that would allow industry and the academy to move forward together.

As to what was being taught in the academy, Urwick felt that—with administrators normally acquiescing—professors were generally teaching what they wanted to teach, instead of what students wanted to learn, and should learn. In particular, Urwick believed that what academics taught were the issues about which they wanted to write. While students were being exposed, as they should be, to a mix of both liberal and professional education, the selection of the ingredients and their proportions was being dictated more by the interest of the faculty than the needs of business. Having advanced well beyond the point at which it was recognized that management is not just common sense, or a collection of standardized and classified experiences, what was being offered was nevertheless a fragmented array of knowledge representative of the unique interest of individual teachers. The consequence, Urwick felt, was a collection of subjects, a curriculum that delighted professors but did little to provide suitable preparation for the students who would one day be managers.

Urwick went on to note that when he was an undergraduate, he had already made up his mind to go into business. He was furious with Oxford, however, because the university did not teach him anything he wished to learn; management was not an accepted discipline at the time. But acceptance was achieved over the years, and management was now a recognized field of study in the academy. Urwick felt, however, that students still could not study what they wanted to learn, if that happened to differ from what teachers believed they should learn. Such a situation would not have been so intolerable if what was offered were in keeping with the needs of business and reflective of a collective judgment as to the required knowledge in the field. But Urwick understood that this was not the case. What was being presented to students was a multiplicity of loosely related courses, most of which were solely selected by academics in keeping with their personal causes and concerns.

### *About the Structure*

Urwick felt that most of the principles of administration, such as those advanced by Fayol, Taylor, Mooney and Reiley, Graicunas, and Follett, are as applicable to the university as they are to the factory. There is a general theoy of administration, according to Urwick, that can be used equally well by industry, government, and the academy. However, Urwick believed it was no[ generally being used by government, which would find that as a result it would not be able to move ahead as fast as it would like, regardless of how well intentioned it may be. Neither was the theory being used as it should be by the academy, even though it formed the basis of what was generally being [aught in the schools.

Urwick felt that significant reliance by the academy on committees, for example, subjected schools to more of the weaknesses of this form of operation than was necessary. Because a committee has neither body nor soul, it normally encourages irresponsibility, assumes authority without any corresponding accountability, and tends to be slow and ineffective. Moreover, committees often suffer from many psychological problems, which include members trying to impress each other, irrelevant discussion, and gamesmanship for gamesmanship's sake. However, committees are useful for considering policy, examining issues, and promoting unity. Thus, although committees can be effective, Urwick believed they must be used selectively—not as the standard primary means of operation.

It was Urwick's feeling that because of the strong attention and commitment of faculty to their disciplines, it was not unusual for a number of other objectives to spring up in the academy that were inconsistent with the general purpose of schools of business. The momentum generated in pursuit of these other objectives was wasted, Urwick felt, in that it was directed at promoting ends that have no bearing on the explicit mission of the academy. Courage is required, Urwick believed, of those who manage the academy to eliminate these elements of unrelated concern, lest their pursuit dissipate significant resources vitally required by the school.

The need for coordination in the academy was also touched upon by Urwick, who believed that as a meaningful procedural element required for proper administration, coordination was relatively lacking. The many interests of the faculty and its ever increasing diversity of specialization generally require very adept leadership to maintain congruence and accord. While operating arrangements can generally be aligned, holding to a singularity of purpose under such circumstances is difficult or even impossible to do. As a result, conformity of thought, purpose, and action is low. Suitable coordination, Urwick believed, was something that cannot be readily achievable without a major change in the way the academy perceives itself, from an aggregation of separate pieces to a cohesive working whole.

The absence of a generally accepted interest within the academy, Urwick felt, was the reason for weak command. Without a critical mass of commonality, the academy was prevented from planning properly, and hence leadership had little or no significance. Additionally, in the presence of a wide multiplicity of differing ends, it is almost impossible to generate a meaningful framework within which an effective command function can be made operational.

As to control, Urwick felt that many academics mistakenly believe that if they have an adequate process in place then they have access to the facts about their undertakings. The existence of an efficient and effective fact-gathering apparatus is one thing, however; what is done with its product is another. Information is important, but unless it is properly used it is not worth too much, particularly in terms of aligning actual performance with planned performance.

Urwick's remarks should not be interpreted as an overall dissatisfaction with the academy. Rather, they should be viewed as thoughts about a collection of individual items that, in his opinion, require attention. Many of the points he cited, particularly those dealing with structure, are recognizable as some of the elements of administration he first advanced in the early 1940s in a series of lectures presented at the Polytechnic, London. These talks for the London Branch of the Institute of Industrial Administration were later rearranged and published in book form (1947). While Urwick's compilation of principles first appeared in an industrial context, he believed them to be generic-seemingly a continuing belief, as shown by his comments on the academy in the 1970s.

Urwick appeared to be somewhat troubled by what he felt were two shortcomings of schools of business. The first was that in general they were not practicing the elements of administration that form the underpinnings of good management. Second, whereas these elements were usually being taught to students (although Urwick appeared to have some reservations as to whether they were being properly sequenced and weighted), they were not being presented in a form that students would normally find useful when they left the academy to manage. Both of these limitations, he suggested, might well be attributable to the fragmented interests of teachers, who were more concerned with the pursuit of their individual specialties than the continued overall development of the field. Significant contributions were being made, but they were being made as ends in themselves, rather than as means toward a better understanding of the principles and practices of administration. A similar concern was implied, approximately 15 years later, by Porter and McKibben (1988) in their inquiry into the state of schools of business and their ability to meet the needs of the future. Interestingly, their study also suggested an ancillary turn of events that seemed to be bothering Urwick as well: a growing separation of the academy and industry. Urwick implied that the dual-track approach that was developing-with one for academics and one for practitioners-was not in the long-term interest of either group. For meaningful growth of both the concepts and applications of administration, developmental unity of the groups was required; neither could really do it acting on its own.

During his lifetime, Urwick would often draw a parallel between medicine and business, expressing the belief that business skill is comparable to medical skill. He felt that the two were practical arts and, as such, required continuing practice. But practice in the absence of study, Urwick believed, is likely to be limited in worth. Conversely, study without practice could well be sterile and misleading. In the years since Urwick's death, medicine has continued to operate with a reliance on a mixture, running health care on a single track. This is perhaps best evidenced by the close union between empirical research and everyday operation. Management, however, appears to have departed from the mix model, setting up a dual-path arrangement—the ivory tower doing one thing while the crystal palace does another.

On balance, Urwick believed, the business academy was doing well. But it still had miles to go before it could sleep.

## Lyndall Urwick's Scientific Management

Introductory management texts sometimes offer a brief history of the management discipline, often identifying the emergence of Frederick Taylor's scientific management as a key developmental event. Typically developments in European organizational theory and practice are acknowledged in terms of writers such as Henri Fayol and Max Weber joining Frederick Taylor in laying the foundations for the classical management school of thought. Invariably, in the aftermath of the Hawthorne Experiments, this classical approach is portrayed as being superseded in the 1920s, 1930s and 1940s by a human relations or behavioural approach that focused on issues such as group and social functioning in organizations, human motivation, and participative decision-making. These latter developments are almost exclusively represented as a reaction to and the antithesis of the classical school. The problem with such textbook treatment of the history of the management discipline is that it usually oversimplifies and obscures what these early theorists actually wrote and advocated. For example, through a detailed analysis of Henri Fayol's writings, Parker and Ritson (2005a) argued that labelling him as a classical theorist fundamentally misrepresents his work. Far from being a narrowly focused classic writer in Taylorist vein, Fayol was a precursor to the subsequent emergence of the human relations movement, as well as systems and contingency theory, elements of management by objectives, total quality management and knowledge management.

On the relatively rare occasion that Lyndall Urwick is referenced in any account of the development of management thought, he is usually identified as a classical management thinker who popularised the works of Henri Fayol in the English speaking world and integrated Fayol's administrative approach with Taylor's scientific management (Davidson and Griffin, 2002). However, Urwick was a prolific management writer whose publishing career spanned six decades, and whose contribution to the practice of management, both professionally and in the academies, was far-reaching and profound. Indeed, when one turns Urwick's original writings, one finds that not only was he attempting to integrate Taylor's scientific management with Fayol's administrative management, but also with elements of the newly emerging human relations movement.

This chapter sets out to revisit the identity and philosophy of Lyndall Urwick as a historic management thinker and prolific management author. Accordingly it sets out to understand his intellectual loyalty to Frederick Taylor, his shifting conception of scientific management, and his contribution to management thought. In doing so, this paper argues that far from being a narrowly focused classical management writer, Urwick actually embarked upon an integrative approach to management practice and theory that to some extent anticipated the subsequent emergence of systems and contingency theory. Though a staunch and unapologetic advocate of Frederick Taylor's work, Urwick employed a broad definition scientific management that allowed him to assimilate and absorb an eclectic and wide range of diverse management approaches in his unique and idiosyncratic vision for scientific management. In addition, this paper contends that by identifying his integrative approach with scientific management, Urwick unwittingly became the originator and victim of stereotypes that have not only obscured the significance of his own work, but also the work of several of the theorists he cited and so greatly admired.

The chapter begins with a brief sketch of Urwick's background and career, his view of the science and art of management, and his intellectual debt to Frederick Taylor. His embracing of other management thinkers' work into his world of scientific management and his response to his critics is then considered. The paper finally addresses Urwick's positioning and contribution to the history of management thought.

### *A Brief Portrait*

Lyndall Urwick had a remarkable career. Notable for its duration, its international reach, its contribution to both thought and practice, and the stream of management literature it produced, it spanned 60 years. Born an only child in England in 1891,i Lyndall Fownes Urwick was educated in Malvern, Boxgrove School Guildford, Repton and then New College Oxford, graduating with a degree in modern history. After initial employment in his father's family glove-making firm, he served as a second lieutenant and then major in World War I, earning the Military Cross and subsequently an Order of the British Empire (OBE). He read Frederick Taylor's *Shop Management* in the trenches and served in several administrative staff officer positions in the military. After a brief period of post-war service as partner, he left his former firm, having been unable to convince his family partners to try his newfound approaches to management. In 1922 he joined the organizing office of Rowntree & Co, chocolate and confectionery manufacturers, there being influenced by two 7 management thinkers, Seebohm Rowntree and Oliver Sheldon (serving a period as Sheldon's assistant). While there, he participated and lectured in the Oxford Management Conferences, assisted Rowntree in establishing informal national Management Research Groups for exchanging ideas on new management developments, and embarked on professional writing in management, by 1927 attracting readership in the USA and the UK (Bedeian, 1972; Jeremy and Shaw, 1986; Matthews and Boyns, 2001).

In 1928, he became director of the world's first international management body, the International Management Institute in Geneva, serving until early 1934 when the Institute closed due to withdrawal of funding by the Institute's sponsor. The Institute's main purpose was the promotion of scientific management, and his work there connected Urwick to a wide range of scientific management and other management thinkers throughout Europe and the USA, not least through his role as honorary secretary of the International Council for Scientific Management. Returning to London, along with Scottish engineer and consultant J.L. Orr, he established the British management-consulting firm Urwick Orr & Partners.

Apart from his absence from the firm due to his government service in World War II, Urwick served as founder, managing partner (1945-51) and chair (1934-61), and subsequently president, even after his move to Australia in the early 1960s. His WWII service included consultant to the British government Treasury, deputy director of the Petroleum Warfare Department, and member of the Mitcheson Committee of the Ministry of Pensions, completing his military involvement at the rank of Lieutenant-Colonel. In his management consulting career, Urwick not only built his firm to national and international prominence, but was also the first president of an informal international association of management consultants, and leader of the British Management Consultants' Association.

In addition to his voluminous writing and publication in the management field, Urwick was prominent in promoting management education and the management profession. He was founding member and then chairman (1947-52) of the British Institute of Management and of its Education Committee. Chair of the education committee of the Institute of Industrial Administration (1944), and Chair of the Ministry of Education Committee on Education for Management (1945-46) (a committee that proposed a national syllabus for teaching management in the UK), and Chair of the Anglo-American Productivity team on

Education for Management in the United States of America (1951). In addition, he was first president of the Federation of European Management Consultants (1960). He was also a driving force behind the 1948 launch of the Administrative Staff College at Henley-on-Thames (now Henley Business School, University of Reading, UK).

His lecture tours and management advisory work, particularly from the 1950s, took him to many countries. He held visiting professorships in business in universities in the USA, Canada and Australia, and on his "retirement" to Australia, he continued his writing, publishing and speaking career. He advised and made presentations to the American Management Association, the Indian Planning Commission for an Institute of Management, and the Australian Institute of Management.

As will already be evident, Urwick was internationally prominent. His awards and accolades were many, mostly achieved during the zenith of his career in the 1950s and 1960s. They included the International Committee of Scientific Management gold medal, the Wallace Clark International Management medal, the American Management Association's and American Society of Engineers' Henry Laurence Gantt memorial gold medal, the Taylor key, the British Institute of Management's Bowie medal, and Knight first class of the Order of St. Olaf (Norway). He was made fellow or honorary member of numerous organizations and associations.

Urwick's last published work appeared in 1980, two years before his death (in 1983) in Sydney, Australia, at the age of 92. He left a legacy of more than 14 books that he authored, co-authored or edited, and hundreds of published journal articles, conference papers, lectures, seminar presentations and addresses covering a plethora of management subjects including scientific management, management history, leadership, control, business/government management and relations, human resource management, office organization, management semantics, organization structures and committees, and management education. The volume and scope of his published output, the extent of his international involvement and impact, and the length of time over which he strode the international stage is arguably unrivalled amongst his peers in the 20th century.

### *Towards a Scientific Art*

Urwick conceived of organizational management as a social philosophy and discipline dictated by what he saw to be an economy based upon power-driven machinery which he wished to study in a fashion borrowed from the physical sciences. For him, the solution to the effective management of society, government and business lay in a scientific approach that addressed their technical leadership, economic control and social direction. Science, he saw as a codified body of knowledge, and argued for its development in management to provide insights into 'the laws and causes which rule the world'. He repeatedly talked of using a scientific 'temper' and method: approaching every management issue through definition, analysis, measurement, experiment and proof, as in the physical or 'exact sciences'. Consistent with his view of management as a social discipline, he advocated a social engineering approach that required managers to think 'scientifically' about themselves and other people.

This social engineering philosophy was prompted by a view of the economic, social and organizational world tailored to the demands of 'power-driven machinery'. For him, the technological revolution had brought an array of changes and forces, primarily through 'machine industry' that required acceptance, discipline, planning, direction, supervision and control. His philosophy of science and management was machine-focused, whereby machinery imposed a mental discipline that emphasized quantitative analysis of objectively determined facts. This analysis of objectively determined facts was essential if managers were to master their machine environment. While occasionally alluding to the organization as being akin to a living biological organism, Urwick (1942, 1947) immediately re-asserted his mechanistic view of the organization, at times referring to his as an 'engineering approach'. Seeing people as the social groups that assisted in production and distribution of economic goods, he therefore aimed to control people as the power behind (or adjuncts to) machines.

Consistent with his predisposition to record and encompass the full spectrum of developing management thought, particularly in the 1930s and 1940s, Urwick attempted to retain his mechanistic social engineering approach to management while formulating a scientific philosophy that purported to be all-embracing. Scientific management, according to Urwick, is an art: the art of managing human beings, practised in accordance with scientific methods and standards. For Urwick, the medical profession was the exemplar for management to follow. The practice of medicine, he argued, is the art of healing: one requiring clinical experience and judgement based on a scientific body of knowledge. Medicine's scientific body of knowledge draws on a range of underlying scientific disciplines such as biology, physiology, anthropology, sociology, individual and social psychology, as well as the physical and statistical sciences. As will be seen in this paper, such a definition allowed Urwick, while continuing to champion a predominantly Taylorist view of scientific management, to claim competing schools of thought as part of his own scientific management philosophy.

## A Taylor Apologist and Proselytiser

Throughout his professional life, and long after most writers had abandoned Frederick Taylor, Urwick advocated Taylorism as a guiding light for management practice. At times, Urwick was an apologist for Taylor's shortcomings, conceding that Taylor failed to 'generalize with sufficient precision', but simultaneously arguing that Taylorism implicitly contained 'substantially every feature which has come to be recognized as essential to modern practice' (Urwick, 1928: 170). As an apologist, he repeatedly claimed that Taylor had been the victim of jealousy amongst his peers, undue rigidity by his disciples, and misunderstandings and misrepresentations by his critics and that he and his ideas had suffered ongoing abuse, particularly from academics in the USA.

Urwick argued that Taylor's use of the term 'scientific' could be understood in broad terms. The term 'scientific management' is usually understood as meaning the "one best way" to manage and control shop floor practice. This "one best way" approach is the meaning we usually associate with Frederick Taylor's work and the principles of scientific management. However, Urwick remained convinced that Taylor had used the term 'scientific' in a quite different sense, one that embraced any systematic and organized body of knowledge when referring to higher levels of organization and their management. In essence, Urwick's approach drew on this second meaning of the word 'scientific', to respond to claims that Taylor's approach only applied engineering solutions to the complexities of managing people. Repeatedly, Urwick denied that Taylor had ever suggested his principles were an exact science. To Urwick, Taylor simply advocated a spirit of scientific enquiry and the study of common organizational problems by people trained in scientific method. Consistent with his own view of scientific management, Urwick promulgated his own understanding of Taylor as a man who had advocated an attitude and philosophy rather than a detailed set methods or devices. Taylor had merely approached management problems scientifically: defining, measuring, analyzing, and producing a stock of knowledge 'with a foundation in the exact sciences and, where exact knowledge ended, still using a scientific methodology in its approach to its problems'. Urwick attributed the origins of his own machine related social engineering philosophy to Taylor, arguing that the latter was simply propounding a broad spectrum approach to the general issue of exercising control over organizational members.

Taylor's approach to the management of people attracted much criticism and remains a controversial approach to management to this date. Whilst admitting that Taylor had undertaken little research into the human element in management, Urwick (1956a) nonetheless defended Taylor by arguing that Taylor had understood its fundamental importance and the limitations of scientific experiment and proof regarding human behaviour. To illustrate, Urwick forgave Taylor for his approach to motivating individuals, one that emphasized monetary piece-rate payments for performance, arguing that this approach merely reflected the conventions of its day. Similarly, Urwick (1956a: 39) admitted to the 'meticulous discipline and training' required by Taylor's approach to management, while at the same time claiming that Taylor had recognized the value of 'giving the individual a sense of growth and opportunity'.

Urwick also acknowledged the strength of union resistance to Taylorism. However, he attributed that resistance not to Taylorism's inherent weaknesses but to a general societal readjustment to peacetime conditions, to incorrect imitations of its methods, to misunderstandings of Taylor's actual practices and experiences, and finally to agitation by professional rivals. Indeed, Urwick pointed out that no strikes had ever taken place in shops in the USA in which Taylor was directly involved. Urwick also blamed initial US union resistance for an antipathy to Taylorism within the British Trade Union Movement, and an accompanying reluctance of British employers to openly embrace its principles (Urwick, 1929). Claiming that British managers' longer term focus had been on 'technical issues', personnel management and industrial psychology, Urwick (1938) and Urwick and Brech (1945b) argued that British management's resistance to Taylor's philosophy lay in an unfounded fear that a pre-existing humanistic perspective would be supplanted by a scientific perspective of organizations and life. Indeed such was the antipathy of British labour and management to Taylorism, that Urwick and Brech (1945b) devoted an entire chapter to examining the detailed history of this rejection under the contradictory title 'The Acceptance of F.W.Taylor by British Industry'. No doubt, Urwick's staunch defence of Taylorism had its origins in debates undertaken during his early management career. Urwick's one-time employer, Seebohm Rowntree, was noted for the strength of his critique and rejection of scientific management. Urwick's exposure to Rowntree's humanitarian concerns and the work of Rowntree's first industrial psychologist may well have motivated Urwick's attempt to humanize Taylorism (Roper, 2001).

Urwick's work proffers a strangely disjointed amalgam of management thought. His is an idiosyncratic reinterpretation scientific management and the thoughts, ideas, beliefs, and philosophies of its founding figure, Fredrick Taylor. The weight of international critique and incontrovertible evidence of British management and labour's rejection of Taylorism induced Urwick to develop both an apologia for Taylor's shortcomings alongside a new interpretation of aspects of his philosophy.

Urwick crafted this interpretation to yield a more humanistic form of scientific management, one that was consistent with pre-existing British managerial practices and his own beliefs. In so doing, Urwick was able to apply the label "scientific management" to a broad range of management thinkers and theorists.

# 13

# Mary Parker Follett

Mary Parker Follett (3 September 1868 – 18 December 1933) was an American social worker, management consultant and pioneer in the fields of organizational theory and organizational behaviour. She also authored a number of books and numerous essays, articles and speeches on democracy, human relations, political philosophy, psychology, organizational behaviour and conflict resolution. Along with Lillian Gilbreth, Mary Parker Follett was one of two great women management gurus in the early days of classical management theory. As such she was one of the first women ever invited to address the London School of Economics, where she spoke on cutting-edge management issues. She also distinguished herself in the field of management by being sought out by President Theodore Roosevelt as his personal consultant on managing not-for-profit, non-governmental, and voluntary organizations. In her capacity as a management theorist, Mary Parker Follett pioneered the understanding of lateral processes within hierarchical organizations (which recognition led directly to the formation of matrix-style organizations, the first of which was DuPont, in the 1920s), the importance of informal processes within organizations, and the idea of the "authority of expertise"—which really served to modify the typology of authority developed by her German contemporary, Max Weber, who broke authority down into three separate categories: legitimate, traditional and charismatic.

Follett was born in Massachusetts and spent much of her early life there. In September 1885 she enrolled in Anna Ticknor's Society to Encourage Studies at Home. In 1898 she graduated from Radcliffe College, but was denied a doctorate at Harvard on the grounds that she was a woman. Over the next three decades, however, she published many works, including:

- *The Speaker of the House of Representatives* (1896)
- *The New State* (1918)
- *Creative Experience* (1924)
- *Dynamic Administration* (1941) (this collection of speeches and short articles was published posthumously)

There is correction in the publishing year of book "Dynamic Administration" it is actually 1st published in 1942 by harper& brothers publisher its a collection of papers of follett which was edited by C.Metcalf and L. Urwick. She recognized the holistic nature of community and advanced the idea of "reciprocal relationships" in understanding the dynamic aspects of the individual in relationship to others. Follett advocated the principle of what she termed "integration," or noncoercive power-sharing based on the use of her concept of "power with" rather than "power over." Her ideas on negotiation, power, and employee participation were highly influential in the development of the fields of organizational studies, alternative dispute resolution, and the Human Relations Movement. She was also a pioneer in the establishment of community centres.

Even though most of Mary Parker Follett's writings remained known in very limited circles until republished at the beginning of this decade (beginning with Pauline C. Graham's first-rate work), her ideas gained great influence after Chester Barnard, a New Jersey Bell exec and advisor to President Franklin D. Roosevelt, published his seminal treatment of executive management, *The Functions of the Executive*. Barnard's work, which stressed the critical role of "soft" factors such as "communication" and "informal processes" in organizations, owed a telling yet undisclosed debt to Follett's thought and writings. In addition, her emphasis on such soft factors paralleled the work of Elton Mayo at Western Electric's Hawthorne Plant, and presaged the rise of the Human Relations Movement, as developed through the work of such figures as Abraham Maslow, Kurt Lewin, Douglas McGregor, Chris Argyris, Dick Beckhard and other breakthrough contributors to the field of Organizational Development or "OD". Her influence can also be seen indirectly perhaps in the work of Ron Lippitt, Ken Benne, Lee Bradford, Edie Seashore and others at the National Training Laboratories in Bethel, New Hampshire, where T-Group methodology was first theorized and developed. Thus, Mary Follett's work set the stage for a generation of effective, progressive changes in management philosophy, style and practice, revolutionizing and humanizing the American workplace, and allowing the fulfilment of Douglas McGregor's management vision—quantum leaps in productivity effected through the humanization of the workplace.

## Mary Parker Follett Quotes

- Law flows from our life, therefore it cannot be above it. The source of the binding power of law is not in the consent of the community, but in the fact that it has been produced by the community. This gives us a new conception of law.
- When we look upon law as a thing we think of it as a finished thing; the moment we look upon it as a process we think of it always in evolution. Our law must take account of our social and economic conditions, and it must do it again to-morrow and again day after to-morrow. We do not want a new legal system with every sunrise, but we do want a method by which our law shall be capable of assimilating from day to day what it needs to act upon that life from which it has drawn its existence and to which it must minister. The vital fluid of the community, its life's blood, must pass so continuously from the common will to the law and from the law to the common will that a perfect circulation will be established. We do not "discover" legal principles which it then behooves us to burn candles before forever, but legal principles are the outcome of our daily life. Our law therefore cannot be based on "fixed" principles: our law must be intrinsic in the social process.
- Some writers talk of social justice as if a definite idea of it existed, and that all we have to do to regenerate society is to direct our efforts towards the realization of this ideal. But the ideal of social justice is itself a collective and a progressive development, that is, it is produced through our associated life and it is produced anew from day to day.

With her concern for creative experience, democracy and for developing local community organizations, Mary Parker Follett is an often forgotten, but still deeply instructive thinker for educators and social animateurs. Mary Parker Follett (1868-1933) occupies a very significant place in the development of thinking and practice around adult and informal education. Her contribution can be seen in three particular arenas. First, her involvement in, and advocacy of, community centres in the first two quarters of the twentieth century did a great deal to establish them as an important social and educational form. Second, her theorizing around the notions of community, experience and the group, and how these related to the individual and to the political domain broke new ground-and was 'far ahead of her time' (Konopka 1958: 29). It provided a key element in the development of the theorizing and practice of groupwork and community development and organization. For example, her argument that democracy could only work if individuals organized themselves into neighbourhood groups, and people's needs, desires and aspirations were attended to was fundamental to the sorts of thinking that emerged. Last, she was able to help key figures like Henry Croly and Eduard Lindeman not only to develop their thinking, but also to access important sources of financial help.

Today, Mary Parker Follett is better known for her pioneering work on management-although her contribution was soon forgotten after her death in 1933 (especially in the USA). She looked to approach organizations as group networks rather than as hierarchical structures, and attended to the influence of human relations within the group. In terms of current debates around management such a perspective is hardly revolutionary -but then it's radicalism and 'soft' orientation stood well outside mainstream.

## Mary Parker Follett-Her Life

Follett was born in 1868 into an affluent Quaker family in Quincy, Massachusetts. She was educated at the Thayer Academy but had to take on a significant role within the family in her teens when her father died (her mother was disabled). In 1892 she entered Society for the Collegiate Instruction of Women in Cambridge, Massachusetts (later Radcliffe College) where she graduated in 1898 in economics, government, law and philosophy. While at Radcliffe she spent a year at Newnham College,

Cambridge. Her research thesis at Radcliffe was published in 1896 as *The Speaker of the House of Representatives* (and quickly became a standard work). From 1900 to 1908 Follett became involved in social work in the Roxbury neighbourhood of Boston (joining the staff of Roxbury Neighbourhood House). She had an independent income and was able to throw herself into the work (in much the same way that Jane Addams and others were able to become immersed in settlement activity). She appears to have had the classic abilities of the informal educator to engage with a wide range of people, to listen and explore what they had to say, and to gain their confidence and esteem.

Roxbury at that point was a diverse neighbourhood both in terms of class and ethnicity. It had many of the classic dynamics of the suburbs-a grid-like design with no strong centre, a relative lack of attachment by its inhabitants and fairly limited local networks. However, Mary Parker Follett saw considerable possibility in the diverse nature of the population. Mixed neighbourhoods have potential, she believed, in that that they can work against the narrowness and exclusiveness of many, more homogenized, communities.

Instead of shutting out what is different, we should welcome it because it is different and through its difference will make a richer content of life... Every difference that is swept up into a bigger conception feeds and enriches society; every difference which is ignored feeds *on* society and eventually corrupts it. (Follett 1918: 40). Follett looked to encourage face-to-face encounter and the development of groups and activities. Diversity became a key ingredient of her vision of community. She believed that all human interaction held potential, and that it needed cultivating. Through such attention creativity and learning could be realized.

From 1908 Mary Parker Follett became involved in the movement to establish community centres in public schools (as chairperson of the Women's Municipal League's Committee on Extended Use of School Buildings). She sought to make 'the centres into institutions for overcoming civic apathy, further mutual understanding among groups, and creating a local framework for the integration of churches, trade associations, lodges and youth groups' (Quandt 1970: 39). In 1911 the committee was able to open the East Boston High School Social Centre as an experiment for the winter. The success of the initiative proved to be a catalyst for the development of other centres. Her experience was to change her view of democracy and the place of local groups radically-and was a major force behind her work on the promotion of local networks and democratic forms in *The New State* (1918).

Later Mary Park Follett was to serve as a member of the Massachusetts Minimum Wage Board, and in 1917 she became vice-president of the National Community Centre Association. The interest in industrial conditions appears to have grown in part from a concern for vocational guidance in connection with evening schools. She was also involved in *The Inquiry* a social reform movement founded by the Federal Council of Churches in America. (The main financial backer was Dorothy Straight-who went on to marry Leonard Elmhurst and to found Dartington Hall in England). At this time (perhaps through Henry Croly) Follett met Eduard Lindeman and became deeply impressed with the direction and quality of his thinking. Lindeman was similarly struck by her 'marvelous mind' (Leonard 1991: 44). Aside from the political direction of her work (her concern with democracy and local group organization) one of the key things to strike Lindeman was Mary Parker Follett's interest in, and commitment to, adult education.

Lindeman and Follett were, according to Stewart (1987: 147), 'an odd couple' and their collaboration was always a little wobbly. She proposed that they wrote a book together-something which Lindeman rejected. However, both acknowledge considerable debts to each other. The exacting, sickly, maidenly, and (to judge from her correspondence with Lindeman) severely neurotic Mary Follett did not always achieve good personal chemistry with the volatile, lusty, and often disorganized Eduard Lindeman. Though her own behaviour could also be erratic, the ethereal Miss Follett required personal and professional surroundings that were predictable, built on ground that was solid-very solid.

Her commitment and quick thinking made a last impression on many that met her (such as Lionel Urwick-who was to later edit her papers on management and administration). From the early 1920s Mary Parker Follett devoted a significant amount of attention to the state of management and administration in industry and public institutions. *Creative Experience* followed in 1924. This book, with its focus on learning, exploration and team, can be seen as a key predecessor of more recent interest in learning organizations.

Follett became a popular lecturer-and it could be argued that one of the reasons that her ideas found a significant response at the time was the passion and charm with which she was able to communicate her thinking. Her writing was accessible and her talks full of examples and commonsense connection. Basically, she took her ideas around community groups and networks and applied them to public and commercial organizations. With the continuing rise of scientific management and reaction to the social obligations that her views placed upon organizations her calls for a more 'human' approach to administration got less of an audience. After her death in 1933, according to Peter F. Drucker, 'she gradually became a 'non-person'. Her ideas were not acceptable in the mainstream of American management and organization thinking of the 1930s and 1940s. In Britain she had still had a significant following. Her various speeches and articles around management, for example were brought together by Henry Metcalf and Lionel Urwick and published in England in *Dynamic Administration* (1941). Gradually, a number of management thinkers and practitioners began to pick up on her work (especially in Japan in the 1960s) and with the emergence of discourses around the learning organization she has become recognized, according to Peter Drucker as a 'prophet of management' quoted by Babcock 1998).

### *The New State*

In *The New State* Mary Parker Follett argued that group organization and local networks provided the key to democratic advance.The study of democracy', she wrote, 'has been based largely on the study of institutions; it should have be based on how men behave together' (1918: 19). The book was begun as an exploration of community and social centres and quickly changed into a much wider analysis. According to Konopka (1958: 28) the crucial elements were as follows:

(1) Social experience is the basis of state structure.

(2) Sovereignty is relative to the capacity to rule oneself, to rule a group or a state.

(3) State structure is the expression of elements of identity in purpose.

(4) The will of a group is not atomic but is the common expression of individual wills.

(5) Rich experience can only come through actual experiences in group life. There must be experience in a variety of groups. Because of the multiplicity of human nature no one group can exhaust the capacity of the modern citizen.

(6) Individual and group are not antitheses.

(7) The individual is the ultimate unit which is more diversified than any group can be.

(8) There is no necessary contradiction between the citizen and the state.

(9) Freedom and determinism are not opposites.

(10) Self and others are not opposites.

In exploring groups and experience in this way Mary Parker Follett draws upon the work of James and others (for example she looks upon the person as 'a complex of radiating and converging, crossing and recrossing energies 1918: 75). She is able to place individuality in a social context and to stress relationship. The individual is created by the social process and is daily nourished by that process. There is no such things as a self-made man. What we possess as individuals is what is stored up from society, is the subsoil of social life.... Individuality is the capacity for union. The measure of individuality is the depth and breadth of true relation. I am an individual not as far as I am apart from, but as far as I am a part of other men. Evil is non-relation. (Follett 1918: 62)

Given this analysis it is no surprise that Mary Parker Follett argued for the deepening of people's capacities for, and commitment to, citizenship through involvement in groups and associations (in this respect she is an important advocate of la vie associative-the educative power of association). 'No one can give us democracy, we must learn democracy', she wrote. To be a democrat is not to decide on a certain form of human association, it is to learn how to live with other men... The group process contains the secret of collective life, it is the key to democracy, it is the master lesson for every individual to learn, it is our chief hope or the political, the social, the international life of the future.

(Follett 1918: 22-23) Neighbourhood education was, thus, one of the key areas for social intervention, and the group a central vehicle. Her own experience in Roxbury and elsewhere had taught her that it was possible for workers to become involved in local groups and networks and to enhance their capacity for action and for improving the quality of life of their members. Group process could be learned and developed by practice. As Konopka (1958; 29) again notes, she 'realized the dual aspect of the group, that it was a union of individuals but it also presented an individual in a larger union'. She argued that progressives and reformers had been wrong in not using the group process. Just what all this meant in educational terms was set out in the appendix to the book 'Training for the new democracy'.

The training for democracy can never cease while we exercise democracy. We older ones need it exactly as much as the younger ones. That education is a continuous process is a truism. It does not end with graduation day; it does not end when 'life' begins. Life and education must never be separated. We must have more life in our universities, more education in our life... We need education all the time and we all need education. (1918: 369). This appendix, according to Stewart (1987: 146) 'one of the earliest of scholarly writings on adult education in the United States'. It is marked by many of the concerns around education from everyday living and lifelong learning that Lindeman was to set out in his *Meaning of Adult Education* (1926) and that came to the fore in the famous 1919 Report in England.

### *Creative Experience*

*Creative Experience* (1924) while carrying forward a number of the themes developed in *The New State* (1918) reflects Mary Parker Follett's growing interest in the problems of industrial relations and the realm of management. She has the same commitment to democracy and encounter, but the focus is now on, as the title suggests, the creative use of experience. In this, David W. Stewart (1987: 145) suggests, her approach was basically that of a pragmatist, 'though she emphasized—and placed higher value on—the creative rather than the verifying aspects of experience'.

Experience is the power-house where purposes and will, thought and ideals, are being generated. I am not of course denying that the main process of life is that of testing, verifying, comparing. To compare and to select is always the process of education... When you get to a situation it becomes what it was plus you; you are responding to the situation plus yourself, that is, to the relation between it and yourself... Life is not a movie for us; you can never watch life because you are always *in* life... [T]he 'progressive integrations,' the ceaseless interweavings of new specific respondings, is the whole forward moving of existence; there is no adventure for those who stand at the counters of life and match samples. (Follett 1924: 133-134) Follett's is a philosophy of engagement and encounter. Through thinking about our experiences, questioning their meaning and truth and looking to the people we are, it is possible to learn. But there can be dangers in this process if approached narrowly.

The people who 'learn by experience' often make great messes of their lives, that is, if they apply what they have learned from a past incident to the present, deciding from certain appearances that the circumstances are the same, forgetting that no two situations can ever be the same... All that I am, all that life has made me, every past experience that I have had-woven into the tissue of my life-I must give to the new experience. That past experience has indeed not been useless, but its use is not in guiding present conduct by past situations. We must put everything we can into each fresh experience, but we shall not get the same things out which we put in if it is a fruitful experience, if it is part of our progressing life... We integrate our experience, and then the richer human being that we are goes into the new experience; again we give ourself and always by giving rise above the old self. . What we have here is the difference in Follett's terms between a 'mechanical and creating intelligence' (*op. cit.*) (which in turn mirrors the distinction Aristotle makes between technical and practical reasoning).

## Power and Management

From the publication of *Creative Experience* to her death in 1933 Mary Parker Follett was best known for her work around the administration and management of organizations. In 1925, she presented an influential paper, 'The Psychological Foundations of Business Administration' to executives at the annual conference of the Bureau of Personnel Administration in New York. She argued that the ideas she had been developing with regard to communities could equally be applied to organizations (we have seen a similar shift in recent years around the notion of social capital). Organizations, like communities, could be approached as local social systems involving networks of groups. In this way Mary Parker Follett was able to advocate the fostering of a 'self-governing principle' that would facilitate 'the growth of individuals and of the groups to which they belonged'. By directly interacting with one another to achieve their common goals, the members of a group 'fulfilled themselves through the process of the group's development'.

Boje and Rosile (2001) suggest that Follett was seeking to temper scientific management with her own science of the situation, 'one in which management and workers together cooperated to define not only productivity but situations of social justice'. Exploring 'the science of the situation' involved both management and workers studying the situation at hand together. Boje and Rosile (2001) argue that she was 'the first advocate of situation-search models of leadership and cooperation'. This was not to some surface activity: 'the willingness to search for the real values involved on both sides and the ability to bring about an interpenetration of these values'.

One of the key aspects of Mary Parker Follett's approach was the 'circular' theory of power she initially developed in *Creative Experience* (1924) Power begins... with the organization of reflex arcs. Then these are organized into a system-more power. Then the organization of these systems comprise the organism-more power. On the level of personality I gain more and more control over myself as I unite various tendencies. In social relations power is a centripedial self-developing. Power is the legitimate, the inevitable, outcome of the life-process. We can always test the validity of power by asking whether it is integral to the process of outside the process.

In terms of organizations this view of power involved managers, workers, and other stakeholders influencing each other. She distinguishes between power-over and power-with. (or co-active power rather than coercive power). What is the central problem of social relations? It is the question of power... But our task is not to learn where to place power; it is how to develop power. We frequently hear nowadays of 'transferring power as the panacea for all our ills¼ Genuine power can only be grown, it will slip from every arbitrary hand that grasps it; for genuine power is not coercive control, but coactive control. Coercive power is the curse of the universe; coactive power, the enrichment and advancement of every human soul.

Follett suggests that 'power-over' is resorted to because 'people will not wait for the slower process of education' (1924: 190). 'Power-with', she argues, 'is what democracy should mean in politics or industry.

### *Conclusion*

While Mary Parker Follett's contribution to management theory has come to be recognized, relatively little attention has been given in recent years to her work around the development of thinking and practice in the field of informal education and lifelong learning. At one level this is not surprising. Just as her ideas around management were out of step with the dominant discourses of the 1930s and 1940s, so her concerns with local democracy, group process and the educative power of associational life do not find a ready response within policy debates today. However, it may well be that her time has come. Recent attention to the decline in civic community, most notably by Robert Putnam, may well encourage people to look at what Follett has to offer. Her arguments for the development of schools as community centres still holds considerable power; her exploration of the nature of experience still offers educators insights; and the case for the development of local groups and networks as the bedrock of democracy (and community) is as strong as ever. Her finishing thought in *The New State* (1918), that the 'Community Centre is the real continuation school of America, the true university of true democracy' is something that we would do well to ponder. We need to extend and deepen associational life.

# 14

# Max Weber

Maximilian Carl Emil "Max" Weber (German pronunciation: (21 April 1864–14 June 1920) was a German lawyer, politician, historian, political economist, and sociologist, who profoundly influenced social theory and the remit of sociology itself. Weber's major works dealt with the rationalization and so-called "disenchantment" which he associated with the rise of capitalism and modernity. Weber was, along with his associate Georg Simmel, a central figure in the establishment of methodological antipositivism; presenting sociology as a non-empirical field which must study social action through resolutely subjective means. He is typically cited, with Émile Durkheim and Karl Marx, as one of the three principal architects of modern social science, and has variously been described as the most important classic thinker in the social sciences.

Weber's most famous work is his essay in economic sociology, *The Protestant Ethic and the Spirit of Capitalism*, which also began his work in the sociology of religion. In this text, Weber argued that religion was one of the non-exclusive reasons for the different ways the cultures of the Occident and the Orient have developed, and stressed that particular characteristics of ascetic Protestantism influenced the development of capitalism, bureaucracy and the rational-legal state in the West.

The essay examines the effects Protestantism had upon the beginnings of capitalism, arguing that capitalism is not purely materialist in Karl Marx's sense, but rather originates in religious ideals and ideas which cannot be solely explained by ownership relations, technology and advances in learning alone. In another major work, *Politics as a Vocation*, Weber defined the state as an entity which claims a "monopoly on the legitimate use of violence", a definition that became pivotal to the study of modern Western political science. His analysis of bureaucracy in his *Economy and Society* is still central to the modern study of organizations. Weber was the first to recognize several diverse aspects of social authority, which he respectively categorized according to their charismatic, traditional, and legal forms. His analysis of bureaucracy thus noted that modern state institutions are based on a form of rational-legal authority. Weber's thought regarding the rationalizing and secularizing tendencies of modern Western society (sometimes described as the "Weber Thesis") would come to facilitate critical theory, particularly in the work of thinkers such as Jürgen Habermas.

### *Biography*

Weber was born in 1864, in Erfurt in Thuringia, Germany, the eldest of seven children of Max Weber Sr., a wealthy and prominent politician in the National Liberal Party (Germany) and a civil servant, and Helene Fallenstein, a Protestant and a Calvinist, with strong moral absolutist ideas. Weber Sr.'s engagement with public life immersed the family home in politics, as his salon received many prominent scholars and public figures. Weber was strongly influenced by his mother's views and approach to life, but he did not claim to be religious himself.

The young Weber and his brother Alfred, who also became a sociologist and economist, thrived in this intellectual atmosphere. Weber's 1876 Christmas presents to his parents, when he was thirteen years old, were two historical essays entitled "About the course of German history, with special reference to the positions of the emperor and the pope" and "About the Roman Imperial period from Constantine to the migration of nations". At the age of fourteen, he wrote letters studded with references to Homer, Virgil, Cicero, and Livy, and he had an extended knowledge of Goethe, Spinoza, Kant, and Schopenhauer before he began university studies. It seemed clear that Weber would pursue advanced studies in the social sciences.

In 1882 Weber enrolled in the University of Heidelberg as a law student. Weber joined his father's duelling fraternity, and chose as his major study Weber Sr.'s field of law. Along with his law coursework, young Weber attended lectures in economics and studied medieval history and theology. Intermittently, he served with the German army in Strasbourg.

In the autumn of 1884, Weber returned to his parents' home to study at the University of Berlin. For the next eight years of his life, interrupted only by a term at the University of Göttingen and short periods of further military training, Weber stayed at his parents' house; first as a student, later as a junior barrister, and finally as a dozent/professor at the University of Berlin. In 1886 Weber passed the examination for "Referendar", comparable to the bar association examination in the British and American legal systems. Throughout the late 1880s, Weber continued his study of history. He earned his law doctorate in 1889 by writing a doctoral dissertation on legal history entitled *The History of Medieval Business Organisations*. Two years later, Weber completed his Habilitationsschrift, *The Roman Agrarian History and its Significance for Public and Private Law*. Having thus become a "Privatdozent", Weber was now qualified to hold a German professorship.

In the years between the completion of his dissertation and habilitation, Weber took an interest in contemporary social policy. In 1888 he joined the "Verein für Socialpolitik", the new professional association of German economists affiliated with the historical school, who saw the role of economics primarily as the solving of the wide-ranging social problems of the age, and who pioneered large scale statistical studies of economic problems. He also involved himself in politics, joining the left leaning Evangelical Social Congress. In 1890 the "Verein" established a research program to examine "the Polish question" or Ostflucht, meaning the influx of foreign farm workers into eastern Germany as local labourers migrated to Germany's rapidly industrialising cities. Weber was put in charge of the study, and wrote a large part of its results. The final report was widely acclaimed as an excellent piece of empirical research, and cemented Weber's reputation as an expert in agrarian economics.

In 1893 he married his distant cousin Marianne Schnitger, later a feminist and author in her own right, who was instrumental in collecting and publishing Weber's journal articles as books after his death. The couple moved to Freiburg in 1894, where Weber was appointed professor of economics at Freiburg University, before accepting the same position at the University of Heidelberg in 1896. Next year, Max Weber Sr. died, two months after a severe quarrel with his son that was never resolved. After this, Weber became increasingly prone to nervousness and insomnia, making it difficult for him to fulfil his duties as a professor. His condition forced him to reduce his teaching, and leave his last course in the fall of 1899 unfinished. After spending months in a sanatorium during the summer and fall of 1900, Weber and his wife traveled to Italy at the end of the year, and did not return to Heidelberg until April 1902.

After Weber's immense productivity in the early 1890s, he did not publish a single paper between early 1898 and late 1902, finally resigning his professorship in fall 1903. Freed from those obligations, in that year he accepted a position as associate editor of the Archives for Social Science and Social Welfare next to his colleagues Edgar Jaffé and Werner Sombart. In 1904, Weber began to publish some of his most seminal papers in this journal, notably his essay *The Protestant Ethic and the Spirit of Capitalism*. It became his most famous work, and laid the foundations for his later research on the impact of cultures and religions on the development of economic systems. This essay was the only one of his works that was published as a book during his lifetime. Also that year, he visited the United States and participated in the Congress of Arts and Sciences held in connection with the World's Fair (Louisiana Purchase Exposition) at St. Louis. Despite his successes, Weber felt that he was unable to resume regular teaching at that time, and continued on as a private scholar, helped by an inheritance in 1907. In 1912, Weber tried to organise a left-wing political party to combine social-democrats and liberals. This attempt was unsuccessful, presumably because many liberals feared social-democratic revolutionary ideals at the time.

During the First World War, Weber served for a time as director of the army hospitals in Heidelberg. In 1915 and 1916 he sat on commissions that tried to retain German supremacy in Belgium and Poland after the war. Weber's views on war, as well as on expansion of the German empire, changed throughout the war. He became a member of the worker and soldier council of Heidelberg in 1918. In the same year, Weber became a consultant to the German Armistice Commission at the Treaty of Versailles and to the commission charged with drafting the Weimar Constitution. He argued in favour of inserting Article 48 into the Weimar Constitution. This article was later used by Adolf Hitler to institute rule by decree, thereby allowing his government to suppress opposition and obtain dictatorial powers. Weber's contributions to German politics remain a controversial subject to this day.

Weber resumed teaching during this time, first at the University of Vienna, then in 1919 at the University of Munich. In Munich, he headed the first German university institute of sociology, but ultimately never held a personal sociology appointment. Weber left politics due to right-wing agitation in 1919 and 1920. Many colleagues and students in Munich argued against him for his speeches and left-wing attitude during the German Revolution of 1918 and 1919, with some right-wing students holding protests in front of his home. Max Weber contracted the Spanish flu and died of pneumonia in Munich on June 14, 1920.

*Achievements*

Weber's most famous work relates to economic sociology, political sociology, and the sociology of religion. Along with Karl Marx and Émile Durkheim, he is regarded as one of the founders of modern sociology. In his time, however, Weber was viewed primarily as a historian and an economist. The breadth of Weber's topical interests is apparent in the depth of his social theory:

The affinity between capitalism and Protestantism, the religious origins of the Western world, the force of charisma in religion as well as in politics, the all-embracing process of rationalization and the bureaucratic price of progress, the role of legitimacy and of violence as offsprings of leadership, the 'disenchantment' of the modern world together with the never-ending power of religion, the antagonistic relation between intellectualism and eroticism: all these are key concepts which attest to the enduring fascination of Weber's thinking. – *Radkau, Joachim Max Weber: A Biography 2005*

Whereas Durkheim, following Comte, worked in the positivist tradition, Weber created and worked – like Werner Sombart, his friend and then the most famous representative of German sociology – in the antipositivist, hermeneutic, tradition. These works pioneered the antipositivistic revolution in social sciences, stressing (as in the work of Wilhelm Dilthey) the difference between the social sciences and natural sciences. We know of no scientifically ascertainable ideals. To be sure, that makes our efforts more arduous than in the past, since we are expected to create our ideals from within our breast in the very age of subjectivist culture. – *Max Weber Economy and society 1909*

Weber presented sociology as the science of human social action; action which he differentiated into traditional, affectional, value-rational and instrumental.

*[Sociology is ]...* the science whose object is to interpret *the meaning of social action* and thereby give a *causal explanation* of the way in which the *action proceeds* and the *effects which it produces.* By 'action' in this definition is meant the human behaviour when and to the extent that the agent or agents see it as *subjectively meaningful...* the meaning to which we refer may be either (a) the meaning actually intended either by an individual agent on a particular historical occasion or by a number of agents on an approximate average in a given set of cases, or (b) the meaning attributed to the agent or agents, as types, in a pure type constructed in the abstract. In neither case is the 'meaning' to be thought of as somehow objectively 'correct' or 'true' by some metaphysical criterion. This is the difference between the empirical sciences of action, such as sociology and history, and any kind of *priori* discipline, such as jurisprudence, logic, ethics, or aesthetics whose aim is to extract from their subject-matter 'correct' or 'valid' meaning. – *Max Weber The Nature of Social Action 1922,*

Weber began his studies of rationalisation in *The Protestant Ethic and the Spirit of Capitalism,* in which he argued that the redefinition of the connection between work and piety in Protestantism, and especially in ascetic Protestant denominations, particularly Calvinism, shifted human effort towards rational efforts aimed at achieving economic gain. In Calvinism in particular, but also in Lutheranism, Christian piety towards God was expressed through or in one's secular vocation. Calvin, in particular, viewed the expression of the work ethic as a sign of "election". The rational roots of this doctrine, he argued, soon grew incompatible with and larger than the religious, and so the latter were eventually discarded. Weber continued his investigation into this matter in later works, notably in his studies on bureaucracy and on the classifications of authority into three types—legitimate, traditional, and charismatic. In these works Weber described what he saw as society's movement towards rationalization.

What Weber depicted was not only the secularization of Western *culture,* but also and especially the development of modern *societies* from the viewpoint of rationalization. The new structures of society were marked by the differentiation of the two functionally intermeshing systems that had taken shape around the organizational cores of the capitalist enterprise and the bureaucratic state apparatus. Weber understood this process as the instititutionalization of purposive-rational economic and administrative action. To the degree that everyday life was affected by this cultural and societal rationalization, tradional forms of life-which in the early modern period were differentated primarily according to one's trade-were dissolved. – *Jürgen Habermas Modernity's Consciousness of Time,*

It should be noted that many of Weber's works famous today were collected, revised, and published posthumously. Significant interpretations of his writings were produced by such sociological luminaries as Talcott Parsons and C. Wright Mills. Parsons in particular imparted to Weber's works a functionalist, teleological perspective; this personal interpretation has been criticised for a latent conservatism.

### *Sociology of Religion*

Weber's work in the field of sociology of religion started with the essay *The Protestant Ethic and the Spirit of Capitalism,* which grew out of heavy "field work" among Protestant sects in America, and continued with the analysis of *The Religion of China: Confucianism and Taoism, The Religion of India: The Sociology of Hinduism and Buddhism,* and *Ancient Judaism.* His work on other religions was interrupted by his sudden death in 1920, which prevented him from following *Ancient Judaism* with studies of Psalms, Book of Jacob, Talmudic Jewry, early Christianity and Islam. His three main themes were the effect of religious ideas on economic activities, the relation between social stratification and religious ideas, and the distinguishable characteristics of Western civilization.

His goal was to find reasons for the different development paths of the cultures of the Occident and the Orient, although without judging or valuing them, like some of the contemporary thinkers who followed the social Darwinist paradigm; Weber wanted primarily to explain the distinctive elements of the Western civilization. In the analysis of his findings, Weber maintained that Calvinist (and more widely, Protestant) religious ideas had had a major impact on the social innovation and development of the economic system of Europe and the United States, but noted that they were not the only factors in this development. Other notable factors mentioned by Weber included the rationalism of scientific pursuit, merging observation with mathematics, science of scholarship and jurisprudence, rational systematization of government administration, and economic enterprise. In the end, the study of the sociology of religion, according to Weber, merely explored one phase of the freedom from magic, that "disenchantment of the world" that he regarded as an important distinguishing aspect of Western culture.

## Spirit of Capitalism

Weber's essay *The Protestant Ethic and the Spirit of Capitalism* (*Die protestantische Ethik und der Geist des Kapitalismus*) is his most famous work. It is argued that this work should not be viewed as a detailed study of Protestantism, but rather as an introduction into Weber's later works, especially his studies of interaction between various religious ideas and economic behaviour. In *The Protestant Ethic and the Spirit of Capitalism*, Weber put forward the thesis that Calvinist ethic and ideas influenced the development of capitalism. In this work, he relied on a great deal of statistics from the era, which indicated the predominance of Protestants among the wealthy, industrial, and technical classes relative to Catholics. He also noted the shift of Europe's economic centre after the Reformation away from Catholic countries such as France, Spain and Italy, and toward Protestant countries such as the Netherlands, England, Scotland and Germany. This theory is often viewed as a reversal of Marx's thesis that the economic "base" of society determines all other aspects of it. Christian religious devotion had historically been accompanied by rejection of mundane affairs, including economic pursuit. Why was that not the case with Protestantism? Weber addressed that paradox in his essay. According to Weber, one of the universal tendencies that Christians had historically fought against, was the desire to profit. After defining the spirit of capitalism, Weber argued that there were many reasons to look for the origins of modern capitalism in the religious ideas of the Reformation. Many observers, such as William Petty, Montesquieu, Henry Thomas Buckle, John Keats, and others had commented on the affinity between Protestantism and the development of the commercial spirit.

Weber showed that certain types of Protestantism – notably Calvinism – favored rational pursuit of economic gain and worldly activities which had been given positive spiritual and moral meaning. It was not the goal of those religious ideas, but rather a byproduct – the inherent logic of those doctrines and the advice based upon them both directly and indirectly encouraged planning and self-denial in the pursuit of economic gain. A common illustration is in the cobbler, hunched over his work, who devotes his entire effort to the praise of God. In addition, the Reformation view "calling" dignified even the most mundane professions as being those that added to the common good and were blessed by God, as much as any "sacred" calling could. This Reformation view, that all the spheres of life were sacred when dedicated to God and His purposes of nurturing and furthering life, profoundly affected the view of work.

To illustrate and provide an example, Weber quoted the ethical writings of Benjamin Franklin: Remember, that *time is money*. He that can earn ten shillings a day by his labor, and goes abroad, or sits idle, one half of that day, though he spends but sixpence during his diversion or idleness, ought not to reckon *that* the only expense; he has really spent, or rather thrown away, five shillings besides.... Remember, that money is the *prolific, generating nature*. Money can beget money, and its offspring can beget more, and so on. Five shillings turned is six, turned again is seven and threepence, and so on, till it becomes a hundred pounds. The more there is of it, the more it produces every turning, so that the profits rise quicker and quicker. He that kills a breeding sow, destroys all her offspring to the thousandth generation. He that murders a crown, destroys all that it might have produced, even scores of pounds. Weber noted that this is not a philosophy of mere greed, but a statement laden with moral language. Indeed, Franklin claimed that God revealed to him the usefulness of virtue. To emphasize the work ethic in Protestantism relative to Catholicism, Weber noted a common problem that industrialists faced when employing precapitalist laborers: agricultural entrepreneurs would try to encourage time spent harvesting by offering a higher wage, with the expectation that laborers would see time spent working as more valuable and so engage it longer. However, in precapitalist societies similar attempts often resulted in labourers spending *less* time harvesting. Labourers judged that they could earn the same amount as previously, while spending less time working and having more leisure. Weber also noted that societies having more Protestants were those that have a more developed capitalist economy.

It was particularly advantageous in technical occupations for workers to be extremely devoted to their craft. To view the craft as an end in itself, or as a "calling" would serve this need well. This attitude was well-noted in certain classes which have endured religious education, especially of a Pietist background.

Weber stated that he abandoned research into Protestantism because his colleague Ernst Troeltsch, a professional theologian, had initiated work on the book *The Social Teachings of the Christian Churches and Sects*. Another reason for Weber's decision was that the essay had already provided the perspective for a broad comparison of religion and society, which he continued in his later works. The phrase "work ethic" used in modern commentary is a derivative of the "Protestant ethic" discussed by Weber. It was adopted when the idea of the Protestant ethic was generalised to apply to the Japanese people, Jews and other non-Christians.

## Confucianism and Taoism

*The Religion of China: Confucianism and Taoism* was Weber's second major work on the sociology of religion. Weber focused on those aspects of Chinese society that were different from those of Western Europe and especially contrasted with Puritanism, and posed a question why capitalism did not develop in China. In *Hundred Schools of Thought Warring States Period*, he concentrated on the early period of Chinese history, during which the major Chinese schools of thoughts (Confucianism and Taoism) came to the fore. By 200 BC, the Chinese state had developed from a loose federation of feudal states into a unified empire with patrimonial rule, as described in the *Warring States Period*. As in Europe, Chinese cities had been founded as forts or leaders' residences, and were the centres of trade and crafts. However, they never received political autonomy and its citizens had no special political rights or privileges.

This is due to the strength of kinship ties, which stems from religious beliefs in ancestral spirits. Also, the guilds competed against each other for the favour of the Emperor, never uniting in order to fight for more rights. Therefore, the residents of Chinese cities never constitute a separate status class like the residents of European cities.

Early unification of the state and the establishment of central officialdom meant that the focus of the power struggle changed from the distribution of land to the distribution of offices, which with their fees and taxes were the most prominent source of income for the holder, who often pocketed up to 50% of the revenue. The imperial government depended on the services of those officials, not on the service of the military (knights) as in Europe.

Weber emphasised that Confucianism tolerated a great number of popular cults without any effort to systematise them into a religious doctrine. Instead of metaphysical conjectures, it taught adjustment to the world. The "superior" man (literati) should stay away from the pursuit of wealth (though not from wealth itself). Therefore, becoming a civil servant was preferred to becoming a businessman and granted a much higher status.

Chinese civilization had no religious prophecy nor a powerful priestly class. The emperor was the high priest of the state religion and the supreme ruler, but popular cults were also tolerated (however the political ambitions of their priests were curtailed). This forms a sharp contrast with medieval Europe, where the Church curbed the power of secular rulers and the same faith was professed by rulers and common folk alike.

According to Confucianism, the worship of great deities is the affair of the state, while ancestral worship is required of all, and the multitude of popular cults is tolerated. Confucianism tolerated magic and mysticism as long as they were useful tools for controlling the masses; it denounced them as heresy and suppressed them when they threatened the established order (hence the opposition to Buddhism). Note that in this context, Confucianism can be referred to as the state cult, and Taoism as the popular religion.

Weber argued that while several factors favored the development of a capitalist economy (long periods of peace, improved control of rivers, population growth, freedom to acquire land and move outside of native community, free choice of occupation) they were outweighed by others (mostly stemming from religion):

- technical inventions were opposed on the basis of religion, in the sense that the disturbance of ancestral spirits was argued to lead to bad luck, and adjusting oneself to the world was preferred to changing it.
- sale of land was often prohibited or made very difficult.
- extended kinship groups (based on the religious importance of family ties and ancestry) protected its members against economic adversities, therefore discouraging payment of debts, work discipline, and rationalisation of work processes.
- those kinship groups prevented the development of an urban status class and hindered developments towards legal institutions, codification of laws, and the rise of a lawyer class.

According to Weber, Confucianism and Puritanism represent two comprehensive but mutually exclusive types of rationalisation, each attempting to order human life according to certain ultimate religious beliefs. Both encouraged sobriety and self-control and were compatible with the accumulation of wealth. However, Confucianism aimed at attaining and preserving "a cultured status position" and used as means adjustment to the world, education, self-perfection, politeness and familial piety. Puritanism used those means in order to create a "tool of God", creating a person that would serve the God and master the world. Such intensity of belief and enthusiasm for action were alien to the aesthetic values of Confucianism. Therefore, Weber states that it was the difference in prevailing mentality that contributed to the development of capitalism in the West and the absence of it in China.

## The Sociology of Hinduism and Buddhism

*The Religion of Nepal: The Sociology of Hinduism and Buddhism* was Weber's third major work on the sociology of religion. In this work he deals with the structure of Indian society, with the orthodox doctrines of Hinduism and the heterodox doctrines of Buddhism, with modifications brought by the influence of popular religiosity, and finally with the impact of religious beliefs on the secular ethic of Indian society.

The ancient Nepalese social system was shaped by the concept of caste. It directly linked religious belief and the segregation of society into status groups. Weber describes the caste system, consisting of the Brahmins (priests), the Kshatriyas (warriors), the Vaisyas (merchants) and the Shudras (labourers). Then he describes the spread of the caste system in Nepal due to conquests, the marginalisation of certain tribes and the subdivision of castes. Weber pays special attention to Brahmins and analyzes why they occupied the highest place in Nepalese society for so many centuries. With regard to the concept of dharma he concludes that the Indian ethical pluralism is very different both from the universal ethic of Confucianism and Christianity. He notes that the caste system prevented the development of urban status groups.

Next, Weber analyses the Hindu religious beliefs, including asceticism and the Hindu world view, the Brahman orthodox doctrines, the rise and fall of Buddhism in Nepal, the Hindu restoration, and the evolution of the guru. Weber asks the question whether religion had any influence upon the daily round of mundane activities, and if so, how it impacted economic conduct. He notes the idea of an immutable world order consisting of the eternal cycles of rebirth and the deprecation of the mundane world, and finds that the traditional caste system, supported by the religion, slowed economic development; in other words, the "spirit" of the caste system militated against an indigenous development of capitalism.

Weber concludes his study of society and religion in India by combining his findings with his previous work on China. He notes that the beliefs tended to interpret the meaning of life as otherworldly or mystical experience, that the intellectuals tended to be apolitical in their orientation, and that the social world was fundamentally divided between the educated, whose lives were oriented toward the exemplary conduct of a prophet or wise man, and the uneducated masses who remained caught in their daily rounds and believed in magic. In Asia, no Messianic prophecy appeared that could have given "plan and meaning to the everyday life of educated and uneducated alike." He argues that it was the Messianic prophecies in the countries of the Near East, as distinguished from the prophecy of the Asiatic mainland, that prevented Western countries from following the paths of China and India, and his next work, Ancient Judaism was an attempt to prove this theory.

### Ancient Judaism

In *Ancient Judaism,* his fourth major work on the sociology of religion, Weber attempted to explain the "combination of circumstances" which resulted in the early differences between Oriental and Occidental religiosity. It is especially visible when the innerworldly asceticism developed by Western Christianity is contrasted with mystical contemplation of the kind developed in India. Weber noted that some aspects of Christianity sought to conquer and change the world, rather than withdraw from its imperfections. This fundamental characteristic of Christianity (when compared to Far Eastern religions) stems originally from ancient Jewish prophecy. Stating his reasons for investigating ancient Judaism, Weber wrote that

> Anyone who is heir to the traditions of modern European civilization will approach the problems of universal history with a set of questions, which to him appear both inevitable and legitimate. These questions will turn on the combination of circumstances which has brought about the cultural phenomena that are uniquely Western and that have at the same time (...) a universal cultural significance.

Further on he adds: "For the Jew (...) the social order of the world was conceived to have been turned into the opposite of that promised for the future, but in the future it was to be overturned so that Jewry could be once again dominant. The world was conceived as neither eternal nor unchangeable, but rather as being created. Its present structure was a product of man's actions, above all those of the Jews, and God's reaction to them. Hence the world was a historical product designed to give way to the truly God-ordained order (...). There existed in addition a highly rational religious ethic of social conduct; it was free of magic and all forms of irrational quest for salvation; it was inwardly worlds apart from the path of salvation offered by Asiatic religions. To a large extent this ethic still underlies contemporary Middle Eastern and European ethic. World-historical interest in Jewry rests upon this fact. (...) Thus, in considering the conditions of Jewry's evolution, we stand at a turning point of the whole cultural development of the West and the Middle East".

Weber analyzes the interaction between the Bedouins, the cities, the herdsmen and the peasants, including the conflicts between them and the rise and fall of the United Monarchy. The time of the United Monarchy appears as a mere episode, dividing the period of confederacy since the Exodus and the settlement of the Israelites in Canaan from the period of political decline following the division of the monarchy. This division into periods has major implications for religious history. Since the basic tenets of Judaism were formulated during the time of Israelite confederacy and after the fall of the United Monarchy, they became the basis of the prophetic movement that left a lasting impression on the Western civilization.

Weber discusses the organization of the early confederacy, the unique qualities of the Israelites' relations to Yahweh, the influence of foreign cults, types of religious ecstasy, and the struggle of the priests against ecstasy and idol worship. He goes on to describe the times of the Division of the Monarchy, social aspects of Biblical prophecy, the social orientation of the prophets, demagogues and pamphleteers, ecstasy and politics, and the ethic and theodicity of the prophets. Weber notes that Judaism not only fathered Christianity and Islam, but was crucial to the rise of modern Occident state, as its influence were as important to those of Hellenistic and Roman cultures. Reinhard Bendix, summarizing *Ancient Judaism*, writes that

free of magic and esoteric speculations, devoted to the study of law, vigilant in the effort to do what was right in the eyes of the Lord in the hope of a better future, the prophets established a religion of faith that subjected man's daily life to the imperatives of a divinely ordained moral law. In this way, ancient Judaism helped create the moral rationalism of Western civilisation.

### *Sociology of Politics and Government*

In political sociology, one of Weber's most significant contributions is his *Politics as a Vocation* essay. Therein, Weber unveils the definition of the state that has become so pivotal to Western social thought: that the state is that entity which possesses a monopoly on the legitimate use of physical force, which it may nonetheless elect to delegate as it sees fit. In this essay, Weber wrote that politics is to be understood as any activity in which the state might engage itself in order to influence the relative distribution of force. Politics thus comes to be understood as deriving from power. A politician must not be a man of the "true Christian ethic", understood by Weber as being the ethic of the Sermon on the Mount, that is to say, the injunction to turn the other cheek. An adherent of such an ethic ought rather to be understood to be a saint, for it is only saints, according to Weber, that can appropriately follow it. The political realm is no realm for saints. A politician ought to marry the ethic of ultimate ends and the ethic of responsibility, and must possess both a passion for his vocation and the capacity to distance himself from the subject of his exertions (the governed).

Weber distinguished three pure types of political leadership, domination and authority:

1. charismatic domination (familial and religious),
2. traditional domination (patriarchs, patrimonalism, feudalism), and
3. legal domination (modern law and state, bureaucracy).

In his view, every historical relation between rulers and ruled contained such elements and they can be analysed on the basis of this tripartite distinction. He also notes that the instability of charismatic authority inevitably forces it to "routinize" into a more structured form of authority. Likewise he notes that in a pure type of traditional rule, sufficient resistance to a master can lead to a "traditional revolution". Thus he alludes to an inevitable move towards a rational-legal structure of authority, utilising a bureaucratic structure. Thus this theory can be sometimes viewed as part of the social evolutionism theory. This ties to his broader concept of rationalisation by suggesting the inevitability of a move in this direction.

Weber is also well-known for his critical study of the bureaucratisation of society, the rational ways in which formal social organizations apply the ideal type characteristics of a bureaucracy. It was Weber who began the studies of bureaucracy and whose works led to the popularization of this term. Many aspects of modern public administration go back to him, and a classic, hierarchically organized civil service of the Continental type is called "Weberian civil service", although this is only one ideal type of public administration and government described in his *magnum opus Economy and Society* (1922), and one that he did not particularly like himself – he only thought it particularly efficient and successful. In this work, Weber outlines a description, which has become famous, of rationalization (of which bureaucratization is a part) as a shift from a value-oriented organization and action (traditional authority and charismatic authority) to a goal-oriented organization and action (legal-rational authority). The result, according to Weber, is a "polar night of icy darkness", in which increasing rationalization of human life traps individuals in an "iron cage" of rule-based, rational control. Weber's bureaucracy studies also led him to his analysis – correct, as it would turn out, after Stalin's takeover – that socialism in Russia would lead to over-bureaucratization rather than to the "withering away of the state" (as Karl Marx had predicted would happen in communist society).

***Economics***

While Weber is best known and recognized today as one of the leading scholars and founders of modern sociology, he also accomplished much in other fields, notably economics, although this is largely forgotten today among orthodox economists, who pay very little attention to his works. The view that Weber is at all influential to modern economists comes largely from non-economists and economic critics with sociology backgrounds. During his life distinctions between the social sciences were less clear than they are now, and Weber considered himself a historian and an economist first, sociologist distant second.

From the point of view of the economists, he is a representative of the "Youngest" German historical school of economics. His most valued contributions to the field of economics is his famous work, *The Protestant Ethic and the Spirit of Capitalism*. This is a seminal essay on the differences between religions and the relative wealth of their followers. In contrast Sombart located the rise of capitalism successively in the Enlightenment ideal of reason and control of nature, Judaism and urbanization. Weber's other main contribution to economics (as well as to social sciences in general) is his work on methodology: his theories of "Verstehen" (known as *understanding* or *Interpretative Sociology*) and of antipositivism (known as *humanistic sociology*).

The doctrine of Interpretative Sociology is one of the main sociological paradigms, with many supporters as well as critics. This thesis states that social, economic and historical research can never be fully inductive or descriptive as one must always approach it with a conceptual apparatus, which Weber termed "Ideal Type". The idea can be summarized as follows: an ideal type is formed from characteristics and elements of the given phenomena but it is not meant to correspond to all of the characteristics of any one particular case. Weber's Ideal Type became one of the most important concepts in social sciences, and led to the creation of such concepts as Ferdinand Tönnies' "Normal Type".

Weber conceded that employing "Ideal Types" was an abstraction but claimed that it was nonetheless essential if one were to understand any particular social phenomena because, unlike physical phenomena, they involve human behaviour which must be interpreted by ideal types. This, together with his antipositivistic argumentation can be viewed as the methodological justification for the assumption of the "rational economic man" (*homo economicus*).

Weber formulated a three-component theory of stratification, with Social class, Social status and party (or politicals) as conceptually distinct elements.

- Social class is based on economically determined relationship to the market (owner, renter, employee etc.).
- Status is based on non-economical qualities like honour, prestige and religion.
- Party refers to affiliations in the political domain.

All three dimensions have consequences for what Weber called "life chances". Weber's other contributions to economics were several: these include a (seriously researched) economic history of Roman agrarian society, his work on the dual roles of idealism and materialism in the history of capitalism in his *Economy and Society* (1914) which present Weber's criticisms (or according to some, revisions) of some aspects of Marxism. Finally, his thoroughly researched General Economic History (1923) can be considered the Historical School at its empirical best.

### *As a Critic of Socialism*

In the final years of his career Weber became vocal critic of socialism, both in European and Bolshevik variants. He saw Lenin's ideal of applying hierarchical mode of organization in the firm on society at large as an attempt to universalize serfdom. He believed that workers in socialist society still would work in hierarchy, but this time in much worse form of it, fused with government power.

Weber developed, independently from Ludwig von Mises, a critique of socialism as an economically impossible system. Weber stated that when socialism abolishes private property in the means of production, it would at the same time abolish market prices and monetary calculation of cost and profit, and that way make a rational planned economy impossible. Socialist central planners can resort to calculation in-kind, but this type of economic coordination would be grossly inefficient. According to Weber, the main reason why a socialist in-kind mode of economic calculation cannot work is because it is unable to solve the problem of imputation (i.e. to determine the relative price of capital goods):

In order to make possible a rational utilization of the means of production, a system of in-kind accounting would have to determine "value"-indicators of some kind for the individual capital goods which could take over the role of the "prices" used in book valuation in modern business accounting. But it is not at all clear how such indicators could be established, and in particular, verified; whether, for instance, they should vary from one production unit to the next (on the basis of economic location), or whether they should be uniform for the entire economy, on the basis of "social utility," that is, of (present and future) consumption requirements? [...] Nothing is gained by assuming that, if only the problem of a non-monetary economy were seriously enough attacked, a suitable accounting method would be discovered or invented. The problem is fundamental to any kind of complete socialization. We cannot speak of a rational "planned economy" so long as in this decisive respect we have no instrument for elaborating a rational "plan".

## On Capitalism

Weber's most famous book is *The Protestant Ethic and the Spirit of Capitalism* (1904-5). It is generally taken as a counter to the Marxist thesis of the primacy of base over superstructure: Weber is supposed to have argued in this book that capitalism in fact developed historically as a result of a *religious* movement, protestantism, specifically Calvinism. The argument is that Calvinism, with its doctrine of predestination-i.e. the doctrine that God eternally decreed the salvation of some and the damnation of others, not in view of the good or evil deeds they would do, but simply 'because he willed it'-that this doctrine made Calvinists anxious about their salvation; that this led them to seek reassurance in attempting to succeed in their economic (and other) undertakings, in the belief that God signifies his favour by giving prosperity to the undertakings of the elect; at the same time the Calvinist did not spend his money on self-indulgence, so had nothing else to do with it but plough it back into the business. And his employees, being Calvinists also, had a sense of their jobs as 'callings' to be done well out of religious duty even for small earthly reward. Hence the 'Protestant ethic'-the famous 'work ethic'-, the drive for economic success, the will to work hard, the habit of not spending on frivolous self-indulgence-all this, originating in theology, provided a 'spirit' for capitalism, the set of motivations and attitudes that led to 'rational investment' of profits continually ploughed back, and to the modern world. I suspect that this is a travesty of Weber's book.

It is certainly a travesty of Calvinism. Any properly catechized Calvinist would have known that it was wrong to seek a sign that he had been saved, and nonsense to find it in economic success. If 17th century Calvinists *were* thinking along those lines, then perhaps Calvinism had been corrupted by the influence of early capitalism; and in that case the economic base might have been the 'independent variable' or initiator of change. As Parkin says: 'The question then arises as to why the doctrine [Calvinism] evolved in the particular manner it did... Weber does not address this problem of what might be called "the transition from Calvinism to Puritanism"'. As Parkin points out, Weber generally supposes that a religion will be held in differing senses by different social strata; if Calvinism underwent some change between John Calvin and the early Calvinist capitalists that Weber studied in his book, then that change should have something to do with the way Calvin's doctrine was *received* in different social strata. 'What seemed to be required was a complementary study designed to demonstrate the effects of the stratification system on the peculiar evolution of early protestantism. Had Weber managed to get round to conducting such a study, he would have had to clarify and expand upon his own brand of materialism and to show how it differed from the Marxist version.... there are enough hints in his work to suggest that his own final position would not have differed very much from a sophisticated Marxist one'.

At any rate, as long as the 'Calvinism' that is supposed to have provided the initiating force for capitalism is *not* the Calvinism of John Calvin, but something already undergoing change caused by unexplained factors, it has not been established that capitalism originated in the realm of ideas, if that is what Weber was trying to prove. Parkin suggests that Weber has two thesis which he never clearly distinguishes, what Parkin calls the 'strong' and the 'weak' thesis. The 'strong' thesis is that Calvinism caused capitalism, the weak thesis is that Calvinism did not (like other religions) *obstruct* the development of capitalism. The strong thesis is that when a certain change occurred in the realm of religious thought, that brought into being the capitalist economic system. The weak thesis is that there were *already* causes at work which did in the end produce capitalism, but that they were obstructed by certain religious ideas, until the change in religious thinking removed the obstacle.

There is another possible interpretation of his thesis: that while capitalism was not brought into being by religious ideas but by other causes that were present already, Calvinism did provide a *legitimation* for this development. On this interpretation Calvinism was not just religion getting out of the way, but religion helping a development it had not originated, by 'legitimating' the work of the other causes. Admittedly, 'legitimation' is the removal of an obstacle, namely of objections that the thing is not legitimate; but it can go beyond that, to call for an attitude of positive approval and assistance.

There is also another distinction to be made: between a 'one-phase' causal relationship, and feedback. (These are not technical terms-I'm inventing them now!) By a 'one-phase' relationship I mean that A causes B, or B causes A, and that is it. Sometimes it is said that 'each reciprocally causes the other', but this is what I call feedback: A > B > A′ > B′ >A″ > B″. In the second phase B reacts on A to transform it into something rather different, A′, which in the third phase transforms B into B′, and so on. Perhaps this is the interaction of capitalism and religion: it may be difficult to know on which side the process *began*, but each progressively transformed the other: perhaps the transformation was the reinforcement or strengthening of capitalism and the corruption or weakening of Protestantism. Indeed by the 19th century Protestantism in Germany had become a convenient support for other social institutions, not a critic or a threat, a shadow of its former self.

If the relationship was one of mutual or reciprocal influence, or feedback, then neither the 'superstructure' *nor* the 'base' was *the* originator of social change. We have rather the sort of thing Mill envisages, 'consensus', but apparently without any 'central chain'.

After the *Protestant Ethic* Weber undertook a series of comparative studies of various cultures and religions. These are discussed in Parkin's chapter, The point of the 'comparative method' is to apply Mill's methods of 'agreement' and 'difference'. Agreement: if these two cases in both of which the phenomenon being investigated is found agree in the following circumstances: [a list], then among those circumstances will be found the cause of the phenomenon.

Difference: case A, case B; similar in all circumstances except that in case A there is circumstance X, not found in B; then if the phenomenon occurs in A and not in B, X is its cause. This is the well-known 'control group' method.

In Weber's studies the phenomenon under investigation is the emergence of capitalism, which he thinks took place only in

Western Europe in early modern times, being exported to other countries (e.g. China, Japan) by invasion from Europe. He examines all the cultural circumstances, looking for cases in other places which were in almost all circumstances similar to early modern Europe, hoping to find what made the difference. The other similar cultures are the 'control'. His argument by the method of difference is that if such and such a culture was like early modern Europe in every respect but one, then that one will be what made the difference, it will be the cause of the emergence of capitalism. What made the difference is religion: the parts of early modern Europe in which capitalism originated had a religion more favourable to rational calculation etc. than other 'control' cultures, otherwise pretty similar, in which capitalism did not originate.

But Mill would have been horrified at such a crude application of his method of difference. It overlooks his warning that 'consensus' means, in social inquiry, that major institutions in one social context cannot really be compared directly with, and pronounced to be similar to, the 'corresponding' institutions embedded in another social context. This is drawing lessons from history in just the way Mill warns against. And as Parkin points out, on closer examination all the institutions in Weber's 'control' cultures turn out to be importantly different from the 'corresponding' European institutions. 'Virtually every institution that falls under Weber's scrutiny-is shown to have an entirely different form and function in the east compared with the west', Parkin. 'If, on Weber's own reckoning, the urban structure, property relations, the legal and administrative system, the political functions of the state, and very much else besides, were completely different as between east and west, it is obviously not possible to test for the separate effect of the religious variable', Parkin.

You will remember that Mill held that social science must explain in terms of psychological laws of the type, 'Someone with such a disposition will in such circumstances act like this', 'Someone with such a disposition will in such circumstances acquire this new disposition'-propositions about individuals, testable over *many* instances (since there are many individuals, whereas there are few 'cultures' or 'societies')-the *circumstances*, however, including the social situation. Mill's psychological propositions are the remote descendants of the 'maxims' used by the sophist-trained speechmakers in Thucydides. Now compared with Mill's approach Weber's method of 'ideal types' is not sufficiently *analytic*. Instead of getting down to many separate psychological generalizations about individuals, Weber, in constructing types, often constructs a *complex* in which are juxtaposed elements that do not have any tight logical or psychological (or other causal) connection. For example, his model of bureaucracy embodies the notion of division of labour, and also the notion of authoritarian subordination: but it is quite possible for a division of labour to be organized by a set of people acting as a 'collective', relating as equals. So in studying the phenomena associated with bureaucratization Weber is not well placed to distinguish what is due to division of labour and what to authoritarianism, since he has lumped these two things together under the one concept, bureaucracy. For example, take his worry that bureaucracy is inimical to freedom, and yet inevitable and inescapable, because bureaucracies are so effective that they displace all non-bureaucratic rivals. If their effectiveness is due to the division of labour, and the threat to freedom is due to authoritarianism, then it might be worthwhile to ask whether you can in practice have one without the other. Is it even possible that a non-authoritarian bureaucracy might be even more effective? Perhaps, after all, division of labour *requires* authoritarianism, but this is something that needs to be thought about. Weber's 'ideal type' is just an abstraction of the Prussian bureaucracy that was *in fact* authoritarian, and the 'ideal type' does not help, but is rather an obstacle, to thinking about the question whether a division of administrative labour has to be organized in an authoritarian way. ('Authoritarianism', by the way, is also an 'ideal type', a complex: it is possible to have authority that is non-authoritarian. But I will not pursue this question.)

To return to Weber on Capitalism. Parkin points out that in constructing the complex 'ideal types' or models he uses in his comparative study of eastern and western cultures, Weber's inclusions and exclusions are pretty arbitrary, slanted toward the conclusion he expects to come to: 'In his characterization of the world religions, Weber sets up a series of ideal-types. Only the most salient features of any belief system are incorporated into the general construct. This necessarily entails the accentuation of some features and the exclusion or devaluation of others. In the case of Calvinism, it is noticeable that Weber heavily underscores those teachings that could be said to be broadly compatible with the capitalist ethos, while discounting those elements that appear to jar with it. When it comes to the other major religions, the opposite procedure is adopted. Elements in Hinduism, Confucianism, Judaism, and the rest, that seem to square quite well with economic rationality are accorded only a peripheral place in the model, while those elements that are at variance with such an outlook are given a central place. As a number of other authorities on these religions have noted, it is perfectly possible to construct ideal-types in which Weber's priorities are reversed'. This is a general problem with the method of constructing ideal-types, in contrast with the method of analyzing into the causally independent elements as Mill recommends. Any complex consisting of diverse elements not tied together by logical or causal relations is only accidentally unified, and could be reconstructed in another way. Investigation carried on by means of such ideal types has had some of its conclusions built in, when the complex was put together.

### Origins of Capitalism

*The General Economic History* is Weber's last work. An account of the theory of capitalism found in it is given by Randall Collins in 'Weber's Last Theory of Capitalism', *American Sociological Review* 45 (1980), pp.925-42. Capitalism is 'rational' in the sense that it bases decisions on calculations of likely return; this presupposes some degree of predictability, in particular a predictable legal system; capitalism also supposes that there are free markets for products and for labour and other factors of production, and that these markets are wide-given wide markets and some predictability innovation in search of profit gets under way.

Among the social preconditions of the original development of capitalism are a predictable legal system, and behind that a state bureaucracy; and (to establish wide markets) a habit of treating all people as having rights and as possible partners in law-regulated commercial dealings. In some societies a strong distinction is made between insiders and outsiders: one does not drive commercial bargains with insiders, and one does not much respect the rights of outsiders. 'Universalistic' religions such as Christianity break down such distinctions. Behind the legal order is the notion of universal citizenship-that residents are mostly citizens with rights, not subjects at the ruler's discretion; universalistic religion favours that. The legal order also requires a bureaucratic state to enforce the law-professional administrators and jurists. The bureaucratic state arose partly by natural selection, because such states can supply larger armies with better weapons. (Weber notes the analogy between capitalism, in which workers do not own the means of production, bureaucracies in which bureaucrats do not own their offices or means of administration, and armies using centrally supplied and team-operated weapons). The bureaucratic state presupposes literacy (which religion may foster), and various other factors. So the chain (or rather web) of causation is traced backward to many factors. Calvinist predestination is not mentioned; protestantism figures as another surge of christian universalism, and as abolishing the monasteries. The abolition of monasteries is important as removing an obstacle, namely the preoccupation of people with the strongest religious motivation with other-worldly ends.

According to Collins 'Weber's constant theme is that the *pattern of relations among the various factors* is crucial in determining their effect upon economic rationalization'. If one factor is by itself, or very much stronger than the others, capitalism will not develop; for example, if the state is too strong by itself it tends to stifle capitalism.

Weber's theory as Collins describes it does not exemplify Mill's project of finding some central chain in the filiation of one stage from another, around which everything else can be organises-a project of which Marx's theory is an example. Rather it sounds like Mill's emphasis on consensus: 'Any one factor occurring by itself tends to have opposite effects, overall, to those which it has in combination with the other factors'. As Collins remarks, 'Weber's position might well be characterized as... seeing history as a concatenation of unique events and unrepeatable complexities'. Collins writes: 'The discipline of historical scholarship reached its maturity around the end of the nineteenth century. Not only had political and military history reached a high degree of comprehensiveness and accuracy, but so had the history of law, religion, and economic institutions not only for Europe and the ancient Mediterranean but for the Orient as will...Weber was perhaps the first great master of the major institutional facts of world history', *ibid.*, p.937. This exaggerates Weber's standing as an historian. Still, it is worth noting that the progress of historical scholarship does not seem favourable to the idea that there is a central chain of causation running through history. (Of course this may be due simply to a reaction on the part of bourgeois scholars against the prevailing materialist versions of this idea-the lessons of historical scholarship are never clear enough to rule out class, religious and other prejudices).

So far we have been considering Weber's view of the origin of capitalism. A few remarks on his view of its future. Once capitalism has come into being and is well established the factors which led to its existence need not be the ones that keep it in existence, and there may be others that tend to destroy it. It may be that there is no incompatibility between Weber's account of the origin of capitalism and Marx's account of its future: though Weber's story weakens the materialist theory of history in its crudest form (Weber's late theory attributes an important role to religious and other ideas, though not as in *The Protestant Ethic*), Marx's prognosis for capitalism is not based on the crude form of the materialist theory of history. In fact it does not seem to be based on any form of the materialist theory of history: Marx's analysis is of what is specific to capitalism, and, if it were valid, could stand apart from any more general theory of history.

As capitalism goes on some of the factors that brought it into being, such as christianity, are eroded by capitalism itself; within this case-perhaps some weakening of the structure. 'The closing words of the book speak of the threat of working class revolution which appears once capitalism matures and work discipline loses its religious legitimation'; Collins. 'In the advanced societies, the skeleton of the economic structure might even be taken over by socialism', *ibid.* This sounds like a possible anticipation of Schumpeter.

### *Expropriation*

On Marx's account, Capitalism presupposes a 'primitive accumulation' that was achieved by forcible expropriation. According to Weber, the expropriation of some may result simply from the competitive advantage others have in a market. If a few become systematic in pursuit of money others will end up as their employees. As capitalism continues to develop expropriation of labourers results from the competitive advantage enjoyed by autocratic management with complete control over productive resources: because of the 'bargaining superiority which management, by virtue of its possession of property, has enjoyed, both on the labour market in relation to the worker, and in the commodity market, by virtue of its capital accounting, and its command over capital gods and credit. In these ways it is superior to any [other] type of competitor'. There need be no forcible expropriation-though Weber acknowledges the existence of 'booty' capitalism and other spoliative kinds.

Weber uses the notion of expropriation in analysing not only economic institutions but also others. Government requires certain material goods. In some states these goods are the property of the staff, in others the staff is separated from the means of administration or coercion. 'This distinction holds in the same sense in which today we say that the salaried employee and the proletarian in the capitalistic enterprise are "separated" from the material means of production'. In the second kind of state the staff are 'non-owners... who do not use the material means of administration in their own right but are directed by the lord', *ibid.*. Feudal states exemplify the first type. The development of the modern state was the expropriation of the feudal lords by the prince. 'The whole process is a complete parallel to the development of the capitalist enterprise through gradual expropriation of the independent producers'. 'The bureaucratization of... the universities is a function of the increasing demand for material means of management.... Through the concentration of such means in the hands of the privileged head of the institute, the mass of researchers and docents are separated from their "means of production" in the same way as capitalist enterprise has separated the workers from theirs.

Weber's *Protestant Ethic* hypothesis, and Marx's 'materialist' hypothesis, have stimulated a good deal of historical research, especially in economic history. What often happens in the study of history is that some imaginative and exciting hypothesis is put forward, with too much assurance, and then several generations of academic historians test it against the facts and gradually decide that the exciting hypothesis was too imaginative. The moral to draw from such experience is, however, not that imagination should be restrained. If it were not for the imaginers the factual researchers would simply drown in fact. But it does seem to me that the project of explaining what caused capitalism by examining its origins in certain places in Europe is a bit like trying to explain what causes thunderstorms by investigating why this one started in a certain part of the country. Perhaps there were in *many* places conditions that could easily have led to the development of capitalism, if conditions had been only slightly different-and perhaps the difference needed was one thing in one place, another thing in another. If what is needed in such situations is just a slight difference, perhaps historians will never be able to discover what slight difference it was that precipitated the development.

# 15

# Peter Drucker

Peter Ferdinand Drucker (November 19, 1909 – November 11, 2005) was a writer, management consultant, and self-described "social ecologist." His books and scholarly and popular articles explored how humans are organized across the business, government and the nonprofit sectors of society. His writings have predicted many of the major developments of the late twentieth century, including privatization and decentralization; the rise of Japan to economic world power; the decisive importance of marketing; and the emergence of the information society with its necessity of lifelong learning. In 1959, Drucker coined the term "knowledge worker" and later in his life considered knowledge work productivity to be the next frontier of management.

### *Personal life and Roots of his Philosophy*

The son of a high-level civil servant in Austria-Hungary – his mother Caroline Bondi had studied medicine and his father Adolf Drucker was a lawyer – Drucker was born in Vienna, the capital of Austria, in a small village named Kaasgraben (now part of the 19th district of Vienna, Döbling). He grew up in a home where intellectuals, high government officials, and scientists would meet to discuss new ideas. After graduating from Döbling Gymnasium, Drucker found few opportunities for employment in post-Habsburg Vienna, so he moved to Hamburg, Germany, first working as an apprentice at an established cotton trading company, then as a journalist, writing for *Der Österreichische Volkswirt* (*The Austrian Economist*). Drucker then moved to Frankfurt, where he took a job at the Daily *Frankfurter General-Anzeiger*. While in Frankfurt, he also earned a doctorate in international law and public law from the University of Frankfurt in 1931. Among his early influences was the Austrian economist Joseph Schumpeter, a friend of his father's, who impressed upon Drucker the importance of innovation and entrepreneurship. Drucker was also influenced, in a much different way, by John Maynard Keynes, whom he heard lecture in 1934 in Cambridge. "I suddenly realized that Keynes and all the brilliant economic students in the room were interested in the behaviour of commodities," Drucker wrote, "while I was interested in the behaviour of people."

Over the next 70 years, Drucker's writings would be marked by a focus on relationships among human beings, as opposed to the crunching of numbers. His books were filled with lessons on how organizations can bring out the best in people, and how workers can find a sense of community and dignity in a modern society organized around large institutions.

As a young writer, Drucker wrote two pieces — one on the conservative German philosopher Friedrich Julius Stahl and another called *"The Jewish Question in Germany"* — that were burned and banned by the Nazis. In 1933, Drucker left Germany for England. In London, he worked for an insurance company, then as the chief economist at a private bank. He also reconnected with Doris Schmitz, an acquaintance from the University of Frankfurt. They married in 1934. (His wedding certificate lists his name as Peter Georg Drucker.) The couple permanently relocated to the United States, where he became a university professor as well as a free-lance writer and business consultant. (Drucker disliked the term "guru," though it was often applied to him; "I have been saying for many years," Drucker once remarked, "that we are using the word 'guru' only because 'charlatan' is too long to fit into a headline.")

In 1943, Drucker became a naturalized citizen of the United States. He taught at Bennington College from 1942-1949, then at New York University as a Professor of Management from 1950 to 1971. Drucker came to California in 1971, where he developed one of the country's first executive *MBA* programs for working professionals at Claremont Graduate University (then known as Claremont Graduate School). From 1971 to his death he was the Clarke Professor of Social Science and Management at Claremont Graduate University. The university's management school was named the "Peter F. Drucker Graduate School of Management" (later known as the "Peter F. Drucker and Masatoshi Ito Graduate School of Management") in his honour in 1987. He taught his last class at the school in 2002 at age 92.

### *Career*

His career as a business thinker took off in 1942, when his initial writings on politics and society won him access to the internal workings of General Motors (GM), one of the largest companies in the world at that time. His experiences in Europe had left him fascinated with the problem of authority. He shared his fascination with Donaldson Brown, the mastermind behind the administrative controls at GM. In 1943 Brown invited him in to conduct what might be called a "political audit": a two-year social-scientific analysis of the corporation. Drucker attended every board meeting, interviewed employees, and analyzed production and decision-making processes.

The resulting book, *Concept of the Corporation,* popularized GM's multidivisional structure and led to numerous articles, consulting engagements, and additional books. GM, however, was hardly thrilled with the final product. Drucker had suggested that the auto giant might want to reexamine a host of long-standing policies on customer relations, dealer relations, employee relations and more. Inside the corporation, Drucker's counsel was viewed as hypercritical. GM's revered chairman, Alfred Sloan, was so upset about the book that he "simply treated it as if it did not exist," Drucker later recalled, "never mentioning it and never allowing it to be mentioned in his presence."

Drucker taught that management is "a liberal art," and he infused his management advice with interdisciplinary lessons from history, sociology, psychology, philosophy, culture and religion. He also believed strongly that all institutions, including those in the private sector, have a responsibility to the whole of society. "The fact is," Drucker wrote in his 1973 *Management: Tasks, Responsibilities, Practices,* "that in modern society there is no other leadership group but managers. If the managers of our major institutions, and especially of business, do not take responsibility for the common good, no one else can or will."

Drucker was interested in the growing effect of people who worked with their minds rather than their hands. He was intrigued by employees who knew more about certain subjects than their bosses or colleagues and yet had to cooperate with others in a large organization. Rather than simply glorify the phenomenon as the epitome of human progress, Drucker analyzed it and explained how it challenged the common thinking about how organizations should be run.

His approach worked well in the increasingly mature business world of the second half of the twentieth century. By that time, large corporations had developed the basic manufacturing efficiencies and managerial hierarchies of mass production. Executives thought they knew how to run companies, and Drucker took it upon himself to poke holes in their beliefs, lest organizations become stale. But he did so in a sympathetic way. He assumed that his readers were intelligent, rational, hardworking people of good will. If their organizations struggled, he believed it was usually because of outdated ideas, a narrow conception of problems, or internal misunderstandings.

During his long consulting career, Drucker worked with many major corporations, including General Electric, Coca-Cola, Citicorp, IBM, and Intel. He consulted with notable business leaders such as GE's Jack Welch; Procter & Gamble's A.G. Lafley; Intel's Andy Grove; Edward Jones' John Bachmann; Shoichiro Toyoda, the honorary chairman of Toyota Motor Corp.; and Masatoshi Ito, the honorary chairman of the Ito-Yokado Group, the second largest retailing organization in the world. Although he helped many corporate executives succeed, he was appalled when the level of Fortune 500 CEO pay in America ballooned to hundreds of times that of the average worker. He argued in a 1984 essay that CEO compensation should be no more than 20 times what the rank and file make — especially at companies where thousands of employees are being laid off. "This is morally and socially unforgivable," Drucker wrote, "and we will pay a heavy price for it."

Drucker served as a consultant for various government agencies in the United States, Canada and Japan. He worked with various nonprofit organizations to help them become successful, often consulting pro bono. Among the many social-sector groups he advised were the Salvation Army, the Girl Scouts of the USA, C.A.R.E., the American Red Cross, and the Navajo Indian Tribal Council.

In fact, Drucker anticipated the rise of the social sector in America, maintaining that it was through volunteering in nonprofits that people would find the kind of fulfilment that he originally thought would be provided through their place of work, but that had proven elusive in that arena. "Citizenship in and through the social sector is not a panacea for the ills of post-capitalist society and post-capitalist polity, but it may be a prerequisite for tackling these ills," Drucker wrote. "It restores the civic responsibility that is the mark of citizenship, and the civic pride that is the mark of community."

### *Criticism*

*The Wall Street Journal* researched several of his lectures in 1987 and reported that he was sometimes loose with the facts. Drucker was off the mark, for example, when he told an audience that English was the official language for all employees at Japan's Mitsui trading company. (Drucker's defence: "I use anecdotes to make a point, not to write history.") And while he was known for his prescience, he wasn't always correct in his forecasts. He anticipated, for instance, that the nation's financial centre would shift from New York to Washington.

Others maintain that one of Drucker's core concepts—"management by objectives"—is flawed and has never really been proven to work effectively. Specifically, critics say that the system is difficult to implement, and that companies often wind up overemphasizing control, as opposed to fostering creativity, to meet their goals.

### *Author*

Drucker's 39 books have been translated into more than thirty languages. Two are novels, one an autobiography. He is the co-author of a book on Japanese painting, and made eight series of educational films on management topics. He also penned a regular column in the *Wall Street Journal* for 20 years and contributed frequently to the *Harvard Business Review, The Atlantic Monthly*, and *The Economist*. He continued to act as a consultant to businesses and non-profit organizations well into his nineties. Drucker died November 11, 2005 in Claremont, California of natural causes at 95.

### Basic Ideas

Several ideas run through most of Drucker's writings:

- Decentralization and simplification. Drucker discounted the command and control model and asserted that companies work best when they are decentralized. According to Drucker, corporations tend to produce too many products, hire employees they don't need (when a better solution would be outsourcing), and expand into economic sectors that they should avoid.
- A profound skepticism of macroeconomic theory. Drucker contended that economists of all schools fail to explain significant aspects of modern economies.
- Respect of the worker. Drucker believed that employees are assets and not liabilities. He taught that knowledge workers are the essential ingredients of the modern economy. Central to this philosophy is the view that people are an organization's most valuable resource and that a manager's job is to prepare and free people to perform.
- A belief in what he called "the sickness of government." Drucker made nonpartisan claims that government is often unable or unwilling to provide new services that people need or want, though he believed that this condition is not inherent to the form of government. The chapter "The Sickness of Government" in his book *The Age of Discontinuity* formed the basis of the New Public Management, a theory of public administration that dominated the discipline in the 1980s and 1990s.
- The need for "planned abandonment". Businesses and governments have a natural human tendency to cling to "yesterday's successes" rather than seeing when they are no longer useful.
- A belief that taking action without thinking is the cause of every failure.
- The need for community. Early in his career, Drucker predicted the "end of economic man" and advocated the creation of a "plant community" where individuals' social needs could be met. He later acknowledged that the plant community never materialized, and by the 1980s, suggested

that volunteering in the nonprofit sector was the key to fostering a healthy society where people found a sense of belonging and civic pride.

- The need to manage business by balancing a variety of needs and goals, rather than subordinating an institution to a single value. This concept of management by objectives forms the keynote of his 1954 landmark *The Practice of Management*.
- A company's primary responsibility is to serve its customers. Profit is not the primary goal, but rather an essential condition for the company's continued existence.
- An organization should have a proper way of executing all its business processes.
- A belief in the notion that great companies could stand among humankind's noblest inventions.

## Awards and Honours

Drucker was awarded the Presidential Medal of Freedom by U.S. President George W. Bush on July 9, 2002. He also received honours from the governments of Japan and Austria. He was the Honorary Chairman of the *Peter F. Drucker Foundation for Nonprofit Management*, now the *Leader to Leader Institute*, from 1990 through 2002. In 1969 he was awarded New York University's highest honour, the NYU Presidential Citation. Harvard Business Review honored Drucker in the spring of 2005 with his seventh McKinsey Award for his article, "What Makes an Effective Executive", the most awarded to one person. Drucker was inducted into the Junior Achievement U.S. Business Hall of Fame in 1996. Additionally he holds 25 honorary doctorates from American, Belgian, Czech, English, Spanish and Swiss Universities. In Claremont, California, Eleventh Street between College Avenue and Dartmouth Avenue was renamed "Drucker Way" in October of 2009 to commemorate the 100th anniversary of Drucker's birth

### *Criticism*

*The Wall Street Journal* researched several of his lectures in 1987 and reported that he was sometimes loose with the facts. Drucker was off the mark, for example, when he told an audience that English was the official language for all employees at Japan's

Mitsui trading company. (Drucker's defence: "I use anecdotes to make a point, not to write history.") And while he was known for his prescience, he wasn't always correct in his forecasts. He anticipated, for instance, that the nation's financial centre would shift from New York to Washington.

Others maintain that one of Drucker's core concepts—"management by objectives"—is flawed and has never really been proven to work effectively. Specifically, critics say that the system is difficult to implement, and that companies often wind up overemphasizing control, as opposed to fostering creativity, to meet their goals.

### *Quotes*

- "In fact, that management has a need for advanced education – as well as for systematic manager development – means only that management today has become an institution of our society."
- "The best way to predict the future is to create it."
- "Management is doing things right; leadership is doing the right things."
- "What's measured improves."
- "Company cultures are like country cultures. Never try to change one. Try, instead, to work with what you've got."
- "Efficiency is doing better what is already being done."
- "Follow effective action with quiet reflection. From the quiet reflection will come even more effective action."
- "People who don't take risks generally make about two big mistakes a year. People who do take risks generally make about two big mistakes a year."
- "The most important thing in communication is hearing what isn't said."
- "The purpose of business is to create and keep a customer."
- "There is nothing so useless as doing efficiently that which should not be done at all."
- "When a subject becomes totally obsolete we make it a required course."
- "Rank does not confer privilege or give power. It imposes responsibility."

- "To focus on contribution is to focus on effectiveness."
- "People in any organization are always attached to the obsolete – the things that should have worked but did not, the things that once were productive and no longer are."
- "Wherever you see a successful business, someone once made a courageous decision."
- "Most of what we call management consists of making it difficult for people to get their work done."
- "You can only manage what you can measure."
- "What everybody knows is frequently wrong."
- "Do not simply cling to your past successes, be willing to change, adopt new ideas and continually review all the different segments of business."
- "success breeds success" "nothing succeeds like success" This statement from "A Class With Drucker" states that if you know you can succeed at something, then automatically you'll have the self confidence to do it. If you have been successful in the past, you have a better chance at being successful again.
- "A leader, any leader, must act for the benefit of others and not for oneself,"

## Invented Management

Little more than six months ago, I was sitting within a foot of Peter F. Drucker's right ear — the one he could still hear from — in the living room of his modest home in Claremont, Calif. Even that close, I had to shout my questions to him, often eliciting a "What?" rather than an answer. Yet when he absorbed my words, his mind remained vigorous even as his body was failing.

He had often said that at his age "one doesn't pray for a long life but for an easy death." Since then he had struggled through a series of ailments, from life-threatening abdominal cancer to a broken hip. Oversize hearing aids plugged into both ears, he had a pacemaker in his chest and needed a walker to get around his ranch home on Wellesley Drive. Over 20-plus years, I often met or spoke to Drucker in the course of reporting any number of business and management stories. On that spring morning in April, in black cotton slippers and socks that barely covered his ankles, Drucker seemed unusually frail and tired — not at all in a mood to ponder his legacy. "I'm not very introspective," he protested in his familiar guttural baritone, thick with the accent of his native Austria. "I don't know. What I would say is I helped a few good people be effective in doing the right things."

Let others now speak for Drucker, who died peacefully in his sleep at home on Nov. 11 at age 95, eight days shy of his 96th birthday: "The world knows he was the greatest management thinker of the last century," Jack Welch, former chairman of General Electric Co. (GE), said after Drucker's death. "He was the creator and inventor of modern management," said management guru Tom Peters. "In the early 1950s, nobody had a tool kit to manage these incredibly complex organizations that had gone out of control. Drucker was the first person to give us a handbook for that."

Adds Intel Corp. (INTC) co-founder Andrew S. Grove: "Like many philosophers, he spoke in plain language that resonated with ordinary managers. Consequently, simple statements from him have influenced untold numbers of daily actions; they did mine over decades." The story of Peter Drucker is the story of management itself. It's the story of the rise of the modern corporation and the managers who organize work. Without his analysis it's almost impossible to imagine the rise of dispersed, globe-spanning corporations.

But it's also the story of Drucker's own rising disenchantment with capitalism in the late 20th century that seemed to reward greed as easily as it did performance. Drucker was sickened by the excessive riches awarded to mediocre executives even as they slashed the ranks of ordinary workers. And as he entered his 10th decade, there were some in corporations and academia who said his time had passed. Others said he grew sloppy with the facts. Meanwhile, new generations of management gurus and pundits, many of whom grew rich off books and speaking tours, superseded him. The doubt and disillusionment with business that Drucker expressed in his later years caused him to turn away from the corporation and instead offer his advice to the nonprofit sector. It seemed an acknowledgment that business and management had somehow failed him.

But Drucker's tale is not mere history. Whether it's recognized or not, the organization and practice of management today is derived largely from the thinking of Peter Drucker. His teachings form a blueprint for every thinking leader (page 106). In a world of quick fixes and glib explanations, a world of fads and simplistic PowerPoint lessons, he understood that the job of leading people and institutions is filled with complexity. He taught generations of managers the importance of picking the best people, of focusing on opportunities and not problems, of getting on the same side of the desk as your customer, of the need to understand your competitive advantages, and to continue to refine them. He believed that talented people were the essential ingredient of every successful enterprise.

### *Renaissance Man*

Well before his death, before the almost obligatory accolades poured in, Drucker had already become a legend, of course. He was the guru's guru, a sage, kibitzer, doyen, and gadfly of business, all in one. He had moved fluidly among his various roles as journalist, professor, historian, economics commentator, and raconteur. Over his 95 prolific years, he had been a true Renaissance man, a teacher of religion, philosophy, political science, and Asian art, even a novelist. But his most important contribution, clearly, was in business. What John Maynard Keynes is to economics or W. Edwards Deming to quality, Drucker is to management.

After witnessing the oppression of the Nazi regime, he found great hope in the possibilities of the modern corporation to build communities and provide meaning for the people who worked in them. For the next 50 years he would train his intellect on helping companies live up to those lofty possibilities. He was always able to discern trends — sometimes 20 years or more before they were visible to anyone else. "It is frustratingly difficult to cite a significant modern management concept that was not first articulated, if not invented, by Drucker," says James O'Toole, the management author and University of Southern California professor. "I say that with both awe and dismay." In the course of his long career, Drucker consulted for the most celebrated CEOs of his era, from Alfred P. Sloan Jr. of General Motors Corp. (GM) to Grove of Intel.

— It was Drucker who introduced the idea of decentralization— in the 1940s — which became a bedrock principle for virtually every large organization in the world.

— He was the first to assert — in the 1950s — that workers should be treated as assets, not as liabilities to be eliminated.

— He originated the view of the corporation as a human community — again, in the 1950s — built on trust and respect for the worker and not just a profit-making machine, a perspective that won Drucker an almost godlike reverence among the Japanese.

— He first made clear — still the '50s — that there is "no business without a customer," a simple notion that ushered in a new marketing mind-set.

— He argued in the 1960s — long before others — for the importance of substance over style, for institutionalized practices over charismatic, cult leaders.

— And it was Drucker again who wrote about the contribution of knowledge workers — in the 1970s — long before anyone knew or understood how knowledge would trump raw material as the essential capital of the New Economy.

Drucker made observation his life's work, gleaning deceptively simple ideas that often elicited startling results. Shortly after Welch became CEO of General Electric in 1981, for example, he sat down with Drucker at the company's New York headquarters. Drucker posed two questions that arguably changed the course of Welch's tenure: "If you weren't already in a business, would you enter it today?" he asked. "And if the answer is no, what are you going to do about it?"

Those questions led Welch to his first big transformative idea: that every business under the GE umbrella had to be either No. 1 or No. 2 in its class. If not, Welch decreed that the business would have to be fixed, sold, or closed. It was the core strategy that helped Welch remake GE into one of the most successful American corporations of the past 25 years.

Drucker's work at GE is instructive. It was never his style to bring CEOs clear, concise answers to their problems but rather to frame the questions that could uncover the larger issues standing in the way of performance. "My job," he once lectured a consulting client, "is to ask questions. It's your job to provide answers." Says Dan Lufkin, a co-founder of investment banking firm Donaldson, Lufkin & Jenrette Inc. (CSR), who often consulted with Drucker in the 1960s: "He would never give you an answer. That was frustrating for a while. But while it required a little more brain matter, it was enormously helpful to us. After you spent time with him, you really admired him not only for the quality of his thinking but for his foresight, which was amazing. He was way ahead of the curve on major trends."

Drucker's mind was an itinerant thing, able to wander in minutes through a series of digressions until finally coming to some specific business point. He could unleash a monologue that would include anything from the role of money in Goethe's Faust to the story of his grandmother who played piano for Johannes Brahms, yet somehow use it to serve his point of view. "He thought in circles," says Joseph A. Maciariello, who teaches "Drucker on Management" at Claremont Graduate University.

Part of Drucker's genius lay in his ability to find patterns among seemingly unconnected disciplines. Warren Bennis, a management guru himself and longtime admirer of Drucker, says he once asked his friend how he came up with so many original insights. Drucker narrowed his eyes thoughtfully. "I learn only through listening," he said, pausing, "to myself."

Among academics, that ad hoc, nonlinear approach sometimes led to charges that Drucker just wasn't rigorous enough, that his work wasn't backed up by quantifiable research. "With all those books he wrote, I know very few professors who ever assigned one to their MBA students," says O'Toole. "Peter would never have gotten tenure in a major business school."

I first met Drucker in 1985 when I was scrambling to master my new job as management editor at *BusinessWeek*. He invited me to Estes Park, Colo., where he and his wife, Doris, often spent summers in a log cabin, part of a YWCA camp. I remember him counseling me to drink lots of water, ingest a super dose of vitamin C, and take it easy to adjust to the high altitude. I spent two days getting to know Drucker and his work. We had breakfast, lunch, and dinner together. We hiked the trails of the camp. And I became intimately familiar with his remarkable story.

Born in Austria in 1909 into a highly educated professional family, he seemed destined for some kind of greatness. The Vienna that Drucker knew had been a cultural and economic hub, and his parents were in the thick of it. Sigmund Freud ate lunch at the same cooperative restaurant as the Druckers and vacationed near the same Alpine lake. When Drucker first met Freud at the age of eight, his father told him: "Remember, today you have just met the most important man in Austria and perhaps in Europe." Many evenings his parents, Adolph and Caroline, would gather the intellectual elite in the drawing room of their Vienna home for wide-ranging discussions of medicine, politics, or music. Peter absorbed not merely their content but worldliness and a style of expression.

When Hitler organized his first Nazi meeting in Berlin in 1927, Drucker, raised a Protestant, was in Germany, studying law at the University of Frankfurt. He attended classes taught by Keynes and Joseph Schumpeter. As a student, a clerk in a Hamburg export firm, and a securities analyst in a Frankfurt merchant bank, he lived through the years of Hitler's emergence, recognizing early the menace of centralized power. When his essay on Friedrich Julius Stahl, a leading German conservative philosopher, was published as a pamphlet in 1933, it so offended the Nazis that the pamphlet was banned and burned. A second Drucker pamphlet, *Die Judenfrage in Deutschland*, or *The Jewish Question in Germany*, published four years later, suffered the same fate. The only surviving copy sits in a folder in the Austrian National Archives with a swastika stamped on it.

Drucker immigrated to London shortly after Hitler became Chancellor, taking a job as an economist at a London bank while continuing to write and to study economics. He came to America in 1937 as a correspondent for a group of British newspapers, along with his new wife, Doris, whom he had met in Frankfurt. "America was terribly exciting," remembered Drucker. "In Europe the only hope was to go back to 1913. In this country everyone looked forward."

So did Drucker. He taught part time at Sarah Lawrence College before joining the faculty at Bennington College in Vermont. He could be a difficult taskmaster. One Bennington student recalled that Drucker said her paper "resembled turnips sprinkled with parsley. I could wring his fat frog-like neck," she wrote in a letter to her parents. "Unfortunately, he is a very brilliant and famous man. He has at least taught me something."

Drucker was a professor of politics and philosophy at Bennington when he was given the opportunity to study General Motors in 1945, the first time he peeked inside the corporation. His examination led to the publication of his groundbreaking book, *Concept of the Corporation*, and his decision, in 1950, to attach himself to New York University's Graduate School of Business. It was around this time that Drucker heard Schumpeter, then at Harvard University, say: "I know that it is not enough to be remembered for books and theories. One does not make a difference unless it is a difference in people's lives."

## Creating a Discipline

He took Schumpeter's advice to heart, beginning a career in consulting while continuing his life as a teacher and writer. Drucker's most famous text, *The Practice of Management*, published in 1954, laid out the American corporation like a well-dissected frog in a college laboratory, with chapter headings such as "What is a Business?" and "Managing Growth." It became his first popular book about management, and its title was, in effect, a manifesto. He was saying that management was not a science or an art. It was a profession, like medicine or law. It was about getting the very best out of people. As he himself put it: "I wrote *The Practice of Management* because there was no book on management. I had been working for 10 years consulting and teaching, and there simply was nothing or very little. So I kind of sat down and wrote it, very conscious of the fact that I was laying the foundations of a discipline."

Drucker taught at NYU for 21 years — and his executive classes became so popular that they were held in a nearby gym where the swimming pool was drained and covered so hundreds of folding chairs could be set up. Drucker moved to California in 1971 to become a professor of social sciences and management at Claremont Graduate School, as it was known then. But he was always thought to be an outsider — a writer, not a scholar — who was largely ignored by the business schools. Tom Peters says he earned two advanced degrees, including a PhD in business, without once studying Drucker or reading a single book written by him. Even some of Drucker's colleagues at NYU had fought against awarding him tenure because his ideas were not the result of rigorous academic research. For years professors at the most elite business schools said they didn't bother to read Drucker because they found him superficial. And in the years before Drucker's death even the dean of the Peter F. Drucker Graduate School of Management at Claremont said: "This is a brand in decline."

In the 1980s he began to have grave doubts about business and even capitalism itself. He no longer saw the corporation as an ideal space to create community. In fact, he saw nearly the opposite: a place where self-interest had triumphed over the egalitarian principles he long championed. In both his writings and speeches, Drucker emerged as one of Corporate America's most important critics. When conglomerates were the rage, he preached against reckless mergers and acquisitions. When executives were engaged in empire-building, he argued against excess staff and the inefficiencies of numerous "assistants to." In a 1984 essay he persuasively argued that CEO pay had rocketed out of control and implored boards to hold CEO compensation to no more than 20 times what the rank and file made. What particularly enraged him was the tendency of corporate managers to reap massive earnings while firing thousands of their workers. "This is morally and socially unforgivable," wrote Drucker, "and we will pay a heavy price for it."

The hostile takeovers of the 1980s, a period that revisionists now say was essential to improve American efficiency and productivity, was for Drucker "the final failure of corporate capitalism." He then likened Wall Street traders to "Balkan peasants stealing each other's sheep" or "pigs gorging themselves at the trough." He maintained that multimillion-dollar severance packages had perverted management's ability to look out for anything but itself. "When you have golden parachutes," he told one journalist, "you have created incentives for management to collude with the raiders." At one point, Drucker was so put off by American corporate values that he was moved to say that, "although I believe in the free market, I have serious reservations about capitalism."

We tend to think of Drucker as forever old, a gnomic and mysterious elder. At least I always did. His speech, always slow and measured, was forever accented in that commanding Viennese. His wisdom could not have come from anyone who was young.

So it's easy to forget his dashing youth, his long devotion to one woman and their four children (until the end, Drucker still greeted his wife of 71 years with an effusive "Hello, my darling!"), or even his deliciously self-deprecating sense of play.

During his early consulting work with DLJ, the partners flew out to California to meet with Drucker at home. After one of his famously meandering monologues, Drucker thought everyone needed a break.

"Well, boys," he said, "why don't we relax for a few minutes? Let's go for a swim."

The executives explained that they hadn't brought their swimming trunks.

"You don't need swimming suits because it's just men here today," replied Drucker.

"And we took off our clothes and went skinny-dipping in his pool," recalls Charles Ellis, who was with the group.

Surely, Drucker never fit into the buttoned-down stereotype of a management consultant. He always favored bright colors: a bottle-green shirt, a knit tie, a royal blue jacket with a blue-on-blue shirt, or simply a woolen flannel shirt and tan trousers. Drucker always worked from a home office filled with books and classical records on shelves that groaned under their weight. He never had a secretary and usually handled the fax machine and answered the telephone himself — he was something of a phone addict, he admitted.

### *Privacy Prevails*

Yet Drucker also was an intensely private man, revealing little of his personal life, even in his own autobiography, *Adventures of a Bystander*, the book he told me was his favorite of them all. Not surprisingly, perhaps, the Drucker Archives at Claremont Graduate University contain only one personal letter from his wife to him. Doris had clipped two images from a 1950s-era newspaper, one of a handsome man in a plaid robe, fresh from a good night's sleep, another of a couple in love, man and woman staring into each other's eyes, over a late evening snack. She glued each black-and-white image onto a flimsy piece of typing paper and wrote the words: "I love you in the morning when things are kind of frantic. I love you in the evening when things are more romantic." It is undated and unsigned.

It was Doris, in her own unpublished memoir, who told the story of how she once locked Drucker in a London coal cellar to hide him from her disapproving mother. As Doris' mother turned the house upside down in a frantic search for a man she thought was sleeping with her daughter, Peter spent the better part of the night crouched in a cold, dark hole. Doris' mother had long hoped her daughter would someday marry a Rothschild or a German of high social standing. The last thing she wanted was for her to marry a light-in-the-pocket Austrian.

In his later years, as his health weakened, so did Drucker's magnetic pull. Although he maintained a coterie of corporate followers, he increasingly turned his attention to nonprofit leaders, from Frances Hesselbein of the Girl Scouts of the USA to Rick Warren, founding pastor of Saddleback Church in Lake Forest, Calif. Warren, author of *The Purpose-Driven Life*, considered Drucker a mentor. "Drucker told me: 'The function of management in a church is to make the church more churchlike, not more businesslike. It's to allow you to do what your mission is,"' Warren said. "Business was just a starting point from which he had this platform to influence leaders of all different kinds."

Still, it was clear Drucker cared deeply about how he would be remembered. He tried in 1990 to discredit and quash an admiring biography of quality guru Deming, whom he seemed to consider a rival. And when Professor O'Toole assessed the influence of Drucker's landmark 1945 study on General Motors, he concluded that the guru not only had had no impact on GM but also became persona non grata at the company for nearly half a century. "I sent it to Peter, and he spent hours going over it with me," recalls O'Toole. "He was a little unhappy with it because he didn't like the conclusion. He felt he had had a big impact at GM. I thought that was either very generous of Peter or else he was kidding himself."

During the same period, Drucker, then 80 years old, penned a severely flawed foreword for a new edition of Alfred Sloan's *My Years with General Motors*. In one passage, Drucker quotes Sloan as saying that the death of his younger brother Raymond was "the greatest personal tragedy in my life." Raymond, however, died 17 years after Alfred. In another section, Drucker noted that the publication of the book had been delayed because Sloan "refused to publish as long as any of the GM people mentioned in the book was still alive. On the day of the death of the last living person mentioned in the book, Sloan released it for publication," wrote Drucker. In fact, Sloan generously heaped praise on 14 colleagues in the preface of his book, and all were still alive when *My Years with General Motors* was first published.

Whether the mistakes were a result of sloppiness or his declining intellectual power is not clear. But Drucker was no longer at the top of his game. The dean of the Drucker school, Cornelis de Kluyver, had reason to believe that Drucker's influence was on the wane — the school was having difficulty attracting big money from potential donors. To gain a $20 million gift for its puny endowment, de Kluyver agreed in 2003 to put another name on the school, that of Masatoshi Ito, the founder of Ito-Yokado Group, owner of 7-Eleven stores in Japan and North America. Students protested, even marching outside the dean's office toting placards decrying the change. An ailing Drucker volunteered to speak directly to the students. "I consider it quite likely that three years after my death my name will be of absolutely no advantage," he told them. "If you can get 10 million bucks by taking my name off, more power to you."

In April, during our last meeting, I asked Drucker what he had been up to lately. "Not very much," he replied. "I have been putting things in order, slowly. I am reasonably sure that I am not going to write another book. I just don't have the energy. My desk is a mess, and I can't find anything."

I almost felt guilty for having asked the question, so I praised his work, the 38 books, the countless essays and articles, the consulting gigs, his widespread influence on so many of the world's most celebrated leaders. But he was agitated, even dismissive, of much of his accomplishment.

"I did my best work early on — in the 1950s. Since then it's marginal. O.K.? What else do you have?"

I pressed the nonagenarian for more reflection, more introspection. "Look," he sighed, "I'm totally uninteresting. I'm a writer, and writers don't have interesting lives. My books, my work, yes. That's different."

# 16

# Robert K. Merton

Robert King Merton (July 4, 1910 – February 23, 2003, born *Meyer R. Schkolnick* to immigrant parents) was a distinguished American sociologist perhaps best known for having coined the phrase "self-fulfilling prophecy," the explanation for how a belief or an expectation, correct or incorrect, affects the outcome of a situation or the way a person or a group will behave. He also coined many other phrases that have gone into everyday use, such as "role model," which first appeared in a study on the socializaton of medical students at Columbia. The term grew from his theory of a reference group, or the group to which individuals compare themselves, but to which they do not necessarily belong. Social roles were a central piece of Merton's theory of social groups. Merton emphasized that, rather than a person assuming one role and one status, they have a status set in the social structure which has attached to it a whole set of expected behaviors. "Unintended consequences" was another one of Merton's terms. These are outcomes that are not the original results intended by the particular action. Merton spent most of his career teaching at Columbia University, where he attained the rank of University Professor.

***Biography***

Robert K. Merton was born to working class Jewish Eastern European immigrants on July 4, 1910, in Philadelphia. His family was not wealthy, but Merton insisted that his childhood did not lack opportunity. He attended a decent public high school, South Philadelphia High School, which allowed him the opportunity to become a frequent visitor of nearby cultural and educational venues including Andrew Carnegie Library, The Academy of Music,

Central Library, and Museum of Arts. In 1994, Merton stated that growing up in poor South Philadelphia provided young people with, "every sort of capital—social capital, cultural capital, human capital, and, above all, what we may call public capital—that is, with every sort of capital except the personally financial."

He started his sociological career under the guidance of George E. Simpson at Temple University in Philadelphia (1927-1931) where he became Phi Kappa Tau. He worked as a research assistant to Simpson on a project having to do with race and media, introducing him to sociology. Under the leadership of Simpson, Merton attended the ASA annual meeting, where he met Pitrim A. Sorokin, the founding chair of the Harvard University Sociology Department. Merton then applied to Harvard and went to work as a research assistant to Sorokin (1931-1936).

He taught at Harvard until 1938, when he became professor and chairman of the Department of Sociology at Tulane University. In 1941 he joined the Columbia University faculty, becoming Giddings Professor of Sociology in 1963. He was named to the University's highest academic rank, University Professor, in 1974 and became a Special Service Professor, a title reserved by the Trustees for emeritus faculty who "render special services to the University," upon his retirement in 1979. He was associate director of the University's Bureau of Applied Social Research from 1942 to 1971. He was an adjunct faculty member at Rockefeller University and was also the first Foundation Scholar at the Russell Sage Foundation. He withdrew from teaching in 1984. In recognition of his lasting contributions to scholarship and the University, Columbia established the Robert K. Merton Professorship in the Social Sciences in 1990.

Merton received many national and international honours for his research. He was one of the first sociologists elected to the National Academy of Sciences and the first American sociologist to be elected a foreign member of the Royal Swedish Academy of Sciences and a Corresponding Fellow of the British Academy. He was also a member of the American Philosophical Society, the American Academy of Arts and Sciences, which awarded him its Parsons Prize, the National Academy of Education and Academica Europaea. He received a Guggenheim Fellowship in 1962 and was the first sociologist to be named a MacArthur Fellow (1983-88).

Móre than 20 universities awarded him honorary degrees, including Harvard, Yale, Columbia and Chicago, and, abroad, the Universities of Leyden, Wales, Oslo and Kraków, the Hebrew University of Jerusalem and Oxford.

In 1994, Merton was awarded the US National Medal of Science, for "founding the sociology of science and for his pioneering contributions to the study of social life, especially the self-fulfilling prophecy and the unintended consequences of social action." He was the first sociologist to receive the prize.

Merton married Suzanne Carhart in 1934, with whom he had one son, Robert C. Merton, winner of the 1997 Nobel Prize in economics, and daughters Stephanie Merton Tombrello and Vanessa Merton. His daughter Vanessa is a Professor of Law at Pace University School of Law. The couple separated in 1968, and Suzanne died in 1992. He married his fellow sociologist Harriet Zuckerman in 1993. Although Merton may have never explained how and why he changed his name from Schkolnick to Merton, according to Craig Calhoun and others who knew the sociologist, the new name evolved from a teenage career as an amateur magician.

Merton was one of Talcott Parsons most devoted students; he participated not only in Parsons' seminars but was also for years an active participant in Parsons informal Sociology group which met in Adams House. Merton has publicly stated that he came to Harvard in order to study with Sorokin but that the thinker who intriqued and inspired him the most was Parsons. Parsons was a junior member of his dissertation committee, the others being Pitirim Sorokin, Carle C. Zimmermann and the historian of science, George Sarton. The dissertation, a quantitative social history of the development of science in seventeenth-century England, reflected this interdisciplinary committee (Merton, 1985).

## Works—Theories of Middle Range

Merton's work is often compared to that of Talcott Parsons. Unlike Parsons, who emphasized the necessary for social science to establish a general foundation, Merton preferred more limited, middle-range theories. Critics of Merton would say that Merton suffered from empiristic inclinations. According to Merton, middle-range theory starts its theorizing with clearly defined aspects of social phenomena, rather than with broad, abstract entities such as society as a whole. Theories of the middle range are firmly supported by empirical data. These theories must be constructed with observed data in order to create theoretical problems and to be incorporated in proposals that allow empirical testing. Middle-range theories, applicable to limited ranges of data, transcend sheer description of social phenomena and fill in the blanks between raw empiricism and grand or all-inclusive theory. In his advocacy of these kinds of theories Merton stands on the shoulders of Émile Durkheim and Max Weber.

### *Clarifying Functional Analysis*

Merton argues that the central orientation of functionalism is in interpreting data by their consequences for larger structures in which they are implicated. Like Durkheim and Parsons he analyzes society with reference to whether cultural and social structures are well or badly integrated. Merton is also interested in the persistence of societies and defines functions that make for the adaptation of a given social system. Finally, Merton thinks that shared values are central in explaining how societies and institutions work,however he disagrees with Parsons on some issues.

Merton persisting talk about "functionalist theory" although the term is misleading and generally useless as a description of any concept school and direction. Merton generally presented a misconception of a nature of Parsons' theory, which he never fully understood or appreciate despite the intellectual influence in general. According to Merton's perception of "functionalism," the functional unity of society which states that all standardized social and cultural beliefs and practices are functional for both society as a whole as well as individuals in society. This outlook maintains that various parts of social systems must show a high level of integration, but Merton argues that a generalization like this cannot be extended to larger, more complex societies. The second claim has to do with universal functionalism. This claim argues that all standardized social and cultural structures and forms have a positive function. Merton argues that this is a contradiction to what is seen in the real world; not every structure, idea, belief, etc, has positive functions. The third claim of functional analysis that Merton argues is that of indispensability. This claim states that the standardized parts of society have positive functions, and also represent indispensable parts of the working whole, which leads to that structures and functions are functionally necessary for society. Here, Merton argues people must be willing to admit that there exist various structural and functional alternatives within society.

His belief in empirical testing led to the development of his "paradigm" of functional analysis. According to Merton, "paradigm," refers to "exemplars of codified basic and often tacit assumptions, problem sets, key concepts, logic of procedure, and selectively accumulated knowledge that guide [theoretical and empirical] inquiry in all scientific fields." In terms of structural functionalism, Merton felt that the focus should be on social functions rather than on individual motives.

### *Dysfunctions*

Merton emphasizes the existence of dysfunctions. He thinks that some things may have consequences that are generally dysfunctional or which are dysfunctional for some and functional for others. On this point he approaches conflict theory, although he does believe that institutions and values can be functional for society as a whole. Merton states that only by recognizing the dysfunctional aspects of institutions, can we explain the development and persistence of alternatives. Merton's concept of dysfunctions is also central to his argument that functionalism is not essentially conservative.

In Merton's writing on dysfunctions, he highlighted problems that tend to keep social systems from meeting all of their functional requirements. In doing this, he was able to point out the details as well as the contradictions of the overall concept. One group's function could serve as another group's dysfunction, and a general incident could turn out to be both functional and dysfunctional for the same group. Merton clarified the concept by stating that a certain degree of social cohesion eases the productivity of a group and is therefore functional, but it can become dysfunctional when it surpasses a certain threshold, because then the members of the group may become equally indulgent and fail to hold each other to high performance standards. In order to help people determine whether positive functions outweigh dysfunctions, and vice versa, Merton developed the concept of net balance. Because the issues are complex and based on a lot of subjective judgement, they cannot be calculated and weighed easily. Therefore, positive functions and dysfunctions cannot be simply added up and objectively determine which outweighs the other. In order to deal with these issues, Merton believed that there must be levels of functional analysis. Rather than solely focusing on the analysis of society as a whole, Merton argued that analysis could and should also be done on an organization, institution or group.

## Manifest and Latent Functions

Some of the crucial innovations that Merton made to sociology include the description of the unanticipated consequences of social action, of latent functions vs. manifest functions, and, as previously mentioned, of dysfunctions. According to Merton, unanticipated consequences are actions that have both intended and unintended consequences. Everyone is aware of the intended consequences, but the unintended are more difficult to recognize, and therefore, sociological analysis is required to uncover what they may be. In his 1936 essay, "The Unanticipated Consequences of Social Action," Merton uncovered the wide field of human activity where things do not go as planned, and paradoxes and strange outcomes are seen. One of these outcomes is the "self-defeating prophecy," which through the very fact of its being publicized, is actually wrong. Merton was able to illustrate this by referencing Karl Marx's prediction that as societies become more modern, the wealth will be concentrated amongst fewer people, and the majority of society would suffer from poverty and misery. This prediction helped to stimulate the socialist movement, which in some countries slowed the development that Marx had predicted. The opposite of the "self-defeating prophecy" then, is the "self-fulfilling prophecy," when an originally unfounded prophecy turns out to be correct because it is believed and acted upon.

Manifest functions are the consequences that people observe or expect, or what is intended; latent functions are those that are neither recognized nor intended. In distinguishing between manifest and latent functions, Merton argued that must dig to discover latent functions. His example from his 1949 piece, "Manifest and Latent Functions," was an analysis of political machines. Merton began by describing the negative consequences of political machines, and then changed the angle and demonstrated how the people in charge of the machines, acting in their own interest, were meeting the social needs not met by government institutions.

Merton made it very clear however, that unanticipated consequences and latent functions are not the same. Latent functions are one type of unanticipated consequences; functional for the designated system. According to Merton, there are also two other types of unanticipated consequences: "those that are dysfunctional for a designated system, and these comprise the latent dysfunctions, and those which are irrelevant to the system which they affect neither functionally or dysfunctionally..non-functional consequences"

Merton sees attention to latent functions as increasing the understanding of society: the distinction between manifest and latent forces the sociologist to go beyond the reasons individuals give for their actions or for the existence of customs and institutions; it makes them look for other social consequences that allow these practices' survival and illuminate the way society works.

Dysfunctions can also be manifest or latent. Manifest dysfunctions of something like a festival include traffic jams, closed streets, piles of garbage, and a shortage of clean public toilets. Latent dysfunctions of the festival might include people missing work after the event to recover.

### *Functional Alternatives*

Functionalists believe societies must have certain characteristics in order to survive. Merton shares this view but stresses that at the same time particular institutions are not the only ones able to fulfil these functions; a wide range of functional alternatives may be able to perform the same task. This notion of functional alternative is important because it alerts sociologists to the similar functions different institutions may perform and it further reduces the tendency of functionalism to imply approval of the status quo.

### *Merton's Theory of Deviance*

Merton's theory on deviance stems from his 1938 analysis of the relationship between culture, structure and anomie. Merton defines culture as an "organized set of normative values governing behaviour which is common to members of a designated society or group." Social structures are the "organized set of social relationships in which members of the society or group are variously implicated." Anomie, state of normlessness, then occurs when there is "an acute disjunction between the cultural norms and goals and the socially structured capacities of members of the group to act in accord with them." In his theory, Merton links anomie with deviance and argues that the discontinuity between culture and structure have the dysfunctional consequence of leading to deviance within society.

The term anomie, derived from Émile Durkheim, for Merton means: a discontinuity between cultural goals and the legitimate means available for reaching them. Applied to the United States he sees the American dream as an emphasis on the goal of monetary success but without the corresponding emphasis on the legitimate avenues to march toward this goal. In other words, Merton believes that all subscribe to the American Dream, but the ways in which people go about obtaining the Dream are not the same because not everyone has the same opportunities and advantages as the next person. This leads to a considerable amount of (the Parsonian term of) deviance. This theory is commonly used in the study of criminology (specifically the strain theory).

Conformity is the attaining of societal goals by socially accepted means, while innovation is the attaining of those goals in unaccepted ways. Innovators find and create their own way to go about obtaining what they want, and a majority of the time, these new ways are considered to be socially unaccepted and deviant. Ritualism is the acceptance of the means but the forfeit of the goals.

Ritualists continue to subscribe to the means, but they have rejected the overall goal; they are not viewed as deviant. Retreatism is the rejection of both the means and the goals. Retreaters want to find a way to escape from everything and therefore reject the goals and the means and are seen as deviant. Rebellion is a combination of rejection of societal goals and means and a substitution of other goals and means. Innovation and ritualism are the pure cases of anomie as Merton defined it because in both cases there is a discontinuity between goals and means.

### *Sociology of Science*

The sociology of science was a field that Merton was very interested in and remained very passionate about throughout his career. Merton was interested in the interactions and importance between social and cultural structures and science. Merton carried out extensive research into the sociology of science, developing the Merton Thesis explaining some of the causes of the Scientific Revolution, and the Mertonian norms of science, often referred to by the acronym "Cudos". This is a set of ideals that are dictated by what Merton takes to be the goals and methods of science and are binding on scientists. They include:

- Communalism-the common ownership of scientific discoveries, according to which scientists give up intellectual property rights in exchange for recognition and esteem (Merton actually used the term Communism, but had this notion of communalism in mind, not Marxism);
- Universalism-according to which claims to truth are evaluated in terms of universal or impersonal criteria, and not on the basis of race, class, gender, religion, or nationality;
- Disinterestedness-according to which scientists are rewarded for acting in ways that outwardly appear to be selfless;
- Organized Skepticism-all ideas must be tested and are subject to rigorous, structured community scrutiny.

The CUDOS set of Mertonian scientific norms is sometimes identified as Communism, Universalism, Disinterestedness, *Originality* (novelty in research contributions), and Skepticism (instead of Organized Skepticism). This is a subsequent modification of Merton's norm set, as he did not refer to Originality in the essay that introduced the norms (The Normative Structure of Science [1942]).

Merton introduced many relevant concepts to the sociology of science, including 'obliteration by incorporation' (when a concept becomes so popularized that its inventor is forgotten) and 'multiples' (on independent similar discoveries). Merton and his colleagues spent much time studying "how the social system of science works in accordance with, and often also in contradiction to, the ethos of science." This newer focus on the social organization of science led Merton to study the reward system in science, priority disputes between scientists, and the way in which famous scientists often receive disproportionate credit for their contributions, whereas lesser known scientists receive less credit than their contributions actually merit. Merton called this phenomenon the Matthew effect. With his study of the Matthew effect, Merton was able to show how the social system of science sometimes deviated structurally from the ethos of science, in this case by violating the norm of universalism.

### *Influences*

Merton was heavily influenced by Talcott Parsons and to a much lesser degree of Pitirim Sorokin. Indeed, Merton's choice of dissertation topic reflect profoundly the interest from Parsons and was not of Sorokin's liking. Hence, Sorokin was strongly opposed to the emphasis of the creativity of Puritanism, which was a central element in Merton's discussion. However, intellectuals like Paul Lazarsfeld influenced Merton to occupy himself with middle-range theories yet Merton general theoretical perspectives was much closer to Parsons than Sorokin. He was also influenced by Lawrence Joseph Henderson, L.J., who taught him something about the disciplined investigation of what is first entertained as an interesting idea. E.F. Gay also played a role in Merton's thought, as did George Sarton, who allowed Merton to work with him at Harvard. Émile Durkheim and Georg Simmel also greatly contributed to Merton's understanding of sociology and to his own ideas.

## A Meeting of Opposites

We think of Peter as embodying three outstanding qualities, each of which spanned or integrated two seeming opposites. (Peter was very fond of dilemmas and paradoxes.) First, his work and career connected theory and empirical research in an era when these were often disengaged activities. While he was originally attracted to "grand theory," he was converted by his graduate training at Columbia University to value theories of the "middle-range." Later, reading extensively in the philosophy of science, he developed a strong interest in formal, deductive theorizing. Throughout his entire career, however, Peter blended abstract ideas and empirical indicators and evidence. He drew from classical theory to select problems, formulate arguments, and improve interpretations. He tested propositions with survey data. But he also worked inductively: He thought with data; he learned from data. He gathered data not just to test theories but to revise and extend them.

A second type of connection was his linking of teaching and research. He was equally devoted to and strong in both. He was a dynamic, intense, even eloquent teacher. He was truly excited by ideas, and as his former students we recall many times when his mind raced ahead of his mouth so that he would become more and more excited and animated—and harder to understand—as the lecture progressed. One of his most popular courses at the University of Chicago was a required seminar on sociological theory.

The "seminar" was often packed by more than 75 doctoral students, all struggling to understand and keep pace with this vigorous lecturer. Students were reminded in his class of the old adage that being a graduate student at Chicago was like trying to drink from a fire hose! Peter's influence as a teacher continued at Columbia, SUNY Albany, and the University of North Carolina. In each setting he taught not what he believed were the settled truths of science but the scientific method as a continual probing of received wisdom and pursuit of new knowledge. He was remarkably willing to see his own work subjected to revision based on new evidence or analysis and so taught his students some of their most powerful lessons by example.

The third integration embodied by Peter was his bridging of the Old World and the new. Born in Vienna, with much courage and good luck, he was able to make his way to America, where he completed his undergraduate and graduate education. Although Peter "escaped" from the Old World, he remained permanently imprinted by it. He embodied an Old World grace and charm. He was somewhat reserved and formal, even shy, in his interactions. His daughters tell of the terror he could inspire in prospective boyfriends while only intending to make small talk. Long after it was fashionable in academic circles, he wore a hat and a tie and often a heavy tweed suit no matter what the weather. And he retained his strong Viennese accent—which, indeed, seemed to get thicker over the years! In Vienna he had planned to study medicine. Yet, in the United States he enthusiastically embraced the new discipline of sociology. He was strongly committed to the conduct of positivist, empirical scientific research, rather than a looser, more humanistic "social thought." And he quickly mastered the skills of the entrepreneurial investigator, designing dataintensive studies and obtaining funding for large-scale projects. At the same time he believed that better scientific knowledge was of fundamental importance for democracy and for addressing social problems. He was as deeply committed to the ideals of a free and open society as to free and open scientific inquiry. And at the end of his life Peter worried deeply that the public conditions for both democracy and free scientific inquiry were being undermined by reactionary antimodernists.

### *A Dramatic Beginning*

Peter Blau was born in Vienna, Austria, in 1918—the year that the Austro-Hungarian Empire fell. He was the son of secular Jews, and he watched with mounting concern the rise of fascism in postwar Austria. As a young student he wrote articles for the underground newspaper of the Socialist Worker's Party, speaking against his government's repressive regime. When he was only 17, he was convicted of high treason and given a 10-year sentence in federal prison. Ironically, he was released soon thereafter, when the National Socialists came to power and lifted the ban on political activity (Blau, 2002).

When Hitler marched into Vienna in 1938, Peter's family elected to stay, although his sister was sent to England on the Kindertransport. Peter, however, attempted to flee across the Czech border. He was captured, tortured, and eventually released, ending up in Prague. Returning to Austria to visit his family, which had been removed to the ghetto, Peter was able with the help of his high school teacher Fritz Redl to obtain an affidavit permitting his emigration to America. He managed to get to France by train, where because he was carrying a German passport, he gave himself in to the Allied forces. He spent time in a French labor camp, but through the intervention of an acquaintance was released when his visa number came up. He immediately left for Le Havre to seek passage on a boat to America (Blau, 2002).

Let us quote a paragraph from Peter's own matter-of-fact account of this terrible, wonderful, truth-is-stranger-than-fiction story.

World War II broke out and the ship on which my passage was booked did not sail. Thousands of people—Americans returning home as well as refugees immigrating—waited in Le Havre for passage, and this turned out to be fortunate for me. While waiting in Le Havre for news about sailing, I met and passed the time with some Americans, one of whom was the graduate of a Midwestern protestant college. He told me that students at his college had collected a fund for a refugee scholarship, but for this scholarship they had no candidate. He asked me whether I would be interested. I could not believe my ears, and I did not believe him, honest as he seemed (and was), but I told him I would be very interested.

The unlikely connection was successfully made, and Peter sailed to the United States and with his refugee scholarship attended Elmhurst College in Illinois, majoring in sociology. In his undergraduate years he was attracted to the work of the grand theorists, ranging from Marx and Durkheim to Freud and Fromm, and his interests were initially more social-psychological than structural. The balance would shift progressively through his career. Following graduation from college, Peter spent three years in the U.S. Army, returning to the combat zone in Europe. Because of his German language skills, he served as an interrogation officer. He later learned that his family had been killed in Auschwitz in 1942.

### *A Remarkable Cohort*

Following the conclusion of World War II, thanks to the GI Bill, Peter was able to continue his education, entering the sociology department at Columbia University in February of 1946—encouraged by his lifelong friend Lewis Coser, who entered a few months before. Attracted to Columbia by the work of Robert S. Lynd (1970), a scholar noted for his work on class and for translating sociological ideas into social reform efforts, Peter quickly fell under the influence of Robert K. Merton, the leading advocate of "middle-range" theory—theory closely related to and guided by empirical research (Merton, 1949). Merton, together with Paul Lazarsfeld, provided an alternative model to the continental tradition of "grand" theory—a tradition still entrenched at Harvard, under the sway of Pitirim Sorokin (1937-1941) and Talcott Parsons (1951). Gathered around Merton and Lazarsfeld were an extraordinary collection of graduate students, many returning veterans who were to be in the forefront of reinventing sociology for the postwar age. In addition to Blau they included Rose and Lewis Coser, James S. Coleman, Alvin W. Gouldner, Elihu Katz, Seymour MartinLipset, Alice K. and Peter S. Rossi, Philip Selznick, Martin A. Trow, and Dennis Wrong.

## A Founder of Organizational Sociology

Several of these scholars—including Coleman, Gouldner, Lipset, and Selznick—joined with Peter to launch the modern field of organizational sociology. All of them conducted insightful theory-driven, empirical studies of either public or private organizations and thus created a solid research foundation for this field of study. One of these studies was Peter's dissertation, carried out under the supervision of Merton. Drawing upon the human relations tradition in industrial sociology, Peter elected to study the behaviour of work groups but with several amendments and refinements. He focused on behaviour within white-collar, administrative systems rather than blue-collar settings. Following the lead of the Columbia anthropologist Conrad Arensberg (1951), he elected to systematically record interaction patterns among workers rather than basing his work exclusively on informal observations and interviews. And he addressed general theoretical questions regarding the bases of status and power, the unanticipated consequences of purposive action, and endogenous sources of bureaucratic change. The resulting study, The Dynamics of Bureaucracy(Blau, 1955), is rightly regarded as a sociological classic (Merton, 1990).

After his graduation from Columbia in 1952, Peter served briefly on the faculties of Wayne State and Cornell universities before moving to the University of Chicago, where he remained until 1970. While there he coauthored a treatise that became one of the foundational texts of the emerging field of organizational sociology (Blau and Scott, 1962). He also launched an ambitious research program—the Comparative Organization Research

Project (CORP), which he continued after moving to Columbia in 1970. This involved a series of large-scale studies in which organizations rather than individuals were the units of analysis. He examined large samples of distinct types of organizations, including public bureaucracies, universities, and manufacturing organizations. Data were variously drawn from informant reports, official records, organization charts, personnel manuals, job descriptions, and performance ratings. The major findings were reported in The Structure of Organizations (Blau and Schoenherr, 1971) and The Organization of Academic Work (Blau, 1973).

One golden nugget resulting from this research program was, we believe, Blau's theory of structural differentiation, in which Blau devised a remarkable series of propositions to account for the complex relation between organizational size and bureaucracy (measured as a proportion of administrative staff to production workers). Based on the empirical studies he had conducted, Blau (1970) proposed that (1) size increases structural complexity (differentiation), which in turn increases pressures for coordination—the addition of administrators. But at the same time (2) size increases scale— the average size of organizational subunits—a development likely to be associated with administrative economies. Hence, size has two analytically distinct effects, which account for the indeterminant and conflicting association observed between size and bureaucratization.

### *A Theory of Social Exchange*

At the same time that Peter was pioneering organizational sociology, he undertook to develop a theory that would provide a more general explanation of the sorts of interactions and relationships he had observed in his field research. This led to the writing of one of his most famous books, Exchange and Power in Social Life(1964). Inspired by Max Weber's treatment of sociology as first and foremost about relationships, by Merton's concept of middle-range theory, and by microeconomic analysis and utility theory, Blau offered a microsociology of strategic interaction that anticipated and influenced the later rise of rational choice theory.

Peter started from the premise that social interaction has value to people, and he explored the forms and sources of this value in order to understand collective outcomes, such as the distribution of power in a society. People enter all social interactions, Peter suggested, for the same reasons they engage in economic transactions: They need something from other people. By contrast with directly economic exchanges, other social exchanges tend to be long-term and to lack metrics by which parties can be clear as to whether their contributions are equal. Among other things, this leads to an escalation of social exchange as people strive to stay out of "debt" not only because of the norm of reciprocity but also because this gives them advantages of autonomy and potentially power. As Peter put it, "An apparent 'altruism' pervades social life; people are anxious to benefit one another and to reciprocate for the benefits they receive. But beneath this seeming selflessness an underlying 'egoism' can be discovered; the tendency to help others is frequently motivated by the expectation that doing so will bring social rewards".

Beginning with his early work on organizations, Peter's work consistently asked the question of who benefits, cui bono? Yet if he focused much attention on his own rewards it wasn't apparent to those who worked with him (perhaps such manifest altruism is only the best strategy). Certainly he received many awards and enormous recognition. He especially delighted in a year at Cambridge as Pitt Professor and a senior fellow of King's College (and brought back to the United States the rather formal custom of announcing a monthly date when he and his wife, Judith, would be "at home" for drinks). But it is crucial to remember that his formative experience was one of escape from the Anschluss, an almost miraculous chance to go to college, and mobility from a humble start in the United States to considerable eminence. Peter's story, in other words, was a very American story of immigration, opportunity, and social mobility. He never forgot this, and remained both humbled and grateful. He knew that both chance and social structure were crucial to his success alongside his own brilliance and enormous capacity for hard work. And he could delight in each honour and achievement as, at least in part, a gift.

### *A Landmark Study in Stratification*

It is appropriate too that Peter's most famous and influential book should address questions of stratification and mobility—and the distinctiveness of the American pattern in each. The American

Occupational Structure, which Peter coauthored with Otis Dudley Duncan, was the most influential quantitative study in the history of American sociology. It offered powerful and novel findings—such as the widespread distribution of mobility in the United States, as great numbers advanced in small steps rather than the few in giant steps, a pattern inconsistent with the country's Horatio Alger myth. The work embodied and popularized major new research methods—notably path analysis—and launched a novel approach to mobility processes that would guide a generation of work, giving rise to an entire school of "status attainment" research. The core question was to what extent factors other than parents' status explained children's status—operationalized mainly as education, occupation, and income. The more parental status explained, the more social inequalities were reproduced across generations.

Over time the enormous status attainment literature often focused on technical questions—to its critics, on explaining ever-smaller amounts of additional variance. This makes it easy to forget what a dramatic shift in the conceptualization and theorization of social inequality and mobility its origins involved. One central theme was thinking in terms of an overall occupational structure, integrating Weberian themes of status and Marxian concerns for economic inequality. There were, of course, critiques—not least of the fact that the initial work dealt with men and not women. More ironically the status attainment literature was criticized as insufficiently attentive to structural factors, too heavily focused on characteristics of individuals that aided in their attainment of higher statuses. Among the critics of this tendency was Peter Blau himself, though characteristically he didn't pause to redo the older study but rather chose to embark on a major new project.

## A Macrosociological Theory of Social Structure

In the early 1970s Peter began an ambitious effort to develop a new macrosociological theory of social structure. This was informed by the Comparative Organizations Research Project, but it was also a significant departure. In many ways it was at odds with his earlier work. Though he had moved away from the mainly social psychological interests of his student days, in his work on exchange theory and social mobility he had sought what came to be called "microfoundations" for macrostructure. He treated social relations as emergent phenomena, not mere collective aggregates of individual phenomena—and his approach to exchange theory differed from that of George Homans (1961) on just this point. But he focused mostly on the directly interpersonal patterns that might explain those found at larger scales. Now, however, he asked the reverse question. How might the macrostructure shape the patterns of more micro relations (Schwartz, 1990)?

Innovative and curious as always, Peter started a dramatically new line of theory building at a stage when many scholars attempt only syntheses of their earlier work (or simply rest on their laurels). Peter's 1974 presidential address to the American Sociological Association was the first major statement of his new theory, later developed in several books. New though the theory was, a key question harkened back to his earlier organizational research: How does size matter? Stimulated by Michels's theory of oligarchy and Simmel's advocacy of a formal sociology attentive to number and scale, Peter began to reason deductively about the implications of group size and rates of in-group and out-group interaction. A simple example: Assuming random interaction, any minority will have more out-group relations than a majority. Every marriage between a Christian and a Jew in the United States, thus, has a bigger impact on the Jewish population. If overwhelmingly white colleges assigned roommates randomly, nearly all black students would have white roommates while most whites would also have white roommates. From such basic effects of relative group size, Peter began to build a complex and systematic account of the social structure of populations.

Though Peter's theoretical strategy changed markedly from his work of the 1950s and 1960s, his new theory was capacious enough to allow for a reconciliation. As he showed in his 1994 book, opportunities were the products of structural contexts—whether they were opportunities for marriage, ethnic group relations, or social mobility. And social relationships were still matters of exchange and power, though they were always situated in and both made possible and constrained by larger structures (Calhoun et al., 1990).

Among other things Peter's theory gave a more structural account of "homophily," the concept coined by his mentor Robert Merton to describe the common observation that people are drawn to others like themselves. This attraction is a product of structure and not only taste, and indeed what seem individual tastes may be partly structurally produced.

Sociologists, for example, are apt to spend a lot of time with other sociologists—and Peter married two fellow sociologists. With his first wife, Zena Smith Blau, he had a daughter, Pamela—herself now married to a sociologist.

His second wife, Judith Blau, is a distinguished sociologist of culture, and their daughter Reva has followed that lead into art and literature. Even those with much in common are not just alike, which is after all the basis for an exchange relationship. Judith and Reva pushed Peter to see how cultural meaning matters alongside strategy and structure. And if there is one thing Peter Blau liked to exchange, it was ideas. He will be remembered for lively intellectual arguments with a twinkle in his eye and sheer pleasure in thinking clearly and well.

### *A Maker of Modern Sociology*

In an extraordinary career of more than 50 years, Peter Blau played a central role not merely in advancing but also in making modern scientific sociology.

Together with his teachers, Merton and Lazarsfeld, themselves only slightly older, he and others of approximately the same generation developed lines of inquiry that became the main branches of sociology, and they developed analytic approaches and a characteristic way of relating theory to research that shaped the "mainstream" of the field as it matured into a stable and cumulative science.

Peter pioneered the sociology of organizations, turning the insights of Weber, Merton, and others into a highly productive research program using methods ranging from ethnographic observation to comparative statistical analysis. He was among the founders of exchange theory and shaped the emergence of rational choice theory. He recast the study of social inequality as an increasingly precise and mainly quantitative inquiry into processes of social differentiation, mobility, and reproduction. He pushed sociologists to make more use of formal, deductive theorizing. He played a leading role in putting the analysis of social structure at the forefront of the sociological agenda and developed one of the most powerful of structural theories. Remarkably, his work from each stage of his career remains not only historically influential but in active, continuous use.

For each of us, as for an enormous range of others, Peter is an inspiration. Not only did he do great work, he also did it with a true love of science, a generous spirit, a mischievous sense of humour, and a deep appreciation for the opportunities chance and social structure gave him.

# 17

# Woodrow Wilson

Thomas Woodrow Wilson (December 28, 1856 – February 3, 1924) was the 28th President of the United States. A leading intellectual of the Progressive Era, he served as President of Princeton University from 1902 to 1910, and then as the Governor of New Jersey from 1911 to 1913. With Theodore Roosevelt and William Howard Taft dividing the Republican Party vote, Wilson was elected President as a Democrat in 1912. In his first term, Wilson persuaded a Democratic Congress to pass the Federal Reserve Act, Federal Trade Commission, the Clayton Antitrust Act, the Federal Farm Loan Act and America's first-ever federal progressive income tax in the Revenue Act of 1913. Wilson brought many white Southerners into his administration, and tolerated their expansion of segregation in many federal agencies.

Narrowly re-elected in 1916, Wilson's second term centred on World War I. He based his re-election campaign around the slogan "he kept us out of the war", but U.S. neutrality was challenged in early 1917 when the German government proposed to Mexico a military alliance in a war against the U.S., and began unrestricted submarine warfare, sinking without warning every American merchant ship its submarines could find. Wilson in April 1917 asked Congress to declare war. He focused on diplomacy and financial considerations, leaving the waging of the war primarily in the hands of the Army. On the home front in 1917, he began the United States' first draft since the US civil war, raised billions in war funding through Liberty Bonds, set up the War Industries Board, promoted labor union growth, supervised agriculture and food production through the Lever Act, took over control of the railroads, enacted the first federal drug prohibition, and suppressed anti-war movements. National women's suffrage was also achieved under Wilson's presidency.

In the late stages of the war, Wilson took personal control of negotiations with Germany, including the armistice. He issued his *Fourteen Points*, his view of a post-war world that could avoid another terrible conflict. He went to Paris in 1919 to create the League of Nations and shape the Treaty of Versailles, with special attention on creating new nations out of defunct empires. Largely for his efforts to form the League, he was awarded the Nobel Peace Prize. In 1919, during the bitter fight with the Republican-controlled Senate over the U.S. joining the League of Nations, Wilson collapsed with a debilitating stroke. He refused to compromise, effectively destroying any chance for ratification. The League of Nations was established anyway, but the United States never joined. A Presbyterian of deep religious faith, he appealed to a gospel of service and infused a profound sense of moralism into Wilsonianism. Wilson's idealistic internationalism, now referred to as "Wilsonianism", which calls for the United States to enter the world arena to fight for democracy, has been a contentious position in American foreign policy, serving as a model for "idealists" to emulate and "realists" to reject ever since.

## Early Life

Wilson was born in Staunton, Virginia on December 28, 1856 as the third of four children of Reverend Dr. Joseph Ruggles Wilson (1822–1903) and Jessie Janet Woodrow (1826–1888). His ancestry was Scots-Irish and Scottish. His paternal grandparents immigrated to the United States from Strabane, County Tyrone, Ireland (now Northern Ireland), in 1807. His mother was born in Carlisle, England, the daughter of Rev. Dr. Thomas Woodrow, born in Paisley, Scotland and Marion Williamson from Glasgow. His grandparents' whitewashed house has become a tourist attraction in Northern Ireland. Descendants of the Wilsons still live in the farmhouse next door to it.

Wilson's father was originally from Steubenville, Ohio, where his grandfather published a newspaper, *The Western Herald and Gazette,* that was pro-tariff and abolitionist. Wilson's parents moved South in 1851 and identified with the Confederacy. His father defended slavery, owned slaves and set up a Sunday school for them. They cared for wounded soldiers at their church. The father also briefly served as a chaplain to the Confederate Army. Woodrow Wilson's earliest memory, from the age of three, was of hearing that Abraham Lincoln had been elected and that a war was coming. Wilson would forever recall standing for a moment at Robert E. Lee's side and looking up into his face.

Wilson's father was one of the founders of the Southern Presbyterian Church in the United States (PCUS) after it split from the northern Presbyterians in 1861. Joseph R. Wilson served as the first permanent clerk of the southern church's General Assembly, was Stated Clerk from 1865–1898 and was Moderator of the PCUS General Assembly in 1879. Wilson spent the majority of his childhood, up to age 14, in Augusta, Georgia, where his father was minister of the First Presbyterian Church.

Wilson was over ten years of age before he learned to read. His difficulty reading may have indicated dyslexia, but as a teenager he taught himself shorthand to compensate. He was able to achieve academically through determination and self-discipline. He studied at home under his father's guidance and took classes in a small school in Augusta. During Reconstruction, Wilson lived in Columbia, South Carolina, the state capital, from 1870–1874, where his father was professor at the Columbia Theological Seminary.

In 1873, he spent a year at Davidson College in North Carolina, then transferred to Princeton as a freshman, graduating in 1879, becoming a member of Phi Kappa Psi fraternity. Beginning in his second year, he read widely in political philosophy and history. Wilson credited the British parliamentary sketch-writer Henry Lucy as his inspiration to enter public life. He was active in the undergraduate American Whig-Cliosophic Society discussion club, and organized a separate Liberal Debating Society. In 1879, Wilson attended law school at the University of Virginia for one year. Although he never graduated, during his time at the University he was heavily involved in the Virginia Glee Club and the Jefferson Literary and Debating Society, serving as the Society's president. His frail health dictated withdrawal, and he went home to Wilmington, North Carolina where he continued his studies.

In January 1882, Wilson started a law practice in Atlanta. One of his University of Virginia classmates, Edward Ireland Renick, invited him to join his new law practice as partner and Wilson joined him in May 1882. He passed the Georgia Bar. On October 19, 1882, he appeared in court before Judge George Hillyer to take his examination for the bar, which he passed easily. Competition was fierce in the city with 143 other lawyers, and he found few cases to keep him occupied. Nevertheless, he found staying current with the law obstructed his plans to study government to achieve his long-term plans for a political career. In April 1883, Wilson applied to the Johns Hopkins University to study for a doctorate in history and political science and began his studies there in the fall.

## Personal Life

Wilson's mother was possibly a hypochondriac and Wilson himself seemed to think that he was often in poorer health than he really was. He did suffer from hypertension at a relatively early age and may have suffered his first stroke at age 39. In 1885, he married Ellen Louise Axson, the daughter of a minister from Rome, Georgia. They had three daughters: Margaret Woodrow Wilson (1886–1944); Jessie Wilson (1887–1933); and Eleanor R. Wilson (1889–1967). Axson died in 1914, and the following year Wilson married Edith Galt, a direct descendant of the famous Native American Pocahontas. Wilson is one of only three presidents to be widowed while in office.

Wilson was an early automobile enthusiast, and he took daily rides while he was President. His favorite car was a 1919 Pierce-Arrow, in which he preferred to ride with the top down. His enjoyment of motoring made him an advocate of funding for public highways. Wilson was an avid baseball fan. In 1915, he became the first sitting president to attend a World Series game. Wilson had been a centre fielder during his Davidson College days. When he transferred to Princeton he was unable to make the varsity team and so became the team's assistant manager. He was the first President to throw out a first ball at a World Series game.

He cycled regularly, including several cycling vacations in the English Lake District. Unable to cycle around Washington, D.C. as President, Wilson took to playing golf, although he played with more enthusiasm than skill. Wilson holds the record of all the presidents for the most rounds of golf, over 1,000, or almost one every other day. During the winter, the Secret Service would paint golf balls with black paint so Wilson could hit them around in the snow on the White House lawn.

### *Academic Career*

He began his graduate studies at Johns Hopkins University in 1883 and three years later he completed his doctoral dissertation, "Congressional Government: A Study in American Politics", and received a Ph.D. in history and political science. For his doctorate, Wilson had to learn German. He received academic appointments at Bryn Mawr College (1885–88) and Wesleyan University (1888–90).

At Wesleyan, he also coached the football team and founded the debate team – it is still called the T. Woodrow Wilson debate team. He then joined the Princeton faculty as professor of jurisprudence and political economy in 1890. While there, he was one of the faculty members of the short-lived coordinate college, Evelyn College for Women. Additionally, Wilson became the first lecturer of Constitutional Law at New York Law School where he taught with Charles Evans Hughes.

Wilson delivered an oration at Princeton's sesquicentennial celebration (1896) entitled "Princeton in the Nation's Service". This phrase became the motto of the University, later expanded to "Princeton in the Nation's Service and in the Service of All Nations". In this speech, he outlined his vision of the university in a democratic nation, calling on institutions of higher learning "to illuminate duty by every lesson that can be drawn out of the past". Wilson was annoyed that Princeton was not living up to its potential, complaining "There's a little college down in Kentucky which in 60 years has graduated more men who have acquired prominence and fame than has Princeton in her 150 years."

## Writings on Government and Politics

Under the influence of Walter Bagehot's *The English Constitution*, Wilson saw the United States Constitution as pre-modern, cumbersome, and open to corruption. An admirer of Parliament, Wilson favored a parliamentary system for the United States. Writing in the early 1880s: I ask you to put this question to yourselves, should we not draw the Executive and Legislature closer together? Should we not, on the one hand, give the individual leaders of opinion in Congress a better chance to have an intimate party in determining who should be president, and the president, on the other hand, a better chance to approve himself a statesman, and his advisers capable men of affairs, in the guidance of Congress

Wilson started *Congressional Government*, his best known political work, as an argument for a parliamentary system, but he was impressed by Grover Cleveland, and *Congressional Government* emerged as a critical description of America's system, with frequent negative comparisons to Westminster. He said, "I am pointing out facts—diagnosing, not prescribing remedies." Wilson believed that America's intricate system of checks and balances was the cause of the problems in American governance. He said that the divided power made it impossible for voters to see who was accountable. If government behaved badly, Wilson asked:

How is the schoolmaster, the nation, to know which boy needs the whipping?... Power and strict accountability for its use are the essential constituents of good government... It is, therefore, manifestly a radical defect in our federal system that it parcels out power and confuses responsibility as it does. The main purpose of the Convention of 1787 seems to have been to accomplish this grievous mistake. The "literary theory" of checks and balances is simply a consistent account of what our Constitution makers tried to do; and those checks and balances have proved mischievous just to the extent which they have succeeded in establishing themselves. Wilson singled out the United States House of Representatives for particular criticism:... divided up, as it were, into forty-seven seignories, in each of which a Standing Committee is the court-baron and its chairman lord-proprietor. These petty barons, some of them not a little powerful, but none of them within reach [of] the full powers of rule, may at will exercise an almost despotic sway within their own shires, and may sometimes threaten to convulse even the realm itself.

Wilson said that the Congressional committee system was fundamentally undemocratic in that committee chairs, who ruled by seniority, determined national policy although they were responsible to no one except their constituents; and that the it facilitated corruption.

### *Evolving Views*

By the time Wilson finished *Congressional Government*, Grover Cleveland was President, and Wilson's faith in the United States government was restored. When William Jennings Bryan captured the Democratic nomination from Cleveland's supporters in 1896, however, Wilson refused to support the ticket. Instead, he cast his ballot for John M. Palmer, the presidential candidate of the National Democratic Party, or Gold Democrats, a short-lived party that supported a gold standard, low tariffs, and limited government. After experiencing the vigorous presidencies of William McKinley and Theodore Roosevelt, Wilson no longer entertained thoughts of parliamentary government for the United States. In his last scholarly work in 1908, *Constitutional Government of the United States*, Wilson said that the presidency "will be as big as and as influential as the man who occupies it". By the time of his presidency, Wilson merely hoped that Presidents could be party leaders in the same way British prime ministers were. Wilson also hoped that the parties could be reorganized along ideological, not geographic, lines. He wrote, "Eight words contain the sum of the present degradation of our political parties: No leaders, no principles; no principles, no parties."

### Public Administration

Wilson also studied public administration, which he called "government in action; it is the executive, the operative, the most visible side of government, and is of course as old as government itself". He believed that by studying public administration governmental efficiency could be increased. Wilson was concerned with the implementation of government. He faulted political leaders who focused on philosophical issues and the nature of government and dismissed the critical issues of government administration as mere "practical detail". He thought such attitudes represented the requirements of smaller countries and populations. By his day, he thought, "it is getting to be harder to run a constitution than to frame one." He thought it time "to straighten the paths of government, to make its business less unbusinesslike, to strengthen and purify its organization, and it to crown its dutifulness". He complained that studies of administration drew principally on the history of Continental Europe and an American equivalent was required. He summarized the growth of such foreign states as Prussia, France, and England, highlighting the events that led to advances in administration.

By contrast, he thought American required greater compromise because of the diversity of public opinion and the difficulty of forming a majority opinion. Thus practical reform to the government is necessarily slow. Yet Wilson insisted that "administration lies outside the proper sphere of politics" and that "general laws which direct these things to be done are as obviously outside of and above administration." He likens administration to a machine that functions independent of the changing mood of its leaders. Such a line of demarcation is intended to focus responsibility for actions taken on the people or persons in charge. As Wilson put it, "public attention must be easily directed, in each case of good or bad administration, to just the man deserving of praise or blame. There is no danger in power, if only it be not irresponsible. If it be divided, dealt out in share to many, it is obscured..." Essentially, the items under the discretion of administration must be limited in scope, as to not block, nullify, obfuscate, or modify the implementation of governmental decree made by the executive branch.

### *President of Princeton University*

The trustees promoted Professor Wilson to president of Princeton in 1902, replacing Francis Landey Patton, whom the Trustees perceived to be an inefficient administrator. Although the school's endowment was barely $4 million, Wilson sought $2 million for a preceptorial system of teaching, $1 million for a school of science, and nearly $3 million for new buildings and salary increases. As a long-term objective, Wilson sought $3 million for a graduate school and $2.5 million for schools of jurisprudence and electrical engineering, as well as a museum of natural history. He achieved little of those ambitious plans because he was not a strong fund raiser, but he did increase the faculty from 112 to 174, most of whom he selected himself on the basis of their records as outstanding teachers. The curriculum guidelines he developed proved important progressive innovations in the field of higher education. To emphasize the development of expertise, Wilson instituted academic departments and a system of core requirements where students met in groups of six with preceptors, followed by two years of concentration in a selected major. He tried to raise admission standards and to replace the "gentleman's C" with serious study. Wilson aspired, as he told alumni, "to transform thoughtless boys performing tasks into thinking men".

In 1906–10, he attempted to curtail the influence of social elites by abolishing the upper-class eating clubs and moving the students into colleges, also known as quadrangles. Wilson's Quad Plan was met with fierce opposition from Princeton's alumni, most importantly Moses Taylor Pyne, the most powerful of Princeton's Trustees. Wilson refused any proposed compromises that stopped short of abolishing the clubs because he felt that to compromise "would be to temporize with evil". In October 1907, due to the intensity of alumni opposition and Wilson's refusal to compromise, the Board of Trustees withdrew its support for the Quad Plan and instructed Wilson to withdraw it.

Even more damaging to Wilson's administration of the University was his confrontation with Andrew Fleming West, Dean of the graduate school, and West's ally, former President Grover Cleveland, a trustee. Wilson wanted to integrate the proposed graduate building into the same area with the undergraduate colleges. West wanted them to remain separate. The trustees rejected Wilson's plan for colleges in 1908, and then endorsed West's alternative in 1909. The national press covered the confrontation as a battle of the elites represented by West versus democracy represented by Wilson. Wilson served as president of the American Political Science Association in 1910. Around this time, Wilson decided to leave his post at Princeton. After considering an immediate resignation, he decided instead to take up invitations to enter New Jersey state politics.

### *Governor of New Jersey*

In 1910 Wilson ran for Governor of New Jersey against the Republican candidate Vivian M. Lewis, the State Commissioner of Banking and Insurance. Wilson's campaign focused on his independence from machine politics, and he promised that if elected he would not be beholden to party bosses. Wilson soundly defeated Lewis in the general election by a margin of more than 49,000 votes, although Republican William Howard Taft had carried New Jersey in the 1908 presidential election by more than 80,000 votes. In the 1910 election the Democrats also took control of the General Assembly. The State Senate, however, remained in Republican control by a slim margin. After taking office, Wilson set in place his reformist agenda, ignoring the demands of party machinery. While governor, in a period spanning six months, Wilson established state primaries. This all but took the party bosses out of the presidential election process in the state. He also revamped the public utility commission, and introduced worker's compensation.

## Election of 1912

Wilson's popularity as governor and his status in the national media gave impetus to his presidential campaign in 1912. He selected William Frank McCombs, a New York lawyer and a friend from college days, to manage his campaign. Much of Wilson's support came from the South, especially from young progressives in that region, especially intellectuals, editors and lawyers. Wilson managed to maneuver through the complexities of local politics. For example, in Tennessee the Democratic Party was divided on the issue of prohibition. Wilson was progressive and sober, but not a dry, and appealed to both sides. They united behind him to win the presidential election in the state, but divided over state politics and lost the gubernatorial election. The convention deadlocked for more than 40 ballots as no candidate could reach the two-thirds vote required to win the nomination. A leading contender was House Speaker Champ Clark, a prominent progressive strongest in the border states. Other contenders were Governor Judson Harmon of Ohio, and Representative Oscar Underwood of Alabama. They lacked Wilson's charisma and dynamism. Publisher William Randolph Hearst, a leader of the left-wing of the party, supported Clark. William Jennings Bryan, the nominee in 1896, 1900 and 1908, played a critical role in opposition to any candidate who had the support of "the financiers of Wall Street". He finally announced for Wilson, who won on the 46th ballot.

In the campaign Wilson promoted the "New Freedom", emphasizing limited federal government and opposition to monopoly powers—positions that he reversed on coming to office.

Wilson enjoyed the support of many black leaders including W.E.B. DuBois and William Monroe Trotter. Wilson's speeches and letters expressed the sentiments of a defender of the underprivileged. In a bitter contest for the Republican nomination, President William Howard Taft defeated former president Theodore Roosevelt, but when Roosevelt walked out of the Republican convention and ran as a third party candidate, Wilson's success in the electoral college was assured. He won 41.8% of the popular vote.

### *First term as President, 1913–1917*

Wilson is the only President to hold a Ph.D. degree and the only President to serve in a political office in New Jersey before election to the Presidency. He was the first person identified with the South to be elected President since Zachary Taylor and the first Southerner in the White House since Andrew Johnson left in 1868. Wilson had a strong base of support in the South. He was the first president to deliver his State of the Union address before Congress personally since John Adams in 1799. Wilson was also the first Democrat elected to the presidency since Grover Cleveland in 1892 and only the second Democrat in the White House since the Civil War. In resolving economic policy issues, he had to manage the conflict between two wings of his party, the agrarian wing led by Bryan and the pro-business wing. With large Democratic majorities in Congress and a healthy economy, he promptly seized the opportunity to implement his agenda. Wilson experienced early success by implementing his "New Freedom" pledges of antitrust modification, tariff revision, and reform in banking and currency matters. He held the first modern presidential press conference, on March 15, 1913, in which reporters were allowed to ask him questions. Wilson's first wife Ellen died on August 6, 1914 of Bright's disease. In 1915, he met Edith Galt. They married later that year on December 18.

### *Federal Reserve 1913*

Wilson secured passage of the Federal Reserve system in late 1913. Wilson had tried to find a middle ground between conservative Republicans led by Senator Nelson W. Aldrich and those, especially the powerful left wing of the Democratic party led by William Jennings Bryan, who opposed all banking schemes and strenuously denounced private banks and Wall Street. The later group wanted a government-owned central bank that could print paper money as Congress required. The compromise, based on the Aldrich Plan but sponsored by Democratic Congressmen Carter Glass and Robert Owen, allowed the private banks a certain influence over the new Federal Reserve, but appeased the populists by placing controlling interest in a central, public board. This Board of Governors included members appointed by the President and approved by Congress who would outnumber the board members selected by bankers. Moreover, Wilson convinced Bryan's supporters that because Federal Reserve notes were obligations of the government, the plan met their demands. Wilson's plan also organized the Federal Reserve system into 12 districts, a structure meant to weaken the influence of the powerful New York banks, a key demand of Bryan's allies in the South and West. This decentralization was a key factor in winning the support of Congressman Glass.

The final plan passed in December 1913. Some bankers felt it gave too much control to Washington, and some reformers felt it allowed bankers to maintain too much power. Several Congressmen claimed that New York bankers feigned their disapproval. Wilson named Paul Warburg and other prominent bankers to direct the new system. While power was supposed to be decentralized, the New York branch dominated the Fed as the "first among equals". The new system began operations in 1915 and played a major role in financing the Allied and American war effort.

### *Economic Views*

In 1913, the Underwood tariff lowered the tariff. The revenue thereby lost was replaced by a new federal income tax (authorized by the 16th Amendment, which had been sponsored by the Republicans). The "Seaman's Act" of 1915 improved working conditions for merchant sailors. A response to the *RMS Titanic* disaster, it also required all ships to be retrofitted with lifeboats. A series of programs were targeted at farmers. The "Smith Lever" act of 1914 created the modern system of agricultural extension agents sponsored by the state agricultural colleges. The agents taught new techniques to farmers. The 1916 "Federal Farm Loan Board" issued low-cost long-term mortgages to farmers.

Child labor was curtailed by the Keating-Owen Act of 1916, but the U.S. Supreme Court declared it unconstitutional in 1918. No major child labor prohibition would take effect until the 1930s. The railroad brotherhoods threatened in summer 1916 to shut down the national transportation system. Wilson tried to bring labor and management together, but when management refused he had Congress pass the "Adamson Act" in September 1916, which avoided the strike by imposing an 8-hour work day in the industry (at the same pay as before). It helped Wilson gain union support for his reelection; the act was approved by the Supreme Court.

### *Antitrust*

Wilson broke with the big lawsuit tradition of his predecessors Taft and Roosevelt as Trustbusters, finding a new approach to encouraging competition through the Federal Trade Commission, which stopped unfair trade practices. In addition, he pushed through Congress the Clayton Antitrust Act making certain business practices illegal (such as price discrimination, agreements prohibiting retailers from handling other companies' products, and directorates and agreements to control other companies). The power of this legislation was greater than previous anti-trust laws, because individual officers of corporations could be held responsible if their companies violated the laws. More importantly, the new laws set out clear guidelines that corporations could follow, a dramatic improvement over the previous uncertainties. This law was considered the "Magna Carta" of labor by Samuel Gompers because it ended union liability antitrust laws. In 1916, under threat of a national railroad strike, he approved legislation that increased wages and cut working hours of railroad employees; there was no strike.

### *War policy—World War I*

Wilson spent 1914 through the beginning of 1917 trying to keep America out of the war in Europe. He offered to be a mediator, but neither the Allies nor the Central Powers took his requests seriously. Republicans, led by Theodore Roosevelt, strongly criticized Wilson's refusal to build up the U.S. Army in anticipation of the threat of war. Wilson won the support of the U.S. peace element by arguing that an army buildup would provoke war.

Secretary of State William Jennings Bryan, whose pacifist recommendations were ignored by Wilson, resigned in 1915. On 18 December 1916 Wilson unsuccessfully offered to mediate peace. As a preliminary he asked both sides to state their minimum terms necessary for future security.

The Central Powers replied that victory was certain, and the Allies required the dismemberment of their enemies' empires. No desire for peace or common ground existed, and the offer lapsed. While German submarines were killing sailors and civilian passengers Wilson demanded that Germany stop, but he kept the U.S. out of the war. Britain had declared a blockade of Germany to prevent neutral ships from carrying contraband goods to Germany. Wilson protested some British violation of neutral rights, where no one was killed. His protests were mild, and the British knew America would not take action.

## Segregation in the Federal Government

In 1912, "an unprecedented number" of African Americans left the Republican Party to cast their vote for Democrat Wilson. They were encouraged by his promises of support for their issues. The issue of segregation came up early in his presidency when, at an April 1913 cabinet meeting, Albert Burleson, Wilson's Postmaster General, complained about working conditions at the Railway Mail Service.

Offices and restrooms became segregated, sometimes by partitions erected between seating for white and African-American employees in Post Office Department offices, lunch rooms, and bathrooms, as well as in the Treasury and the Bureau of Engraving and Printing.

It also became accepted policy for "Negro" employees of the Postal Service to be reduced in rank or dismissed. And unlike his predecessors Grover Cleveland and Theodore Roosevelt, Wilson accommodated Southern opposition to the re-appointment of an African American to the position of Register of the Treasury and other positions within the federal government. This set the tone for Wilson's attitude to race throughout his presidency, in which the rights of African Americans were sacrificed, for what he felt would be the more important longer term progress of the common good.

### *Election of 1916*

Renominated in 1916, Wilson used as a major campaign slogan "He kept us out of the war", referring to his administration's avoiding open conflict with Germany or Mexico while maintaining a firm national policy. Wilson, however, never promised to keep out of war regardless of provocation. In his acceptance speech on September 2, 1916, Wilson pointedly warned Germany that submarine warfare that took American lives would not be tolerated, saying "The nation that violates these essential rights must expect to be checked and called to account by direct challenge and resistance.

It at once makes the quarrel in part our own." Wilson narrowly won the election, defeating Republican candidate Charles Evans Hughes. As governor of New York from 1907–1910, Hughes had a progressive record, strikingly similar to Wilson's as governor of New Jersey.

Theodore Roosevelt would comment that the only thing different between Hughes and Wilson was a shave. However, Hughes had to try to hold together a coalition of conservative Taft supporters and progressive Roosevelt partisans and so his campaign never seemed to take a definite form. Wilson ran on his record and ignored Hughes, reserving his attacks for Roosevelt. When asked why he did not attack Hughes directly, Wilson told a friend to "Never murder a man who is committing suicide."

The result was exceptionally close and the outcome was in doubt for several days. Because of Wilson's fear of becoming a lame duck president during the uncertainties of the war in Europe, he created a hypothetical plan where if Hughes were elected he would name Hughes United States Secretary of State and then resign along with the vice-president to enable Hughes to become the president.

The vote came down to several close states. Wilson won California by 3,773 votes out of almost a million votes cast and New Hampshire by 54 votes. Hughes won Minnesota by 393 votes out of over 358,000. In the final count, Wilson had 277 electoral votes vs. Hughes 254. Wilson was able to win reelection in 1916 by picking up many votes that had gone to Teddy Roosevelt or Eugene V. Debs in 1912.

## Second term as President, 1917–1921

### *Decision for War, 1917*

Before entering the war in 1917, the U.S. had made a declaration of neutrality in 1914. During this time of neutrality, President Wilson warned citizens not to take sides in the war in fear of endangering wider U.S. policy. In his address to congress in 1914, Wilson states, "Such divisions amongst us would be fatal to our peace of mind and might seriously stand in the way of the proper performance of our duty as the one great nation at peace, the one people holding itself ready to play a part of impartial mediation and speak the counsels of peace and accommodation, not as a partisan, but as a friend." The U.S. maintained neutrality despite increasing pressure placed on Wilson after the sinking of the British passenger liner RMS Lusitania with American citizens on board.

This neutrality would deteriorate when Germany began to initiate its unrestricted submarine warfare threatening U.S. commercial shipping. When Germany started unrestricted submarine warfare in early 1917, despite the promises made in the Arabic pledge and the Sussex pledge, and attempted to enlist Mexico as an ally, Wilson took America into World War I as a war to make "the world safe for democracy". He did not sign a formal alliance with the United Kingdom or France but operated as an "associated" power. He raised a massive army through conscription and gave command to General John J. Pershing, allowing Pershing a free hand as to tactics, strategy and even diplomacy.

Woodrow Wilson had decided by then that the war had become a real threat to humanity. Unless the U.S. threw its weight into the war, as he stated in his declaration of war speech on April 2, 1917, western civilization itself could be destroyed. His statement announcing a "war to end all wars" meant that he wanted to build a basis for peace that would prevent future catastrophic wars and needless death and destruction. This provided the basis of Wilson's Fourteen Points, which were intended to resolve territorial disputes, ensure free trade and commerce, and establish a peacemaking organization. Included in these fourteen points was the proposal of the League of Nations.

### *War Message*

Woodrow Wilson delivered his *War Message* to Congress on the evening of April 2, 1917. Introduced to great applause, he remained intense and almost motionless for the entire speech, only raising one arm as his only bodily movement. Wilson announced that his previous position of "armed neutrality" was no longer tenable now that the Imperial German Government had announced that it would use its submarines to sink any vessel approaching the ports of Great Britain, Ireland or any of the Western Coasts of Europe. He advised Congress to declare that the recent course of action taken by the Imperial German Government constituted an act of war. He proposed that the United States enter the war to "vindicate principles of peace and justice in the life of the world as against selfish and autocratic power". He also charged that Germany had "filled our unsuspecting communities and even our offices of government with spies and set criminal intrigues everywhere afoot against our national unity of counsel, our peace within and without our industries and our commerce". Furthermore, the United States had intercepted a telegram sent to the German ambassador in Mexico City that evidenced Germany's attempt to instigate a Mexican attack upon the U.S. The German government, Wilson said, "means to stir up enemies against us at our very doors". Wilson closed with the statement that the world must be again safe for democracy. With 50 Representatives and 6 Senators in opposition, the declaration of war by the United States against Germany was passed by the Congress on April 4, 1917, and was approved by the President on April 6, 1917.

### *The Fourteen Points*

In a speech to Congress on January 8, 1918, Wilson articulated America's war aims. It was the clearest expression of intention made by any of the belligerent nations. The speech, authored principally by Walter Lippmann, translated Wilson's progressive domestic policies into comparably idealistic equivalents for the international arena: self-determination, open agreements, international cooperation. Promptly dubbed the *Fourteen Points*, Wilson attempted to make them the basis for the treaty that would mark the end of the war. They ranged from the most generic principles like the prohibition of secret treaties to such detailed outcomes as the creation of an independent Poland with access to the sea.

### *Home Front*

To counter opposition to the war at home, Wilson pushed the Espionage Act of 1917 and the Sedition Act of 1918 through Congress to suppress anti-British, pro-German, or anti-war opinions. He welcomed socialists who supported the war and pushed for deportation of foreign-born radicals. Citing the Espionage Act, the U.S. Post Office refused to carry any written materials that could be deemed critical of the U. S. war effort. Some sixty newspapers were deprived of their second-class mailing rights. His wartime policies were strongly pro-labor. He worked closely with Samuel Gompers and the AFL, while suppressing antiwar groups trying to impede the war effort. The American Federation of Labor, the railroad brotherhoods and other 'moderate' unions saw enormous growth in membership and wages during Wilson's administration. There was no rationing, so consumer prices soared. As income taxes increased, white-collar workers suffered. Appeals to buy war bonds were highly successful, however. Bonds had the result of shifting the cost of the war to the affluent 1920s.

Wilson set up the first western propaganda office, the United States Committee on Public Information, headed by George Creel (thus its popular name, *Creel Commission*), which filled the country with patriotic anti-German appeals and conducted various forms of censorship. In 1917, Congress authorized ex-President Theodore Roosevelt to raise four divisions of volunteers to fight in France-Roosevelt's World War I volunteers; Wilson refused to accept this offer from his political enemy. Other areas of the war effort were incorporated into the government along with propaganda. The War Industries Board headed by Bernard Baruch set war goals and policies for American factories. Future President Herbert Hoover was appointed to head the Food Administration which encouraged Americans to participate in "Meatless Mondays" and "Wheatless Wednesdays" to conserve food for the troops overseas. The Federal Fuel Administration run by Henry Garfield introduced daylight savings time and rationed fuel supplies such as coal and oil to keep the US military supplied. These and many other boards and administrations were headed by businessmen recruited by Wilson for a dollar a day salary to make the government more efficient in the war effort.

### *Other Foreign Affairs*

Between 1914 and 1918, the United States intervened in Latin America, particularly in Mexico, Haiti, Cuba, and Panama. The U.S. maintained troops in Nicaragua throughout the Wilson administration and used them to select the president of Nicaragua and then to force Nicaragua to pass the Bryan-Chamorro Treaty. American troops in Haiti, under the command of the federal government, forced the Haitian legislature to choose the candidate Wilson selected as Haitian president. American troops occupied Haiti between 1915 and 1934. Wilson ordered the military occupation of the Dominican Republic shortly after the resignation of its President Juan Isidro Jimenes Pereyra in 1916. The U.S. military worked in concert with wealthy Dominican landowners to suppress the *gavilleros*, a *campesino* guerrilla force fighting the occupation. The occupation lasted until 1924, and was notorious for its brutality against those in the resistance.

After Russia left the war following the Bolshevik Revolution of 1917, the Allies sent troops there to prevent a German or Bolshevik takeover of allied-provided weapons, munitions and other supplies, previously shipped as aid to the pre-revolutionary government. Wilson sent armed forces to assist the withdrawal of Czech and Slovak prisoners along the Trans-Siberian Railway, hold key port cities at Arkangel and Vladivostok. Though not sent to engage the Bolsheviks, the U.S. forces engaged in several armed conflicts against forces of the new Russian government. Despite the apparent innocuousness of Wilson's motives, revolutionaries in Russia resented the American intrusion. As Robert Maddox puts it, "The immediate effect of the intervention was to prolong a bloody civil war, thereby costing thousands of additional lives and wreaking enormous destruction on an already battered society." Wilson withdrew most of the soldiers on April 1, 1920, though some remained until as late as 1922.

In 1919 Wilson guided American foreign policy to "acquiesce" in the Balfour Declaration without supporting Zionism in an official way. Wilson expressed sympathy for the plight of Jews, especially in Poland and in France. In May 1920, after the Senate passed a resolution unanimously expressing sympathy for Armenia's suffering, Wilson sent a proposal to Congress to establish an American mandate over Armenia. It failed in the Senate with only 23 votes for and 52 against. He later requested an appropriation to underwrite a loan to Armenia, but got no response from Congress.

### *Peace Conference 1919*

After World War I, Wilson participated in negotiations with the stated aim of assuring statehood for formerly oppressed nations and an equitable peace. On January 8, 1918, Wilson made his famous *Fourteen Points* address, introducing the idea of a League of Nations, an organization with a stated goal of helping to preserve territorial integrity and political independence among large and small nations alike. Wilson intended the Fourteen Points as a means toward ending the war and achieving an equitable peace for all the nations. He spent six months in Paris for the 1919 Paris Peace Conference (making him the first U.S. president to travel to Europe while in office). He worked tirelessly to promote his plan. The charter of the proposed League of Nations was incorporated into the conference's Treaty of Versailles.

For his peace-making efforts, Wilson was awarded the 1919 Nobel Peace Prize, however, he failed to even win US Senate support for ratification. The United States never joined the League. Republicans under Henry Cabot Lodge controlled the Senate after the 1918 elections, but Wilson refused to give them a voice at Paris and refused to agree to Lodge's proposed changes. The key point of disagreement was whether the League would diminish the power of Congress to declare war. During this period, Wilson became less trustful of the press and stopped holding press conferences for them, preferring to use his propaganda unit, the Committee for Public Information, instead.

A poll of historians in 2006 cited Wilson's failure to compromise with the Republicans on U.S. entry into the League as one of the 10 largest errors on the part of an American president. The extensive restrictions in the Treaty of Versailles left the German populace with a resentment against the treaty and ultimately contributed to the rise of Adolf Hitler and World War II. When Wilson traveled to Europe to settle the peace terms, he visited Pope Benedict XV in Rome, making Wilson the first American President to visit the Pope while in office.

### *Post War: 1919–20*

Wilson's administration did not plan for the process of demobilization at the war's end. Though some advisers tried to engage the President's attention to what they called "reconstruction", his tepid support for a federal commission evaporated with the election of 1918. Republican gains in the Senate meant that his opposition would have to consent to the appointment of commission members. Instead, Wilson favored the prompt dismantling of wartime boards and regulatory agencies. Demobilization proved chaotic and violent. Four million soldiers were sent home with little planning, little money, and few benefits. A wartime bubble in prices of farmland burst, leaving many farmers bankrupt or deeply in debt after they purchased new land. Major strikes in steel, coal, and meatpacking followed in 1919. Serious race riots hit Chicago, Omaha and two dozen other cities. As the election of 1920 approached, Wilson imagined that a deadlocked Democratic convention might turn to him as the only candidate who would make U.S. participation in the League of Nations the dominant issue. He imagined and sometimes pretended he was healthy enough for the effort, but several times admitted that he knew he could not survive a campaign. No one around the President dared tell him that he was incapable and that the campaign for the League was already lost. At the Convention in late June, 1920, some Wilson partisans made efforts on his behalf and sent Wilson hopeful reports, but they were quashed by Wilson's wiser friends.

### *Incapacity*

The immediate cause of Wilson's incapacitation was the physical strain of the public speaking tour he undertook to obtain support for ratification of the Covenant of the League of Nations. In Pueblo, Colorado, on September 25, 1919 he collapsed. Then, on October 2, 1919, he suffered a serious stroke that almost totally incapacitated him, leaving him paralyzed on his left side and blind in his left eye. He was confined to bed for weeks, sequestered from nearly everyone but his wife and his physician, Dr. Cary

Grayson. For at least a few months, he used a wheelchair. Later, he could walk only with the assistance of a cane. The full extent of his disability was kept from the public until after his death on February 3, 1924.

With few exceptions, Wilson was kept out of the presence of Vice President Thomas R. Marshall, his cabinet and Congressional visitors to the White House for the remainder of his term. His wife, Edith, served as his steward, selecting issues for his attention and delegating other issues to his cabinet heads. Eventually, Wilson did resume his attendance at cabinet meetings, but his input there was perfunctory at best. This was one of the most serious cases of presidential disability in American history and was later cited as an argument for the 25th Amendment.

## Administration, Cabinet and Supreme Court Appointments

Wilson's chief of staff ("Secretary") was Joseph Patrick Tumulty 1913–1921, but he was largely upstaged after 1916 when Wilson's second wife, Edith Bolling Wilson, assumed full control of Wilson's schedule. The most important foreign policy advisor and confidant was "Colonel" Edward M. House until Wilson broke with him in early 1919.

## Civil Rights—African Americans

Wilson did not interfere with the well-established system of Jim Crow and backed the demands of Southern Democrats that their states be left alone to deal with issues of race and black voting without interference from the North, ensuring there would be no challenge to the raft of laws passed to disenfranchise African Americans across the region. While president of Princeton University, Wilson discouraged blacks from even applying for admission, preferring to keep the peace among white students than have black students admitted.

Many black leaders supported Wilson in the 1912 election. However their rejoicing over Wilson's victory was short-lived as segregationist white Southerners took control of Congress and many executive departments. As President of the United States, Wilson ignored complaints that his cabinet officials had established official segregation in most federal government offices, in some departments for the first time since 1863. New buildings and facilities were built to house black workers separately. "His administration imposed full racial segregation in Washington and hounded from office considerable numbers of black federal employees." Wilson and his cabinet members fired many black Republican office holders in political appointee positions, but also appointed a few black Democrats to such posts.

W. E. B. Du Bois, a leader of the NAACP, campaigned for Wilson and in 1918 was offered an Army commission in charge of dealing with race relations; DuBois accepted, but he failed his Army physical and did not serve. Wilson drafted hundreds of thousands of blacks into the army, giving them equal pay with whites, but kept them in all-black units with white officers. When a delegation of blacks protested the discriminatory actions, Wilson told them "segregation is not a humiliation but a benefit, and ought to be so regarded by you gentlemen." In 1914, he told *The New York Times*, "If the colored people made a mistake in voting for me, they ought to correct it."

Wilson was highly criticized by African Americans for his actions. He was also criticized by such hard-line segregationists as Georgia's Thomas E. Watson, who believed Wilson did not go far enough in restricting black employment in the federal government. The segregation introduced into the federal workplace by the Wilson administration was kept in place by the succeeding presidents and not officially ended until the Truman Administration. Woodrow Wilson's "History of the American People" explained the Ku Klux Klan of the late 1860s as the natural outgrowth of Reconstruction, a lawless reaction to a lawless period. Wilson noted that the Klan "began to attempt by intimidation what they were not allowed to attempt by the ballot or by any ordered course of public action".

### *White Ethnic Groups*

Wilson had harsh words to say about immigrants in his history books, but after he entered politics in 1910, Wilson worked to integrate immigrants into the Democratic party, the army, and American life. During the war, he demanded in return that they repudiate any loyalty to enemy nations. Irish Americans were powerful in the Democratic party and opposed going to war as allies of their traditional enemy Great Britain, especially after the violent suppression of the Easter Rebellion of 1916. Wilson won them over in 1917 by promising to ask Great Britain to give Ireland its independence. At Versailles, however, he reneged and the Irish-American community vehemently denounced him. Wilson, in turn, blamed the Irish Americans and German Americans for lack of popular support for the League of Nations, saying,

There is an organized propaganda against the League of Nations and against the treaty proceeding from exactly the same sources that the organized propaganda proceeded from which threatened this country here and there with disloyalty, and I want to say, I cannot say too often, any man who carries a hyphen about with him carries a dagger that he is ready to plunge into the vitals of this Republic whenever he gets ready. ' Wilson refused to meet with Éamon de Valera, the President of Dáil Éireann (the revolutionary Irish Republic), during the latter's 1919 visit to the United States.

President Wilson nominated to the Supreme Court Louis Brandeis, the first Jewish American to ever hold this position. Wilson's appointment started a long line of Jewish justices who would serve on the nation's highest court in the future.

### *Death*

In 1921, Wilson and his wife retired from the White House to a home in the Embassy Row section of Washington, D.C. Wilson continued going for daily drives and attended Keith's vaudeville theater on Saturday nights. Wilson was one of only two Presidents (Theodore Roosevelt was the first) to have served as president of the American Historical Association. Wilson died in his S Street home on February 3, 1924. He was buried in Washington National Cathedral. He is the only president buried in Washington, D.C.

Mrs. Wilson stayed in the home another 37 years, dying on December 28, 1961. It was the day she was to be the guest of honour at the opening of the Woodrow Wilson Bridge near Washington, D.C. She died with her favorite dog, Rooter, at her bedside. Mrs. Wilson left the home to the National Trust for Historic Preservation to be made into a museum honoring her husband. The Woodrow Wilson House opened as a museum. It was designated a National Historic Landmark in 1964 and listed on the National Register of Historic Places in 1966.

The USS Woodrow Wilson (SSBN-624), a Lafayette-class ballistic missile submarine, was the only ship of the United States Navy to be named for Wilson. She later was converted into an attack submarine and redesignated SSN-624. The Woodrow Wilson School of Public and International Affairs was founded at Princeton in 1930, created in the spirit of Wilson's interest in preparing students for leadership in public and international affairs.

In 1929, Wilson's image appeared on the $100,000 bill. The bill, now out of print but still legal tender, was only used to transfer money between Federal Reserve banks. In 1944, Darryl F. Zanuck of 20th Century Fox produced a film titled *Wilson*. It looked back with nostalgia to the commander-in-chief of World War I.

# Bibliography


Acton, H.B., 1955, *The Illusion of the Epoch*, London: Cohen and West.

Anderson, Benedict: *Imagined Communities: Reflections on the Origin and Spread of Nationalism*. London, Verso, 1991.

Arthur, C.J., 1986, *Dialectics of Labour*, Oxford: Basil Blackwell.

Avineri, Shlomo, 1970, *The Social and Political Thought of Karl Marx*, Cambridge: Cambridge University Press.

Bender, Barbara: *Landscape: Politics and Perspectives*. Providence and Oxford, Berg, 1993.

Bottery, M. : *The Ethics of Educational Management: Personal, Social and Political Perspectives on School Organization*, London, Cassell, 1992.

Carver, Terrell, 1982, *Marx's Social Theory*, New York: Oxford University Press.

Cohen, G.A., 2001, *Karl Marx's Theory of History: A Defence*, Oxford, Oxford University Press.

DeLong, G. F.: *The Dutch in America, 1609-1974*, Boston, Twayne Publishers, 1975.

Harris, H. S.: *Hegel's Development: Towards the Sunlight 1770-1801*, Oxford, Clarendon Press, 1972

Helen Wallace: *Interlocking dimensions of European integration*, Basingstoke, Palgrave, 2001.

Herbert; Murray Dry: *The Anti-Federalist*, Chicago: University of Chicago Press, 2006.

Hilbert, D.R. : *Color and Color Perception: A Study in Anthropocentric Realism*, Stanford, CSLI, 1987.

Hook, Sidney, 1950, *From Hegel to Marx*, New York: Humanities Press.

Ian Steven Lustick: *Trapped in the War on Terror*, Philadelphia, University of Pennsylvania Press, 2006.

Jacobsen, Hans-Adolf: *Karl Haushofer: Leben und Werk*, Harald Boldt Verlag, Boppard 1979.

Kamenka, Eugene,1962, *The Ethical Foundations of Marxism*, London: Routledge and Kegan Paul.

Macpherson. C. B.: *The Political Theory of Possessive Individualism: Hobbes to Locke*, Oxford, Oxford University Press, 1962.

# Index

□□□